Microfinance and Development in Emerging Economies

Microfinance and Development in Emerging Economies: An Alternative Financial Model for Advancing the SDGs

BY

NISHI MALHOTRA

Assistant Professor, OP Jindal Global University

United Kingdom – North America – Japan – India – Malaysia – China

Emerald Publishing Limited
Howard House, Wagon Lane, Bingley BD16 1WA, UK

First edition 2023

Reprints and permissions service
Contact: permissions@emeraldinsight.com

British Library Cataloguing in Publication Data
A catalogue record for this book is available from the British Library

ISBN: 978-1-83753-827-0 (Print)
ISBN: 978-1-83753-826-3 (Online)
ISBN: 978-1-83753-828-7 (Epub)

Printed and bound by CPI Group (UK) Ltd, Croydon, CR0 4YY

INVESTOR IN PEOPLE

I dedicate this book to my parents, sister and the Indian Armed forces. Above all I thank the almighty God and our priest for his blessings.

Table of Contents

List of Figures and Tables

List of Abbreviations

APES	Aadhaar Enabled Payment System
APMC	Agricultural Produce Market Committee
BHIM	Bharat Interface for Money
CBLO	Collateralized Borrowing and Lending Obligation
CMC	Computer Maintenance Corporation
CMIE	Centre for Monitoring Indian Economy
CPI	Consumer Price Index
CSC	Common Service Centres
DAY	Deendayal Antyodaya Yojana
FINTECH	Financial Technology
FPO	Follow on Public Offer
ICT	Information and Communications Technology
ILO	International Labour Organization
KYC	Know Your Customer
LPG	Liquefied Petroleum Gas
MFI	Microfinance Institution
MNREGA	Mahatma Gandhi National Rural Employment Guarantee Act
MYRADA	Mysore Resettlement and Development Agency
NABARD	National Bank for Agriculture and Rural Development
NACH	National Automated Clearing House
NEFT	National Electronic Funds Transfer
NFS	National Financial Switch
NHM	National Health Mission
NICS	National Institute for Career Service
NOFN	National Optical Fibre Network
NPCI	National Payments Corporation of India
NRLM	National Rural Livelihood Mission
PAC	Producer Agricultural Companies

RBI	Return on Investment
RBV	Resource Based View
ROI	Return on Investment
RUPAY	Rupee and Payment
SBLP	Self Help Group Bank Linkage Programme
SDG	Sustainable Development Goal
SEBI	Securities and Exchange Board of India
SHG	Self Help Group
SSDG	State Portal and State Service Delivery Gateway
SWAN	State Wide Area Network
TAM	Technology Acceptance Model
UID	Unique Identity Number
UN	United Nation
UNDP	United Nation Development Programme
VRIO	Value, Rarity, Imitability and Organization

About the Author

Dr. Nishi Malhotra has completed her PhD from Indian Institute of Management, Kozhikode in Finance, Accounting and Control in the domain of the Analysis of Self-help Group Bank Linkage programme. She has completed her MBA (full time) from MDI Gurgaon (Management Development Institute, Gurgaon) and BCOM (Hons) from Sri Ram College of Commerce, Delhi University. She has qualified for UGC NET in Commerce and has authored more than 16 research papers across various ABDC – B, and C category journals. She has also authored papers in the *Journal of Human Values*, *Q1* and Scopus-listed journals. She is publishing a book with Emerald Publishing in the domain of Microfinance and published two academic reference books on income tax laws and cost accounting. She has been a topper throughout her school from Class II till Class XII.

Preface

This book talks about the issues developing economies face in achieving sustainable development goals of poverty reduction. Within the developmental paradigm of poverty reduction through microfinance, this book highlights the temporal shift in policy framework prescribed by the United Nations and World Bank to tackle the issue of poverty, with customisation for developing nations. This book highlights the uniqueness of the microfinance programme adopted by India in terms of the blend of democratic participation of the poor within the framework of self-reliance through the generation of profits. Various microfinancing initiatives aimed at promoting self-reliance through financial literacy, entrepreneurship, skill development and financial discipline enforced through monitoring and supervision are at the forefront of the success of these initiatives. This book, for the first time, discusses in detail the uniqueness of the innovative welfare schemes adopted by the Indian Government.

Acknowledgement

I dedicate this book to my parents; without their help, I would not have been able to publish this book. I want to thank the almighty for all the encouragement. Above all, I would like to thank the Government of India and the state of Kerala. Thanks to the Emerald Publishing team for making this possible. I am grateful for the outstanding support from Emerald. In particular, I would like to thank Lisa Goodrum – Commissioning Editor – Responsible Management.

Chapter 1

Poverty in Emerging Economies

Handicraft Industry in Nepal – Paradigms of Poverty

Lasting peace cannot be achieved unless large population groups find ways to break out of poverty. Across cultures and civilizations, Yunus and Grameen Bank have shown that even the poorest of the poor can work to bring about their development. *The Noble Committee*

Microfinance and Development in Emerging Economies, 1–21
Copyright © 2023 Nishi Malhotra
Published under exclusive licence by Emerald Publishing Limited
doi:10.1108/978-1-83753-826-320231001

Social Perspective

In Nepal, within the hinterlands and hamlets, quietly nestled in the Himalayas, the self-help groups comprised the women members who weave pashmina shawls, Palpali Dhaka products that include handkerchiefs, jewellery, handmade paper products, wood craft, singing bowls and khukuri knives, glass beads and hemp products. With the digitisation of the villages in Nepal, the level of commerce has increased to a large extent. This has led to the transformation of Nepalese society into a knowledge society. This has led to a reduction in poverty. In Nepal, approximately 50% of the population lives below the poverty line, and most do not have access to basic amenities, including education, clean drinking water, sanitation, etc. It is a small kingdom in which the monarchy has a special place, and the economy mainly depends on agriculture, tourism and other allied activities. Due to a subsistence economy, most families depend on agriculture for survival. Low education is the main reason for poverty among rural citizens. Besides, a high poverty level exists among Nepal's downtrodden castes and creeds. This includes the caste such as Sarkai, Damai and Kami. The story of poverty is extremely high among people from lower castes, downtrodden religions and sects leading to caste discrimination and gross inequalities. This marginalisation leads to social exclusion as the poor people from the lower caste cannot access the wells to fetch water. Thus, the problem of poverty is dependent on root causes which might be demographics. Besides individual factors, contextual factors also lead to poverty. These people do not have rights, including land ownership and entitlement to possess various assets. Poverty is a chronic problem that fraught the economic growth in the villages of Nepal.

Introduction

Globally, 1.7 billion people live below the poverty line. These people cannot access economic resources and collateral to obtain credit. Moreover, the banks do not have any information about the creditworthiness of the poor, which leads to the problem of underdevelopment globally. There are multiple definitions of poverty, but the most accepted explanation is in terms of per-day expenditure on consumption by the household. The World Bank has defined poverty as per capita expenditure of less than $1.90 to $3.10 per day. Further, the statistics and earlier research propagate that poverty is more prevalent among households with three or more children and in rural areas and regions. Extreme poverty is the root cause of all the social problems and ills. It is imperative to eradicate poverty to achieve economic growth and development objectives. Developing nations worldwide have adopted the sustainable development goal of poverty reduction. Approximately 193 countries have adopted the sustainable development framework, including 169 different Global targets, including poverty reduction. In 1901, for the first time, Dadabhai Naroji estimated poverty in India based on the cost of subsistence. India adopted the poverty line estimation based on the recommendations of the National Planning Committee, based on the living standard followed by the Bombay Plan 1944. In the past, the task of estimating poverty was given to various committees, which include the Dandekar and Rath in 1971, the Y.K. Alagh task force in 1979, and the working group of 1962 in the estimation of poverty. Recently, this task has been given to Lakdawala report in 1993, and Rangarajan Committee report in 2014. India has adopted a multidimensional approach to measuring poverty, which includes various indicators such as nutrition, child-adolescent mortality, schooling, attendance, cooking gas, electricity, housing, ownership of assets, bank accounts, education, health, nutrition, access to sanitation, and clean drinking water. By 2030, India and other emerging nations of the world will have adopted the vision of zero poverty. But with the existing challenges and new emerging social challenges, the achievement of this goal looks like a distant dream. With the advent of COVID-19, the gains made in reducing poverty in the last decade have been lost. Recent research and estimates suggest that approximately 68 million to 130 million people might be pushed into the vicious circle of poverty (Wang & Zhou, 2020). The current rate of global poverty hovers around roughly 9.2%, and with the existing scenario, achieving a poverty rate of 3% looks like a distant goal. Poverty is a multidimensional and complex problem with various causes, such as inadequate schooling, low income, and low life expectancy, with gender and regional disparities. Poverty is often defined as a market failure when the market's demand and supply forces cannot achieve the equitable distribution of resources. Many books and literature describe poverty as a structural failure. ILO (International Labour Organisation) defines 'social injustice' as the root cause of the problem of poverty. This social injustice further leads to disharmony and violence in society. The World Bank has laid down two goals. The first goal is eradicating poverty, and the second is achieving shared prosperity. Approximately 15.09% of the world's poor living in abject poverty are staying in the developing nations of South East Asia. Many countries in these developing nations have adopted the goal of poverty reduction through financial inclusion and microfinancing (Saha & Qin, 2023). For the study, it is hypothesised that poverty essentially implies a lack of access to resources due to a lack of capabilities, including access to financial resources. Thus, poverty is defined as the level of financial exclusion and the inability to access financial resources due to the lack of collateral and information about the creditworthiness of the poor. The SDG (Sustainable Development Goal) includes a target indicator as 1.2, which defines poverty as reducing at least by half the proportion of women, men and children of all ages who live below the poverty level.

Definition of Poverty

Poverty has been defined as the feeling of deprivation and lack of well-being among people. It is often described as members lacking resources and capabilities to meet their consumption needs. The resources and capabilities are usually defined as members not having enough income or resources to meet their daily consumption needs. Often the starting point to measure and monitor poverty is to estimate the income earned or economic resources possessed by the members of a household. The World Bank has given a benchmark of $1.90 to $3.10 per day as the threshold to measure poverty levels among community members (World Bank, 1990a, 2001, 2015, 2017a, 2017b). However, it includes various other dimensions, such as health, education, and consumption. The Indian Government has adopted the sustainable development goal of poverty reduction through financial inclusion and women empowerment. As per Amartya Sen (1980), poverty arises when people lack key capabilities in terms of adequate education, income and employment to meet their needs. This deprivation further leads to insecurity and low self-confidence, and self-esteem. In this book, we have adopted a consumption benchmark of $3.10 per day as the benchmark indicator of poverty. Entitlement rights and the right to own property and resources form the genesis of the problem of poverty. Poor people are often socially excluded and are deprived of the right to hold and exchange things. This is often referred to as exchange entitlements (Sen & Foster, 1997). The people below the poverty line do not have the right to exchange resources and items. Not only do they lack resources and endowments, but they are also excluded from exchanging things and accessing financial resources in the form of credit and debt. Thus, per the famous economist Amartya Sen, it becomes essential to analyse the ownership of resources and the rights to exchange entitlements and resources (UNDP, 1991). Human Development Report defined poverty as the ability to avail and make choices. It includes the ability to live a life of dignity. Freedom from poverty is often described as the ability to live a long and healthy life. It is referred to as the ability to exercise political choices and political freedom with a guarantee of human rights. United Nations Economics and Social Council (1988) has defined poverty as freedom from insecurities, deprivations and exclusions. Defining poverty and designing policy interventions to combat poverty is extremely important. Most of the earlier research cites that poor people do not have access to financial services and do not own any property or physical assets to access financial services. They do not have any collateral which can enable them to access credit.

Moreover, banks and financial institutions do not have any information about the creditworthiness of poor people. This leads to the financial exclusion of the poor, which further leads to the inability to avail of suitable employment opportunities. Fig. 1 provides a basis for the classification of various causes of

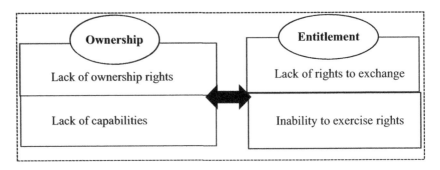

Fig. 1.   Reasons for Poverty. *Source:* By the Author.

poverty. Poverty could be either due to the lack of ownership of physical assets or due to the lack of ability to exercise the rights or entitlement, leading to deprivation.

Social exclusion refers to the exclusion of process and outcome. In the process, social exclusion refers to the exclusion of the members from participating in social, economic, political and cultural activities. Amartya Sen defined social exclusion as the denial of freedoms and the inability of persons to take advantage of opportunities because of policy initiatives. Thus, broadly defining poverty, the background factors could be constitutive that are inherently bad, such as social exclusion, caste discrimination, racial discrimination and policy initiatives that abstain specific individuals from enjoying freedom. Or the factors could be instrumental, which are not inherently bad but can lead to consequences such as lack of access to credit markets.

Poverty Reduction and Women Empowerment

Poverty reduction is one of the sustainable development goals, and gender inequality is one of the primary reasons for the increasing poverty levels in the nation. Various studies highlight that households where women have their entrepreneurship ventures tend to have higher income and lower poverty levels. Similarly, many other factors impact the level of poverty. Poverty is a multidimensional concept and a puzzle that is influenced by and leads to many other problems, such as income inequality, unemployment, vulnerability to disasters, poor health, climate change and lack of education. This view mainly attributes poverty to various macroeconomic factors.

Where Is the Bedrock of Poverty?

Is gender inequality the bedrock and the key to achieving sustainable development? It is imperative to improve the participation of women in day-to-day decision-making. As far as the financial inclusion of the poor is concerned, there is a presence of gender inequalities. From the literature analysis, it becomes apparent that approximately 40% of poor women do not have any access to financial services. And 20% of the female population do not have any access to bank accounts. It is imperative to make women aware of their fundamental rights. There is a need to develop gender-friendly goals to develop smart products and services that cater to the unique needs of women. Information asymmetry is one of the major challenges faced by women in India. Women in rural India do not have any information about the financial products and services available in the market. Organisations must undertake capacity-building initiatives such as training and skill-building initiatives to facilitate women's empowerment. In different parts of the nation, the women members face difficulty accessing financial services. In most households, the women members report crimes inflicted upon them as domestic violence or lack of autonomy. Women generally do not have access to financial resources and depend on their parents, households, friends and informal networks to access finances and funds. There is a need to make changes in the regulations and laws and make them women-friendly. In most cases, the women depend on their husbands to access money and economic resources. The members of big traditional families are generally more inclined to have a male child than a female child. Over time, women in India are repeatedly being afflicted with various crimes such as poverty, rape, and attempts to demand dowry. The major reason behind these increasing social problems is the presence of disparities and the presence of a patriarchal system of governance. In patriarchal societies, there is a need to promote the equitable distribution of resources by providing them access to equitable opportunities. The Indian Government has undertaken various schemes and initiatives, including Government transfers and social welfare schemes such as the Sukanya Smridhi scheme to promote the empowerment of the girl child and promote the holistic development of women. Women need to be empowered by promoting autonomy in financial planning and decision-making. Within the social context of a village, the women members lack access to any physical collateral, which prevents them from accessing formal credit. Moreover, the extant literature highlights that women with higher levels of financial literacy can better manage their households and stand up for women's rights in the family. They can better fight the menace of domestic violence and promote harmony among family members. Attaining gender equality is one of the sustainable development goals, and gender equality further leads to economic growth. Various studies establish that a higher education level among women leads to lower inequalities and poverty. Women's economic and social independence leads to the reduction of economic inequality and higher employment opportunities. One of the major reasons for poverty among the people at the lower levels is the lack of women's empowerment. The levels of social exclusion are extremely high among the women members due to the lower level of education and various forms of behavioural and cultural biases. Various strands of literature define women's empowerment as gaining control over their lives by accessing choices in the strategic context. In this regard, it is essential to understand how access to financial services impacts women's lives at the bottom of the pyramid. One such initiative is the unique group lending initiative started by NABARD in 1992. This initiative provides access to financial services to the poor people at the bottom of the pyramid. In accessing the loans from the self-help group, the members need not have access to the physical collateral or any information about the poor. A homogenous set of people from a common background or geography generally forms these groups. These members already have information about each other and thus provide a guarantee. Through social capital, the poor members of the group get access to financial services in the form of loans and credit. Thus, the self-help groups ensure access to financial services for women in the unorganised sector. Individual-level factors impact poverty, including education, income, access to financial resources, ownership of assets, family demographics and psychographics. Similarly, macroeconomic factors such as climate change, economic resources, governance and availability of clean water and sanitation impact poverty. Besides the individual-level factors, various other contextual factors, such as the level of crimes, climate change, environmental quality and socio-economic infrastructure, impact the country's poverty levels. The existing studies have cited various elements that are important for fighting poverty. These factors include education and training, resilience to climate change, economic resources and basic needs, financial support, governance and social support.

Poverty Due to Factors of Constitutive Relevance

Impact of Socio-Cultural Factors

Social exclusion is a mechanism or process by which specific communities and people are excluded and disadvantaged due to the discrimination they face in terms of gender, race, religion, caste, age, etc. In a society, the rules govern the behaviour of the community members. Through a process of negotiation, these rules and laws become customs. These customs govern the behaviour of individuals and give rise to the social attitudes and values in a particular society. The state then enforces these laws in the form of constitutional mandates. However, in some cases, the loopholes in the existing laws lead to discrimination and exclusion of certain groups. A straightforward example of social exclusion is discrimination among the members of society based on their place of domicile or birth. There is no mechanism to control the exploitation of the discriminated group. Poverty is a complex problem with multiple dimensions. Various socio-cultural factors such as religion, custom, family background, norms and values impact the poverty level in emerging economies. The social environment of a person has a profound impact on the economic prosperity and wellness of a person. Besides, the economic definition of poverty means an individual living at less than $1.90 to $3 a day. But poverty can also be defined as societal poverty. Societal poverty implies the ill-treatment of an individual at the hands of state agencies and society. The primary research highlights that people who lack access to financial resources are at risk of cultural exclusion. India is a diverse nation with people from diverse social backgrounds living together. Various negative cultural factors, such as prevalent customs, traditions and casteism, lead to vulnerability and increased poverty among the people at the bottom of the pyramid. Looking through the lens of social stratification of society, poverty is most prevalent among the economically disadvantaged sections of society, including people from scheduled castes and tribes. Minority communities are excluded from participation in economic activities and social activities. This discrimination and social exclusion lead to the problem of the vicious trap of poverty. Social exclusion leads to the denial of fundamental human rights among the members of society. Through the lens of entitlement theory, poor people are excluded, marginalised and relegated from participation in social activities. Social exclusion leads to exclusion from the right to life of dignity. It also leads to various discriminatory forces such as racism, casteism and unenforced civil rights. Different authors propagate that the lack of distributional rights is at the heart of the prevalence of poverty. India is a diverse country with multiple cultures and customs. Poverty is the cause and consequence of social exclusion. Customs have a significant role in impacting the economic and social well-being of the nation's diaspora.

Thus, though poverty in developing countries such as India has declined in absolute terms, in cultural terms, or in terms of exclusion, poverty has increased. This is adequately reflected in the increasing social crimes like dowry deaths, suicides due to higher debt levels, and social ostracisation. Social inequalities in society have increased manifold. Greek historian Aristotle has defined poverty as the inability to undertake significant economic activities. Further, Adam Smith has described poverty as the inability to face the public without shame. Most of the seminal literature on poverty has highlighted the relevance of customs and traditions in determining the economic status of the members of society. Thus, practices have a significant role in determining a country's economic status.

Within the Indian constitution, *the fundamental right to equality* is enshrined as a basic right, and theoretically, the caste system has been completely abolished. However, the ground reality is very different. Until recently, the caste system classified millions of people as untouchables and Harijans as outcastes. The people from the lower classes are denied work and access to basic amenities such as drinking water and shops, leading to economic inequalities and extenuating poverty. In a developing economy, within the theoretical framework of a financial system based on a rhetoric of equality, the rich and poor compete for limited economic resources. Due to the existing social setup with vast social inequalities, the wealthy class dominates and claims ownership of natural resources leading to the social exclusion of the poor. Thus, the neoclassical theories of a free-market economy do not apply to developing nations fraught with inequalities. Poverty in poor economies is a product of market failure due to the existing social pressures, norms and cultures. The media and other international agencies and institutions have undertaken many social movements to subvert the perils of caste-based discrimination and the subjugation of fundamental rights. An example of such a celluloid movement is *Dalit cinema* in India, which has been operating since the 1960s. These movies lead to a public debate about the social realities existing among the poorest sections of society. The entire film genre is dedicated to the cause of the oppressed and poor, who struggle hard to make a living. Popular cinema, since the 1950s, has made a subtle effort to give voice to the struggles of the poor sections of society.

Inequality and Relational Poverty

Relational poverty refers to a phenomenon when poor people are unable to participate in society or community. Much to the dismay, before the coming of Indian cinema and in the pre-independence era, the scenario in terms of class stratification was highly pathetic. Indus valley civilisation that existed 2,500 years ago is a testimony to the social stratification within the society. India is a diverse country with a rich culture, with a diverse history of rulers and kingdoms. Aryans from Central Asia introduced the caste system in India to control their vast kingdom in Southeast Asia. The narratives and chronicles from the Gupta Empire to the rule of Harshvardhan Raya in Southern India tell tales of how our holy scriptures granted a divine right to the ruling class and the priest class to control the general population through class stratification. Vedic scriptures, including the four Vedas, Upanishads and Bhagavad Gita, elucidate the existence of various courses and thousands of castes. Ancient Hindu manuscripts such as Vedas and Puranas, dating around 1700–1100 BCE, mention caste distinctions. From 200 BCE to 200 CE, Bhagavad Gita highlighted the importance of caste in India. The *Laws of Manu* and *Manu Smriti* highlighted the significance of the *Varna System*. The scriptures propagated the origin of humankind from the body parts of an *Adipurush*.

Untouchables, or the Dalits in Hindu society, were considered the most menial and lowest category of human beings. They were out-casted from Indian culture and were not allowed to be part of the social system. These members of society were involved in menial jobs like *scavenging animal carcasses, leather work, or killing pests.* Despite the historical glories of a golden age, after annexation to the British Empire, the gory realities of class stratification emerged as extreme subjugation of the marginalised sections and minorities. The advent of the British empire in 1757 with the establishment of British rule under administrators like Job Charnock, who adopted Indian customs and exploited the Indian social fabric of caste stratification, laid to extreme exploitation of the marginalised (Riser, 2009). It is the cradle of Asian culture and religions such as Hinduism, Sikhism and Islam and adopted multiple faiths like Christianity. Our nation has acceptance and tolerance for various beliefs and traditions. This diversity has led to social equality and the demolition of the ivory towers of the upper caste. Still, the communal strifes and conflicts pose significant hindrances to the country's development. The testimony to the contribution of cultural and subjective norms to the level of poverty in the country is the plight of *tribes in India.*

Though most social researchers believe that the lack of capabilities is the cause of poverty, the fact is that deprivation is the cause of failure and social exclusion. As aptly described by the Noble Prize-winning economist Amartya Sen, the notion of capabilities is individualistic and negates the social context of poverty. In an emerging economy with myriad inequalities, poverty is a product of social exclusion and deprivation. The central point to be noted here is that every kind of deprivation is not exclusion. Exclusion emerges from the problem of relatedness. When individuals are not permitted to relate to others, it leads to poverty. This is generally in the form of denial to let an individual participate in community activities. In a culturally diverse nation like India, which is the cradle of civilisation, the marginalised communities generally comprise cults and people who have been practicing a particular form of art for centuries. These people earn their livelihoods from family art or practice like sculpture making, weaving, beads work, handicrafts, snake charmers, etc. In modern society, the state's rules govern day-to-day life through customs and norms. But the implementation of these norms in the form of legal acts leads to the loss of cultural rights for these tribes, leading to social exclusion and accentuating poverty among the members of these groups. One such example is the *Qalandar* community of Karnataka. The members of this community make their living from the rearing of snakes and animal shows. However, despite such acceptance, they are subjected to harassment and lack opportunities to make a living by practicing art. Modern society tortures and discriminates against the legal existence of these communities, leading to large-scale poverty among people. This is also called the *constitutive relevance* of social exclusion.

Similarly, the *Kalbelias or Jogi Nath*, the snake charmer community of Rajasthan, live in the hamlets far away from the mainstream. The outsiders are not allowed to visit these hamlets and villages. In the *Bejati* village in Uttarakhand, caste discrimination is prevalent in this hamlet. The untouchables in this village mainly pursue traditional and artisanal work, which comprises vocations such as *Ordh, Lohar, Tamta, Dholi*, etc. They are not allowed to enter and have meals with the upper-class members in their villages and hamlets. The paradox of this community is that they have peacefully accepted the mandate and customs prevailing in an unjust society. Without Government support in the form of quotas in jobs and Government transfers, they are unwilling to fight for their rights. This further leads to poverty and misery in this community. Similarly, in the Attappady tribal block of Kerala state, the *Adiya* and *Paniya* tribe in the Wayanad district face abject poverty and a lack of dignified life. Attappady is one of the most culturally diverse districts, home to 27,121 tribes, out of which Irula is the most prominent tribe, followed by the Muduga and Kurumba groups. 25% of the tribal households live below the poverty line in abject poverty, and a vast majority do not even hold a ration card. Many of the kiths and kins of the fisherfolk community suffer from wasting, stunting and malnourishment. Thus, considering the social fabric of a diverse country like India, the problem of poverty is multidimensional. Cultural and subjective norms have a significant impact on the level of poverty in a particular community. These people who belong to small communities or in occupations that are looked down upon or frowned upon generally face a lot of humiliation and exclusion at the hands of state and institutional machinery. This is a form of *constitutive relevance*[1] of social exclusion. This is constitutive relevance as it restricts the capability of specific individuals to participate in day-to-day activities. Inherently, it is highly inhuman and immoral.

Poverty Due to Factors of Instrumental Importance

Impact of Financial Inclusion

One of the studies by the Asian Development Bank found that it's mostly the low-income and micro-sector enterprises that cannot afford and thus are financially excluded. The disadvantaged members of society or the members who lack access to financial services due to the lack of collateral and information about the creditworthiness of the poor are unable to participate in the functioning of the economy. The United States brought forward the notion of financial inclusion in 2005. The year 2005 was declared the International Year of Financial Inclusion. Reserve Bank of India (RBI), in April 2005, defined financial inclusion as a policy measure to ensure access to financial services for the poor. Most of the financial literature highlights the cost of poverty that the poor impose on society. This cost is mainly in the form of social costs and underdevelopment, and retardation of economic growth. Financial inclusion enables poor people to participate in economic and financial decision-making regarding consumption and investments. Financial inclusion ensures access, availability and usage of financial services for the poor. Most of the financial exclusion in the underdeveloped world is primarily involuntary, as the members of the society do not have access to financial services due to the lack of financial infrastructure, financial income, resources and capabilities, and market failures, including imperfections. Many earlier studies have looked into the dimension of financial inclusion and poverty Burgess and Pande (2005) found that expanding the rural financial infrastructure through bank branches helps reduce poverty and income inequalities in the economy. Mainly, the opening up of bank branches in rural regions helps to reduce poverty. Thus, most financial literature has consensus that financial development through financial inclusion reduces poverty and leads to economic growth. Various approaches to measuring poverty are given by Ruggeri Laderchi et al. (2003), including the participatory, social exclusion, capability and monetary approaches. Moreover, various financial techniques highlight that financial development and inclusion help increase the capacity to absorb financial shocks, smooth consumption and invest in health and education.

Various studies highlight that financial inclusion helps reduce income inequality in low-income countries by ensuring the equitable distribution of resources. Similarly Brune et al. (2011) finds that financial access through universal bank accounts reduces poverty among poor nationals. Honohan (2008) has highlighted that income inequalities and social underdevelopment lowers financial access and lead to poverty. Thus, many studies emphasise that financial exclusion leads to poverty. Usha Tharot report in 2007 has highlighted the role of banks and formal financial institutions, like Post Offices, in promoting financial inclusion among the poor. According to the literature, financial inclusion leads to access to financial resources, thus reducing inequalities, promoting savings among the poor and promoting economic growth.

Without access to financial services, poor people often resort to accessing finance from informal channels such as money lenders and shopkeepers. Besides the lack of financial infrastructure, the lack of financial literacy is the other reason for the financial exclusion of the poor. Many models and measurement techniques measure the poverty ratio as a function of financial inclusion and deepening. Endogenous growth theory highlights how financial development leads to a higher level of economic growth in the country. Approximately 734 million people live in extreme poverty, and they do not have access to financial services. Also, these people do not have the required level of financial literacy to access financial services. Thus, various supply-side and demand-side challenges inhibit access to financial services for the poor. Most unbanked people suffer from different demand-side challenges, including psychological barriers and exclusion, and condition exclusion, which includes the lack of financial literacy and education. Despite having access to financial infrastructure, in terms of access to financial services, many individuals in India cannot use financial services due to a lack of financial literacy. Most of these studies using various techniques highlight that financial inclusion leads to a reduction in income inequalities. Financial inclusion enables poor people to access financial credit, avail of investment opportunities and earn income through the promotion of savings among the poor. Thus, most of the literature and studies highlight that financial inclusion helps reduce inequalities, broaden access to credit, nurture entrepreneurial activities, and increase consumption and investment activities among the poor members of society. Through the various Government schemes such as subsidies and government transfers, financial inclusion helps to reduce the inequalities among the poor and thus reduce poverty. Financial inclusion benefits the poor people of rural society, particularly the young and the women. Financial deepening and financial inclusion through financial inclusion have a far-reaching impact on the development of the economy. One such scheme that has led to financial development through financial inclusion is (Pradhan Mantri Jan Dhan Yojana). This scheme has led to the universal bank opening under this scheme. This financial development and inclusion help to reduce socio-economic risk by promoting equitable distribution of resources and promoting the outreach of financial services to the poor. Financial inclusion helps poor women break the vicious cycle of poverty by promoting higher returns on investment.

The Trade-Off Between Profitability and Social Objectives – Mission Drift

In the 1960s, for the first time, the Indian state introduced the concept of financial inclusion. Until the 1990s, most financial initiatives aimed at providing microfinance to the poor were subsidy-based. However, in the 1990s, after the liberalisation of the economy, emphasis was paid to promoting sustainable finance. The focus of microfinance is fast shifting from subsidised microfinance to the market provision of finance to the poor. The literature highlights the dual mission of financial institutions, which includes achieving the goal of financial sustainability and achieving higher profits and return on investment (ROI). The roots of the concept of mission drift lie in two approaches to financial inclusion: the 'financial system' and the poverty lending programme. The financial systems approach emphasises large-scale outreach to the economically active poor – borrowers who can repay microloans from household and enterprise income streams and savers. It focuses on institutional self-sufficiency (Robinson & World Bank, 2001). The financial system approach mainly aims at building financial intermediation for the poor without financial support or subsidy. At the same time, the poverty lending approach concentrates on reducing poverty by providing access to concessional and subsidised credit for the poor. This credit is offered to poor borrowers at extremely lower rates of interest. The major objective of this approach is to enhance the well-being of the poor by providing monetary and social support. The Grameen Bank, run by Mohammad Yunus, has propagated this approach. Most banks and financial institutions do not find it worthy of lending to the poorer sections of society due to the lack of adequate profits. Thus, most formal and microfinance institutions face a trade-off between the outreach of microfinance to the poorest of the poor and financial sustain-ability through sufficient profits and returns on investment. One of the funda-mental poverty/sustainability questions is whether services can be delivered at an affordable cost to clients. Case studies and community studies highlight the importance of cost structures and delivery methodologies of microfinance institution.

This form of poverty exists when the members of society are financially excluded. This is the case of *instrumental* relevance, as it restricts the ability of the individual to participate. A case in point is the exclusion of the members of society from participating in the credit markets, which reduces the capacity of the members to take advantage of the additional economic opportunities. India is an agricultural nation, with the majority of the people in rural India depending on agriculture for their livelihood. These people lack collateral, and banks and financial institutions do not have any information about the creditworthiness of the poor. This leads to financial exclusion and thus leads to loss of livelihood and abject poverty among the poor. Not only are these farmers excluded from credit markets, but the existing regulatory laws, such as APMC (Agricultural Produce Mandi Act), do not enable these farmers to access free markets for their agri-cultural produce. The farmers in India are generally marginalised, and their land holdings are tiny. They suffer from information asymmetry and do not have any information about the market prices prevailing in the agricultural markets. They suffer financial exclusion, as they cannot access free markets and depend on the commission agents to sell their agricultural produce. This exclusion is also instrumental as it excludes the farmers from getting a fair price for their agri-cultural produce. This exclusion prevents poor farmers from taking advantage of income-earning opportunities. The exclusion of this form, where the loopholes in the existing regulations avoid an individual from participating in financial deci-sions and processes, is mainly passive. Only 1/3rd of the farmers have access to the agricultural markets, and only 65% have access to institutional credit. Most of the time, the agricultural markets lack the infrastructure facilities such as warehouses to store agricultural produce. This leads to chronic poverty and retards economic growth and economic development.

Digitisation and Modernisation of the Ghazipur Mandi

The Ghazipur flower market is famous for the sale of its beautiful flowers. This market is set for modernisation to provide a platform for farmers to sell their agricultural produce at a fair price. With the digitisation of the agricultural markets, the auction process has been automated. Electric and digital boards have been installed in all the Mandis to ensure the right price for agricultural produce. Further, the Delhi Government is planning the expansion of the infrastructure through the establishment of cold storage and a warehouse to facilitate the sale and purchase of agricultural produce. This modernisation of markets will facili-tate the provision of fair market prices to all the farmers for their produce. Despite all the efforts, the poor farmers must sell their agricultural produce

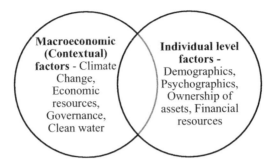

Fig. 2.   Factors Impacting the Level of Poverty. *Source:* By Authors.

through the commission agents. They are able to get fair prices due to the digitisation of the markets and the electronic display of the prevailing market prices. There is some hope that the digitisation of markets might eliminate the presence of intermediaries. These farmers are small farmers, and they are unable to get access to credit due to the lack of collateral. The banks and financial institutions do not have information about the creditworthiness of the poor. Fig. 2 provides the primary classification of the different forms of social exclusions that lead to the problem of poverty. A social exclusion with constitutive relevance is inherently bad and negative and leads to poverty. A case in point is caste discrimination, the denial of certain social classes from visiting the well and public places. And the instrumental relevance has consequences that are not bad but have effects, such as a lack of access to credit markets (Fig. 3).

Sustainable Development Goals and Poverty

UN (United Nations) has adopted the agenda of sustainable development to leave no one behind by 2030. The first sustainable development goal is to eradicate poverty in all forms. Thus, poverty poses a significant barrier and obstacle to achieving equality for all. Most of the sustainable development goals, such as zero Hunger, good health and well-being, quality education, and clean water and sanitation, are impacted by the sustainable development goal to reduce poverty. The end of poverty by 2030 is the major goal for the world. Various reports show that more than 700 million people live below the poverty line and struggle to fulfil basic requirements. And most of the poor live in Southern Asia and Sub-Saharan Africa. The problem of poverty is vicious as the people are linked to each other. Their level of poverty impacts the level of social cohesion and leads to an increase in social tensions. As per the latest research, promoting social equality by enabling a social environment and empowering individuals by providing safe drinking water, health, and sanitation services, education, and training is important. An integrated approach to sustainable development goals will help reduce the nation's poverty levels.

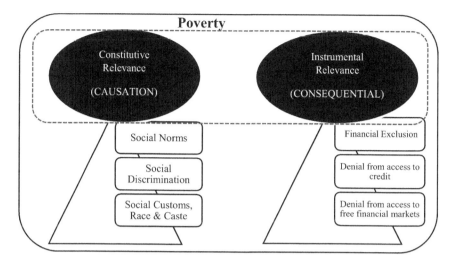

Fig. 3.   Sources of Poverty. *Source:* By the Author.

Fig. 4 briefly describes the various stakeholders involved in the reduction of poverty approach. The Government, community, family, and the public are all involved in implementing the policy initiatives towards poverty reduction. To reduce poverty at an individual level, policy initiatives are needed to ensure good health and education, reduce malnutrition, reduce child labour, reduce child trafficking, ensure the supply of clean drinking water and reduce gender inequality through the development of sustainable cities.

Dimensions of Poverty

UN SDGs have adopted the first sustainable development goal as poverty. Through the analysis of the literature, it was analysed that poverty manifests itself in the form of insufficient income, lack of appropriate work environment, lack of recognition for the work, social and organisation mistreatment, mental and physical harassment, struggle, and social isolation. The existing definition of poverty is narrow, as it not only implies the lack of income, hunger, shelter and clothing, health and sanitation and education. But in broader terms, it also means the vulnerability of poor people to external events beyond their control. For the people living in poverty, it becomes apparent that only financial income is not essential to determine the poverty level, but there is a need to include other factors such as freedom, social cohesion, and the natural form of governance. To overcome poverty, it is important to explore opportunities, facilitate the empowerment of the various sections, and enhance security. Thus, we can say that the definition of poverty includes three dimensions: (1) Freedom, (2) Social Cohesion (3) an Honest form of Governance (Fig. 5).

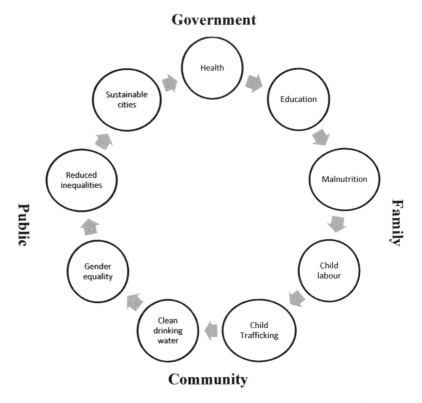

Fig. 4.   SDG (Sustainable Development Goals) Approach to Poverty.
Source: By the Author.

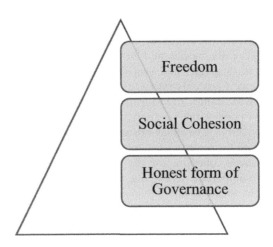

Fig. 5.   Broad Definition of Poverty.

(1) *Freedom:* Poverty is defined as freedom from deprivation. This implies that a person has sufficient capability in the form of situational context and possession of property rights that enable the person to lead a free life. Material possession includes the ownership of assets and physical artefacts. These allow a person to enjoy a free life. A person's capabilities depend on the level of education and skills that person possesses, and he will be able to lead a free life. A person's situational context and situation refer to the social contract that a person has with society. This enables a person to lead a life free from physical violence and fears. To exercise and enjoy freedom, an individual should have a social relationship with his society. He should possess faith and be sensitive to other people's rights in the community. They should have social capital and attitude to fulfil their commitments towards society. Thus, not only do the individuals possess the resources as capabilities but are so socially and culturally embedded in their social context that achieving the economic goals and objectives is not difficult for them.

(2) *Social Cohesion:* Social cohesion comprises various dimensions, including social inclusion, social mobility, and social capital. Social cohesion refers to the level of connectedness and solidarity among the group members. It refers to a person's sense of belongingness with other members of society. Social inclusion is the process of ensuring equal opportunities for people across sections of society. It is also the process of improvement, which includes improving the ability, dignity, and opportunity of the disadvantaged and marginalised sections of society. Certain people are excluded because they are destitute and discriminated against based on identity, ethnicity, race, religion, gender, age and level of disability. Thus, the ability of a person to access education enables a person to access the requisite opportunity, enabling a person to lead a life of dignity. Social exclusion is mainly the result of the existing lattice of power relations among the members of society. It leads to disparity among the various sections of the people. Social capital refers to the level of relationship that exists among the various areas of society. It refers to the bonding and the relationships that an individual possesses with the other members of the community. Social mobility refers to the shift in the status of a person from one social class to another social class. The change in social status can be either intergenerational or intragenerational.

(3) *Honest form of Governance:* Despite various social welfare initiatives, poverty and its adverse impact on the poor have not declined. The income growth for the poor has not been inclusive. Various factors, including the mix of political, economic, and institutional features of good governance, impact the level of governance in an economy. The control of corruption is facilitated through effective regulatory management and improving the ability and capability of the poor through financial literacy and social intermediation. In a democracy, it becomes even more critical to maintain the pillars of democracy in the form of participatory governance and transparency in government. It includes the conduct of public affairs in a

responsible manner and the management of resources. These principles of good governance include fair conduct of elections, representation and participation, responsiveness to change, efficiency, and effectiveness in governance, openness and transparency, the rule of law, the conduct of business in an ethical manner, the show of competence and clarity, innovation and honesty to change, sustainability and a long-term orientation, sound financial management, sensitivity to the human rights, cultural diversity, and social cohesion and accountability. To ensure democratic and free governance, the election must be conducted freely and fairly. Besides that, there should be a representation of the members and participation in all the activities. A free society should be open and transparent with due responsiveness to change. The social system should improve the effectiveness and efficiency of the integrated social system. It should exhibit sensitivity to the culture and openness of the other social systems.

Strategies for Poverty Reduction

Thus, poverty is a significant challenge that has vast repercussions for humankind. It manifests in the form of lack of adequate food, clean drinking water, health and sanitation facilities, lack of employment opportunities, with a need to undertake a sufficient amount of economic and institutional reforms to improve the efficiency and effectiveness of the microcredit programmes. There are various strategies to attain poverty reduction, which include the following:

(1) Increasing income through the economic growth
(2) Expanding employment opportunities for the poor
(3) Improving utilisation of economic resources through reforms
(4) Prioritising the basic needs of the poor
(5) Promoting microfinance programme to ensure financial inclusion
(6) Promoting entrepreneurship
(7) Providing private capital aid through Government transfers
(8) Improving the marketing systems
(9) Capacity building

The strategies for poverty reduction are aimed at promoting equitable economic growth. It includes promoting economic development through an increase in investment expenditure that leads to a rise in income. Employment opportunities for individuals need to be increased to promote inclusive economic growth. The need of the poor, who are below the poverty line, needs to be enhanced through financial inclusion and access to financial resources. There is a need to promote entrepreneurship and business acumen. To meet the financial needs of the poor, there is a need to provide state support in the form of government transfers and subsidies.

Moreover, the marketing systems and infrastructure need to be bolstered to promote the equitable distribution of economic resources. In the case of the agricultural markets, the poor farmers do not have information about the prices of the commodities. There is a need to disseminate information about market prices to the people at the bottom of the pyramid. The digitisation or electrification of the agricultural markets enables economic growth and development to promote poverty reduction.

Importance of Capacity Building

To reduce poverty, there is a need for concrete action on the part of developing nations to improve the economic performance and efficiency of the citizens. The nations often lack the capacity, human resources, or capital to implement economic reforms. Additional human resource and capacity is the key to poverty reduction. Institutional capacity involves several initiatives, which include the following:

(1) The ability to plan and manage the finances and budgets
(2) The ability to fight corruption
(3) To enable the smooth function of the regulatory authority
(4) To promote free and smooth market operations

Reducing poverty requires creating an enabling environment and developing skills to ensure effective financial management. There is a need to build the capacity to deliver the necessary services to the poor at the bottom of the pyramid.

Conclusion

Emerging economies suffer poverty, which is typically associated with market failure. 60% of the impoverished live in developing nations. Donations and subsidies managed poverty until 1990. Since the 1991 'post-Washington consensus', governments worldwide have accepted the sustainable development paradigm through sustainable finance, which prohibits charity or contribution to the needy. Shock therapy-based neoliberalism and market capitalism characterised it. Unlike their western counterparts, most poor people worldwide lack physical collateral and financial services like financial accounts and banking. This is a big issue for emerging nations. Banks won't help the poor. India managed poverty using pro-poor, developmental, and democratic participatory banking. This approach relied on market pricing and resource transfer, multilateral initiatives, democratic engagement, articulating the poor's viewpoint, and boosting entrepreneurship. Microfinance and community initiatives become poverty-reduction solutions. The government wants the poor to hold the state accountable through participatory programs like joint liability organisations. This was a departure from capitalism and corporate socialism, where transnational corporations serve the markets with the sole goal of profits, relying on weak state regulation and negotiation with civil society, which includes academia, which creates knowledge, markets, banks, and financial institutions, which protect it, often leading to speculation, accumulation, and disparity. Developing nations need a paradigm shift to satisfy the demands of the poor through millennium development. Developing countries must create a policy roadmap to reduce poverty and enable women to attain financial inclusion. The blueprint of the strategic map adopted by the state of India to achieve inclusive growth is based on an integrated approach to ensure equitable development through sustainable initiatives in the domain of education, training, health, gender equality, and clean drinking water.

Summary

Poverty is referred to as deprivation and lack of well-being. The economic bench-mark for poverty is an individual who spends less than US$1.90 and US$3.00 per day. The reason for poverty could be constitutive, which is inherently wrong, or instrumental, which can lead to dire consequences. Further, poverty could be due to macroeconomic factors such as climate change and economic resources or micro-economic factors such as demographics like gender. UN Sustainable Development Goals highlight the importance of poverty reduction. Various stakeholders, such as the Public, the Government, the Community, and the Family, are involved in poverty reduction. Initiatives in the area of poverty reduction, such as reduction of child trafficking, reduction of child labour, provision of clean drinking water, reduction in child trafficking, child labour reduction in malnutrition, and improvement of health and education are being undertaken in emerging economies to reduce poverty.

Note

1. Recent research focuses on classifying the types of social exclusion to be constitutive relevance and instrumental relevance as per Sen, A. (1980). Equality of What?. In *The Tanner Lecture on Human Values, I* (pp. 197–220). Cambridge: Cambridge University Press.

References

Burgess, R., & Pande, R. (2005). Do rural banks matter? Evidence from the indian social banking experiment. *American Economic Review, 95*(3), 780–795.

Honohan, P. (2008). Cross-country variation in household access to financial services. *Journal of Banking and Finance, 32*, 2493-2500. https://doi.org/10.1016/j.jbankfin.2008.05.004

Riser, K. S. (2009). The political intensification of caste: India under the Raj. *Penn History Review, 17*(1), 3.

Robinson, M., & World Bank. (2001). *The microfinance revolution: Sustainable finance for the poor.* http://lst-iiep.iiep-unesco.org/cgi-bin/wwwi32.exe/[in=epidoc1.in]/?t2000=014052/(100)

Ruggeri Laderchi, C., Saith, R., & Stewart, F. (2003). Does it matter that we do not agree on the definition of poverty? A comparison of four approaches. *Oxford Development Studies, 31*(3), 243–274. https://doi.org/10.1080/1360081032000111698

Saha, S. K., & Qin, J. (2023). Financial inclusion and poverty alleviation: An empirical examination. *Economic Change and Restructuring, 56*, 409–440.

Sen, A. (1980). Equality of What?. In *The Tanner Lecture on Human Values, I* (pp. 197–220). Cambridge University Press.

Sen, A., & Foster, J. E. (1997). *On economic inequality.* Clarendon Press and Oxford University Press.

UNDP. (1997). *Human development report.* Oxford University Press.

United Nations, Economic and Social Council. (1988). International Co-operation and Co-ordination within the United Nations System – Consumer Protection – Report of the Secretary-General.

Wang, Y. P., & Zhou, X. N. (2020, January 30). The year 2020, a milestone in breaking the vicious cycle of poverty and illness in China. *Infectious Diseases of Poverty, 9*(1), 11. https://doi.org/10.1186/s40249-020-0626-5

World Bank. (1990a). *World development report 1990: Poverty.* Oxford University Press.

World Bank. (2001). *World development report 2000/2001: Attacking poverty.* Oxford University Press.

World Bank. (2015). *Global monitoring report 2014/2015: Ending poverty and sharing prosperity.* World Bank.

World Bank. (2017a). *Monitoring global poverty: Report of the commission on global poverty.* World Bank.

World Bank. (2017b). *Closing the gap: The state of social safety nets 2017.* Technical report. World Bank.

Chapter 2

Social Capital as a Key to Sharing Prosperity

Flower Industry and Village Community of Meghalaya

Social capital is the new gold. Add value to others, value others,
and you will be valued.

By *Lynn Ujiagbe*

Social Perspective

*The villagers in the phulancha gaon of Nikamwadi harvest chrysanthemum and
marigold. The beautiful spectacle is spread as far as eyes can see, and there are
flower carpets. In the village situated in the Krishna basin, the agriculturists grow
sugarcane and turmeric. The fields are lush green with blooming marigold jhendu,
multi-coloured shevanti, Poornima white, Aishwarya Yellow, Pooja purple and
Pitamber Yellow. Similarly, the Mawlynnong village in Meghalaya is the cleanest
village with a well-developed flower community. The town has a beautiful community of florists, and the village residents work together to keep the city clean. A*

Microfinance and Development in Emerging Economies, 23–46
Copyright © 2023 Nishi Malhotra
Published under exclusive licence by Emerald Publishing Limited
doi:10.1108/978-1-83753-826-320231002

village set by the Anglican Christian Church community, this village is a perfect example of social capital and social transformation. The village's alleys are adorned with ornamental shrubs and tall areca nut palm lines. This is the village where the achingly beautiful universe meets against the blue skies and the scarlet vines, pink Jacobina, scarlet vine. In the Eden Garden of the east, the swathes of beautiful flowers and valley of happy flowers greet the visitors with the breeze of fresh air. The aerial roots of the rubber tree and the lush carpet of pine needles speak volumes of the care and grit with which the community nurtures this village. It is a testimony to the care and force of group dynamics and community. The town has an ethereal sense of quiet and serenity. Without any government help, the Khasi community has created a model of an ideal society. The abundance of flowering orchids and vines dangling down from the trees with bell-shaped flowers create an ambiance that speaks volumes about the ancestral culture and new history of this community. Social capital in the form of community relationships and values can be nurtured to achieve a sense of self-determination among community members.

Introduction

Poverty is a complex challenge faced by most of the underdeveloped and developing economies of the world. In India, approximately 228.9 million people live below the poverty line (Asian Development Bank, 2011). It is perhaps the only nation in the world where 19.7% of female-headed households are poorer than male-headed households. And 90% of the families live in rural regions. One of the significant challenges faced by India is to reduce poverty in all forms by half. As per various studies, inclusive growth is the only solution to mitigate poverty and other disparities. Poor people who live below the poverty line do not have access to physical collateral, and there is no information about the creditworthiness of the poor. This leads to the problem of financial exclusion and retardation of economic growth. To resolve this problem, NABARD introduced the Self-help group bank linkage programme in 1992. Self-Help Group Bank Linkage Program (SBLP) is a revolutionary initiative that formally linked group members – many of whom had never had a bank account before – to formal financial services in a sustainable and scalable manner. SHG Bank Linkage Programme is destined to become the country's dominant system of mass-outreach banking for the poor. In a decade, it became the dominant mode of microfinance in India, and the model has successfully encouraged significant savings and high repayment rates. According to the author, a group's social capital refers to the social relationships that exist among its members. In a group, social relationships keep the group members together and ensure trust and reciprocity. The strength of this form of capital is the prior information about the other members of the group. In a group, the member peer selects each other, leading to reduced adverse selection. Ex ante peer selection of the members and ex post peer monitoring and enforcement reduces the likelihood of default in the payment of loans. According to the study, group members tend to know one another and use peer pressure or the horizontal link among the members to push members to make frequent payments.

Social capital reduces the cost of microfinancing through the reduction of transaction costs in terms of monitoring and enforcement costs. Peer pressure refers to the interactions between members who are jointly liable while the individual is only partially liable (Van Bastelaer & Leathers, 2006; Maclean, 2010). Social capital is social collateral that assists in strengthening the group's sustainability through financial activities. The World Bank (2000) highlights the importance of social relationships and networks in achieving financial goals and objectives. It refers to utilising institutional linkages, structures and procedures, such as bookkeeping, meetings and adherence to NABARD's Panchsutras, to achieve a group's financial and institutional sustainability goals. The social capital in the case of specific anti-social programs is extremely negative.

Description of Self-Help Group Linkage Programme

Savings Help Groups was started in India by the Women members of SEWA International under the leadership of Ela Bhatt. In 1985, NGO based out in Southern India, Mysore Resettlement and Development Agency (MYRADA) in 1985. NABARD, jointly with the Canadian International Development Agency (CIDA), funded action research in 1987 into CMGs formed by the Bangalore-based NGO MYRADA. In 1987, NGO PRADAN introduced Savings Groups for Poverty alleviation in Rajasthan. In 1989, IFAD promoted Informal Borrowing and Lending programme. From 1987 to 1990, the Government was busy promoting and supporting Non-Government Organisations (NGOs). Nationalisation of banks was done in 1969–1971, Mandatory System of Priority Lending in 1972, Establishment of Rural Banks in 1982, and Piloting and Mainstreaming of the SHG Movement in 1992–1996. Most self-help groups were formed based on 'saving first and credit later'. In 1992, the government recognised the self-help group as an alternative credit model. This model was based on the principle of graduation, here it refers to how SHG moves up the ladder in terms of income and the factors that can promote it. SHG Bank Linkage involves partnerships between the SHG, NGOs and banks (Badatya & Puhazhendi, 2002).

Poverty and Social Contract Under SBLP

Protagoras, Epicurus, John Locke, Jean-Jacques Rousseau and Immanuel Kant all defined self-help groups as a social contract. A self-help group is a grouping of homogenous members with a common background. These members are homogenous in terms of profession or neighbourhood. The banks are wary of lending to the poor due to the lack of collateral and information about the creditworthiness of the poor. Globally, microfinance through group lending has changed the face of micro-lending. Formal financial institutions are wary of lending to the poor due to the high cost of microfinancing. Due to this reason, most of the poor are coerced to borrow from moneylenders. By doing away with the requirement to borrow using physical collateral, the group enables the members of the group to get access to financial services. In a group, the members undertake a mutual guarantee in the form of a joint liability to pay on behalf of each other in case of default. A social contract describes everyone's consent and agreement to enforce collective commitments. The preferential terms of a group lending contract facilitate the formation of the group through peer selection and the group's operation through peer monitoring and enforcement. In a self-help group, the members agree to undertake joint liability for the group. The banks extend credit to the poor members of the group in terms of collective liability. In case of default by an even member, if other members cannot pay the loan, the entire group will be denied the loan. Social capital in a social contract is a form of externality that promotes trust and reciprocity in the group. Thus, the micro borrowers, who stay at the bottom of the pyramid and would otherwise be denied any loan, are financially included through a self-help group linkage programme. The growing literature in the domain of behavioural economics propagates that the existing social ties or social capital are the primary factor that leads to the success of the group lending programme. Based on peer monitoring, in a joint liability group, the ability of the member to borrow depends on the repayment of the loan by the other members of the group. The set of interactions among the group members that originate from the set of relationships among the group members leads to financial inclusion through cooperative action. Srivastava and Samanta (2015) use six aspects to define social capital: 'Group and Networks', 'Trust and Solidarity', 'Collective Action and Collaboration', 'Social Cohesion' and 'Information and Communication'. In this context, 'Trust and Solidarity' refers to interpersonal behaviour that fosters better cohesion, 'Collective Action' refers to the ability of people to work together, 'Social Cohesion' refers to conflict mitigation, and 'Information and Communication' refer to how social capital helps to improve access to information. In a group, the members enter into a social contract.

The Paradox of Moral Hazard in a Group Lending Scenario

In a group lending scenario, the loans are provided to the micro borrowers, who do not have any physical collateral, and financial institutions do not have information about the creditworthiness of the poor. The banks and financial institutions do not find it commercially viable to provide loans to the poor due to the high cost of screening, monitoring and enforcement. It is presumed that the social contract of a joint liability group enables an individual to borrow in a group with joint liability. The social contract of a joint liability group is based on a debt covenant, that in case of default, all the members will be responsible for paying on behalf of the defaulter. In case of default, the bank will decline to extend credit to the group members. However, there is an increasing debate about the higher propensity to default among group members with social connections. There are increasing instances where the family member colludes to default on the loan strategically. In 1992, NABARD introduced the self-help group linkage programme. In this programme, the loans are extended to homogenous groups in terms of profession and geographic proximity.

Since the groups are not based on social connections, the group members are motivated to work together and monitor each other to maximise the group's profits. Initially, at the time of the group formation, the members of the same profession pre-select other members with the same degree of risk. This screening of the members in a group based on riskiness helps to reduce the moral hazard among the members of the group. Also, after the group's formation, the members monitor each other to ensure the repayment of loans and enforcement of the social contract. Thus, the self-help groups in India, formed through pre-selection and screening of the members based on prior information about the riskiness of the member, leads to a reduction in adverse selection. Also, the social contract among the members for lending from banks based on the joint liability of the group reduces the instances of moral hazard.

Case Study of Banswara Village

Microfinance considers the seasons and rhythms of rural life, and villagers prefer to meet on evenings related to the lunar cycles and many banks. Case in point Banswara asks villagers to repay their loans when the tree is called the Flame of Forest Blooms. Self Help Groups acknowledge the importance of the harvest and sowing seasons and provide for repayment as per the seasons and natural events. Internal Loans from the SHG vary widely. SHG offers various benefits to the members, who are mainly illiterate and landless. SHGs have helped to increase the income and assets of the members of the SHGs. SHGs help reduce the interest rates charged by Money Lenders and extend credit to the poorest; SHGs help form groups for the poorest of women, and with NGO support, SHGs, help promote social development.

Role of Social Capital as Collateral

Social capital in a group lending scenario enables an individual member to access loans by using social collateral. A joint liability group members share social relationships and networks with the other group members. They have preliminary information about the other group members due to their professional affiliation or the typical neighbourhood. Due to prior knowledge, the members in the group can peer, monitor each other and peer select each other, leading to a reduction of moral hazard and adverse selection. The social capital in the group is present in the form of horizontal relationships among the group members, who already know each other, or in the form of a vertical relationship between bankers and borrowers. Social capital can further be classified as cognitive or behavioural. Cognitive, social capital refers to the shared norms, rules, subjectiveness, trust and connectedness among the group members. Affective social capital refers to relational capital in social relationships among group members (Fig. 1).

The vertical relationships among the members exist in the form of relationships among the borrowers and the lenders. And the horizontal relationship exists among the members of the same group. Financing the poor or providing credit to the poor is fraught with the problem of ownership of assets and entitlement to

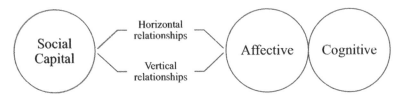

Fig. 1.   Social Capital in a Group Lending. *Source:* By the Authors.

exchange. From the literature analysis, it becomes apparent that the group's collective power improves the ownership rights of assets. Together, the group members can negotiate with the banks and financial institutions for the right to get microcredit. Various policy initiatives also help the members of the group to assess microcredit.

Systems View of Social Capital (Empowerment Strategy)

Social capital has been defined as the collateral among the members of the groups based on some form of social collateral and relationships among the members. The strategy to leverage social capital has been defined as the *Empowerment Zone Strategy*. The poor members leverage social ties and relationships to empower the people at the bottom of the pyramid. The closed social capital in a group comprises shared norms and institutional processes. The members of the group formulate the rules to govern the functioning of the group. Together the members of the group formulate rules for savings and credit. They get together to save money regularly over some time. Once they have saved enough through the pooling of internal resources, the banks link social capital to the group members. This functional capital in the form of closed and linking capital is essential in providing finance to the people at the bottom of the pyramid. The credit provided by the banks often acts as a catalyst and a tool of financial intermediation (Fig. 2).

Social capital has been defined as the set of internal cultures and values that govern the functioning of a collective and community-based organisation. The interactions and the exchange of importance among the members of the society lead to the bonding and consolidation of a financial community. Social capital leads to the transmission of knowledge about the creditworthiness of the group members. This further reduces opportunism and the risk of market failure in a collective initiative like group lending. Collective action mitigates the risk of adverse selection and moral hazard about a group. Thus, it can be presumed that social capital comprises relationships that lead to interaction among the members of the groups. This interaction leads to information sharing and mitigates the free-riding problem. This web of interactions among the members leads to the social contract through the consensus about the debt covenants. This facilitates access to financial resources, loans, and credit. Through the social contract based on prior information about each other, the members start trusting each other, leading to reciprocity and promoting cooperation by reducing opportunistic

Empowerment Zone Strategy

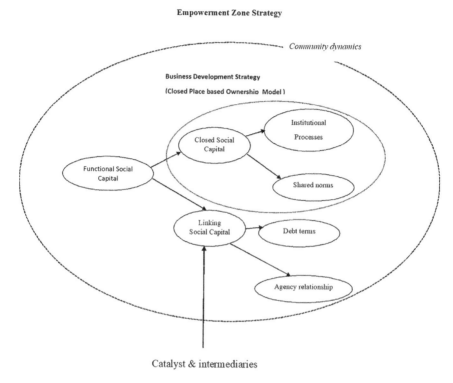

Fig. 2.   Systems View of Social Capital. *Source:* By the Authors.

behaviour. Social capital refers to the shared norms, relationships and values gained by the common social background in terms of neighbourhood and occupation. It can also originate through the possession of a common skill set. Social capital is often confused with the term grapevine, but this is not so. Social capital is a broader term than the informal communication network. The difference is consensus on rules and norms to refrain from doing certain things and following certain shared criteria. These rules and norms pertaining to corporate governance and disclosure of the financial operations of a community lending group play an important role in promoting the financial sustainability of the groups (Fig. 3).

Social capital is generally based on the proposition that the relationships among the community members are essential for achieving the stated goals. And social networks form an important part of social networks. Social networks and relationships are the mechanisms that lead to collaboration, cooperation and harmony among group members. Generally, economists are sceptical that social capital that originates among people under birth or family connections is not constructive and can lead to strategic default. On the other hand, the social capital that arises by virtue of skill, sweat and hard work often leads to a higher degree of social connectedness. This social connectedness enables the poor people at the

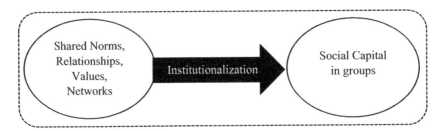

Fig. 3.   Social Capital Through the Institutionalisation of Shared
Norms. *Source:* By the Author.

bottom of the pyramid to achieve economic goals. Extant literature highlights
that social capital resides in the individuals who use this social capital for the
maximisation of utility and self-interest. Moreover, social capital is generated
under the social structure in which the group operates.

Metaphor of Capital

In defining social capital, the term capital refers to the capabilities that have a
transformative ability. In the case of social capital, which comprises social networks, the capital indeed has a transformative ability. It can leverage the existing
relationships to facilitate the entitlement to exchange social goods. Capital can be
either endowed or transferred as a legacy, or time might be spent by an individual
using his skill, time and hard work to generate social capital. Generally, social
capital is not conferred; it is earned or nurtured through hard work, skills and
time. Social capital has the property to make humans more productive and is also
an act of manufacturing. The actors in a social network contribute towards
manufacturing the social capital through their web of interactions, beliefs, attitudes and values. Thus, defining social capital as a source of transformative
abilities is essential to determine the sources and consequences. The source of
social capital is the networks and relationships, i.e., the social capital is relational
and structural. And social capital has certain consequences, which can be positive
and negative. In a positive sense, social capital can lead to cooperation, trust and
reciprocity. Social capital is an act of manufacturing, where the member's networks deliberately indulge in creating shared affiliations and understandings to
facilitate the exchange and creation of entitlement rights (Fig. 4).

Social capital originated through structural sources such as networks and
affiliations, which comprise educational associations, professional collaboration
and other groups. Social capital is manufactured mainly through communication
and information flowing through the networks. Structural social capital is
constitutive and is brought into existence through a deliberate attempt such as
legislation. Relational social capital is naturally occurring, and there is no need
for a conscious contract or agreement to establish such capital. An example of

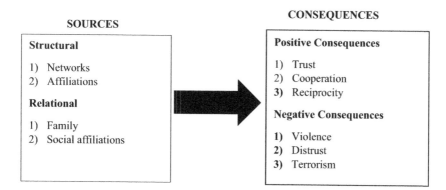

Fig. 4.   Operational Mechanism for Social Capital. *Source:* By the
Authors.

relational capital is social capital, which originated through family relations such
as relationships between family members.

Structuralist Approach to Social Capital

Social capital resides within the structure of the social groups. These social groups
are groups that are bound by some social factors. The social factors include
norms, laws, activities and practices, social institutions, social practices, social
conventions and the nature of the social context. It refers to the set of rules and
regulations that create an edifice of social customs that remain stable over time.
The social factors constitute a social structure, or the social factors contribute to
the formation of social groups. The social network structure determines the
hierarchy of relations within the group. In this context, the self-help groups have a
decentralised structure. A group of 8–10 people is a socio-economic structure
aimed at promoting savings among the people. These kinds of social networks
and structures are not naturally occurring, and they are more constitutive.
Generally, an NGO or Self-Help Promoting Institution (SHPI) hand holds a
self-help group to start their operations and promote savings and investments.
These groups are not naturally occurring, and the SHPI helps the group members
to constitute a group. The SHPI is instrumental in forming constitutive groups.
These groups have an unwritten constitution in terms of debt covenants, nature of
liability for the group, rate of interest to be charged to the members, the amount
of regular savings, and debt repayments. There are democratically elected cashiers
and group leaders that work as nodes in the group. Thus, one of the essential
features of the groups is that they are externally constituted. However, the groups
are constitutively dependent on the social factors that include the existing relations among the members of the groups in terms of homogeneity of profession
and domicile. Thus, the group is not a gerrymandered collection of people in a

natural environment. Rather the group members are selected on the basis of homogeneity of profession or occupation. This social ontology of the groups enables the operationalisation of the peer pressure and peer monitoring mechanism.

Dimensions of Social Capital

Social capital refers to the level of associations between individuals, organisations, beliefs and attitudes that leads to affiliation. This affiliation can be leveraged to get access to financial resources or other resources. The type of affiliation that form social capital comprises (1) relational social capital, (2) structural social capital and (3) affective social capital. Relational social capital contains structural artefacts, and affective social capital refers to reciprocity. Relational social capital is also referred to as the causal aspect of social capital, and affective social capital refers to trust, reciprocity and exchange, which is the effect of social capital. Structural social capital is again the causal factor. Still, a substantial part of the social capital can be seen in the network relations and institutions like groups, affiliations, and club memberships. It is more defined and hierarchal in the form of the roles, rules and processes to be followed. Some researchers also define social capital as bonding, linking and bridging. The bonding social capital refers to the relationship between various individuals. The linking relationship refers to the related groups, and the bridging relationships refer to the relationship of individuals to the banks or other entities.

On the other hand, relational social capital cannot be seen and can only be felt and seen. This is more a matter of subjectivity. This is related to the mental perceptions of the individuals. The individual belief systems and mental makeup of the person impact it. The norms among the members are referred to as relational social capital. These norms can be social in the form of customs or cognitive.

Case Study of the Dhokra Community in India

Dhokra is one of the most ancient art forms practiced in West Bengal near Bikna village. This art is a form of metal cast art that is practiced using lost wax. These Dhokra artists are generally from a nomadic community that practices a common art and have been staying together for ages. Generally, the artists involved in Dhokra art make metal wares, including figurines of animals, gods, goddesses, and animals like bulls, horses and elephants. This art is almost on the verge of extinction, and most artists struggle to make a living. This art is generally practiced by the artisan, who is extremely poor and illiterate and stays on the city's outskirts. They do not communicate with city dwellers and do not have access to financial services; in an interview with an NGO supporting these Dhokra artists, to form themselves into a group and helped them access financial services through linkages with the banks. The NGO head expressed concern about the plight of these artisans. And he elaborated that these artists generally are financially illiterate and they do not have any financial acumen. But they have strong bonding among themselves. They have been practicing this form of art for an extended period, so they are aware of the craftsmen ship and the financial character of other members. They stay in an integrated hamlet and hence are in close proximity. This is called social capital and enables the members of a Dhokra group to access loans from the banks based on their existing relationships. Though their work is seasonal, with Government support in the form of international exhibitions, this community on the verge of extinction has a scope to do well and prosper. They develop trust and choose the other members of the group based on prior knowledge about the risk propensity of the members. They share common social values and have skills in their hand, passed on from generation to generation. The unique designs and improvisations are known to the members, who spend time teaching others in the group the handicraft. Thus, this art form exemplifies how social capital can contribute to protecting our legacy and heritage.

Social Capital and Exchange

Social capital resides in individuals, groups, organisations and communities. An example of social capital in an individual is Ela Bhatt. An example of social capital in a group is the Grameen Bank. The social capital among the group members plays an essential role in facilitating the exchange. This propensity to exchange is often derived from the presence of structural social capital. Structural social capital refers to the existence of network relations among the members of the lending groups in the form of horizontal relationships among the members of the community and vertical relationships that exist among the superiors and the subordinates. And shared cognitive capital refers to the shared understanding of the language and codes among the community members. It relates to the interpretation of the shared reality among the group members.

Example of Social Capital in Paniya Tribe

The Paniya tribe is found in Kerala's Kozhikode, Wayanad, Kannur and Malappuram districts. Today tribes form 16% of the total population of this district (Bluhm et al., 2014). The *Paniya* tribe is the largest and has been recognised as the Scheduled Tribes. Paniya means someone who does the labour or is a manual worker. The common belief is that they originated from a hilltop called *Ippimala.* They seem to have developed from twin brothers and sisters co-joined as twins. In the local language, this couple is known as Ippimala Muttasi and Ippimala Mutappe. Some texts also mention that the Paniya tribe was brought to Kozhikode, Wayanad, through a ship that came and landed on the Malabar Coast. The house of a Paniya is called a *pire* or *kudumbu.* And the house of the Paniya tribe, made with bamboo and leaf trees, is known as the *paadi.* The women from the *Paniya* tribe wear different ornaments, including earrings, known as *oolay.* These earrings are made using coconut palm leaves with *lucky red seeds* known as *manjadikuru.* Another kind of earring is the *choonthumani.* They play musical instruments called *chenni* and *thudi.* This particular tribe has harnessed social capital in the form of prior information about each other. Social capital refers to the presence of the web of social interactions among the members of the group. Local communities play an essentially important role in resource management and decision-making. Various internal and external factors impact the aim or objective of poverty reduction. Internal factors that impact the achievement of the community goals. These internal factors include the socio-economic attributes, governance structure, accountability and endowment of natural resources. The external factors include the forest policy, proximity to the markets, political context and regional governance structures. Internal and external factors play a significant role in the achievement of the objectives of the community. Most of the local communities in the nation have extremely high levels of poverty. The communities' management of the forests is a far more effective approach to forest management. Due to the diverse nature of organisations, there is a need for forest conservation and community management.

Example of Social Capital in Organisations

Organisations are social entities with multiple relationships with suppliers and vendors, competitors and external agencies, including the state government. These entities or organisations indulge in the web of relational interactions with the other organisation members. Organisations can nurture long-term relationships with other stakeholders. The members of an organisation have Intra organisational and inter-organisational relationships. This is often referred to as bridging capital. To leverage the bridging capital, it is essential to leverage the norms of the group and the norms of the network to leverage the capital. Inter-organisational relationships refer to the relationships with the other and external vendors, and intra-organisational relationships refer to the relationships with the internal agencies such as the departmental agencies. In a collectivist culture, the human being is identified as the relational being, and social affiliation is essential in determining the meaning of the actions. Contextual factors become essential in a collectivist culture. The organisation exchange depends on the power distance, which determines the level of social interactions. In a closed organisation, the lower level of power distance enables the community members to interact closely with each other. This is often referred to as horizontal coordination, leading to democratic and consultative governance. The informal interactions among the members of the collectives are often referred to as horizontal social capital. This social capital promotes exchange among the members in the form of credit offtake. In an open society, the power distance between the community members is quite wide. And the power relations are generally hierarchal. Example of such organisational structures is MFI (Microfinance institutions) or Bank linkages, where the members have a vertical relationship with the members of the society. The members of society, who do not have capabilities and entitlements, are part of a relational setup. They have an interdependent relationship with the community or the collectivist arrangement in which they are embedded.

Social Capital and Information Flow Through the Networks

One of the major positive aspects of social capital is that it reduces the information asymmetry among borrowers and lenders. In the case of a social group, the members have access to soft information about the members of the group, which makes lending easy. The prior information about the group members leads to trust and reciprocity, which further leads to access to financial capital from formal financial institutions. Thus, the main reason for forming the groups is the existence of soft information. When the groups start functioning, the members start saving together. This leads to the generation of complex information in the form of records of savings, attendance, and meeting minutes. Thus, in the case of group lending, the generation of information through the maintenance of books of accounts can be used to generate the index for measuring social capital. The source of information that can be used to promote internal lending through the group members and external borrowing from banks can be summarised as (1) soft information and (2) hard information.

Fig. 5 explicitly states that the source of social capital in a collectivist and community context is soft information in the form of ex-ante information and prior information about the group members. And complex information is generated in the form of accounts regarding the savings and repayment of loans. This is an important part of corporate governance and is a mechanism to achieve financial sustainability in a group.

Case Study of a Self-Help Group in India

The group leader selects members with the skill set, gives them livelihood, and attaches them to the group. All the members of the group are acquaintances. In

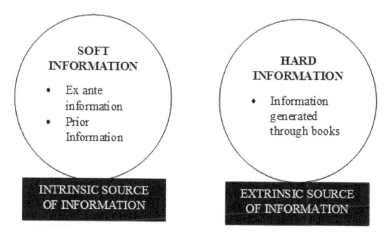

Fig. 5.   Information as Source of Social Capital. *Source:* By the Authors.

the group, members get a livelihood, and we feel that the Government is not cooperative in providing the loan. The bank loan is cheap in terms of the interest rate. Giving a loan is tedious, and bank officials are wary of lending to the members. They are very arrogant and do not know their work. We do not try for loans; we generate a surplus from handicrafts and have ISO certification and a barcode. We feel that a loan is feasible for people who do not have funds. Meetings are conducted regularly every week. Group formation and sustenance are other things. We make members self-reliant; we give them livelihood. Firstly, we provide them with livelihood and teach them savings habits. All the members are salaried people, and then we pool savings from their salaries. The members maintain the money dealings and minutes of meetings, savings accounting, and debit credit vouchers are done.

Then loan appraisal forms, personal files, and passbooks are maintained. I am a caretaker, and there is a woman leader. We are covered under Ajeevika and manufacture handicrafts, pickles, chips, curd, etc. We sell our products through the website. During COVID-19, we started manufacturing food products, but the sale of food products did not stop even during COVID-19. We have insurance for each person, so if any person dies, he gets an insurance claim. We open a bank account for each person at the Bank of India. The rate of interest for each person is 1%. We maintain the books of account. Our company is registered under Startup India. Members discuss the problems with each other. Meetings help to evaluate the amount of savings and loans taken. Leaders are rotated yearly; the women members select two years and new members. The women only know about the rules and regulations, and the member is seen before determining the member's creditworthiness. In the market, we know the member's reputation, as members are jointly responsible and individually responsible for their loans.

Social Capital in the Context of Microfinance in India

Self-help groups are collective organisations of 8–20 individuals, generally comprising women. These organisations are semi-formal institutions. DAY NRLM (National Rural Livelihood Mission) is the main programme established to develop and empower the micro-poor, particularly women. In India, women's self-help groups work together towards achieving common goals such as financial autonomy and achieving group goals of operational sustainability. Exploring the relationship between the operation of self-help groups and social capital formation becomes extremely important. In the Indian context, till the 1990s, most of the self-help groups were donor and subsidy based. Still, after the 1990s, with liberalisation, the emphasis was on replacing donor and subsidy-based finance with sustainable finance. Social capital can be claimed to be the missing link in the development of rural India. In self-help groups, social capital refers to the personal, familial, and professional networks that lead to trust, cooperation and reciprocity. Through the networking process, the groups formulate the rules for governing the societies and the self-help groups. The self-help groups are approximately 10 members who interact and work together to achieve the group goals. Within the self-help groups, the social capital can be defined as:

(1) *Relationship among the members of the group* – The members of the group select each other based on the homogeneity of profession, domicile, or neighbourhood. These members screen out the members who are not safe and form a group with only safe members
(2) *Relationships among the group and the government body*: The members of the group form relationships with the members of the state apex bodies
(3) *Relationships among the group members and the community* – The members of the group forge relationship between the members of the group and the community agencies.

Social capital is discussed as an individual concept throughout the literature regarding trust, cooperation and reciprocity. It can often be referred to as network relations within the community. Or it can be referred to as a societal concept in the form of shared norms and customs. This could be in the form of cultural capital, which refers to shared usage and traditions. The payoffs to the social capital depend on the type of contract among the people. Thus, the *social contract* is the primary vehicle through which social capital is exercised to ensure access to financial services. The social contract comprises the joint liability for the group, individual liability for the own loan, and acceptance of the group norms, viz., attendance, conducting meetings, repayment of loans, peer selection, peer monitoring and contract enforcement through peer sanctions. The graphical description of the social contract that gives rise to the social capital and thus the financial inclusion of the micro-poors is given in Fig. 6.

The social contract enables the members of the self-help groups to access financial services and credit (see Fig. 6). It reduces the cost of screening and monitoring the loans the individual gives. It leads to a reduction in transaction costs and makes lending viable for the members of the group. The joint liability of the group enables the group members to access financial services without the physical collateral. The formal institutions do not have information about the creditworthiness of the poor, and the joint liability refers enables the member to

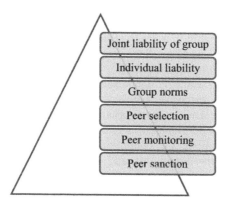

Fig. 6.   Constituents of Social Contract. *Source:* By the Authors.

access financial services. However, the members might strategically decline to repay the loans if the output generated by the group is lesser than the individual's liability. Due to the joint liability, the group members might collaborate to exercise peer pressure to maintain the financial discipline of the group. At the stage of group formation, the member's peer selects the other members who are homogenous with the existing members in the group. This helps to reduce the default in the group. Further, the group members monitor each other to achieve the group objectives. And in case of default, the sanctions are exercised to ensure financial discipline in the group.

Social Organisation and Role in Promoting Social Capital

In an economy, social organisations are essentially part of informal groups and are not governed by society's institutions. These organisations also include those involved in social activities, such as the legal and social environments. The resource-based view (RBV) and bricolage are the foundations of these organisations. The primary goal of most of these organisations is to achieve a competitive edge by utilising valuable, inimitable and rare organisational (VRIO) resources. These groups provide solidarity, allowing the organisation to participate in a democratic, participatory process. Social capital is the sum of norms, networks and social ties among community members. It refers to a collection of social networks that improve a community's social well-being.

Social capital is based on direct and indirect ties. Social capital as a resource actor derives from specific structures and then uses it to pursue interests; changes in a relationship create it (Adler & Kwon, 2002; Putnam, 1993, 2001). Social capital is the aggregate of various relationships and personal resources that are owned by the members of a community. It refers to the network of the set of institutionalized relationships of mutual acquaintance or recognition. From external ties, one definition describes social capital as a resource derived from structures. The other defines it as resources linked to relations. Social capital is not a single entity but a variety of different entities having two characteristics in typical. They all consist of a specific aspect of social structure and facilitate the action of individuals within that structure. Social capital has been defined as ability due to membership in a group (Halpern, 2005). This definition highlights the internal ties of the members. Social capital as the existence of a specific set of informal values or norms shared among group members that permits cooperation among them. More researchers define social capital is a 'a culture of trust and tolerance, in which extensive networks of voluntary associations emerge' (Inglehart, 1997). The size of a social organisation's network also affects its social capital. In community development, social capital has been defined as the norms, network and trust among the community members to facilitate cooperation among members of the community and to facilitate the achievement of community objectives (Mohan & Mohan, 2002). Complementary to both views, social capital is the sum of the network and the assets mobilised through the network (Pretty & Ward, 2001; Robison et al., 2002). One of the significant phases in the strategic management of an organisation is organisational appraisal and environmental appraisal. It comprises the strategic direction of the resources and capabilities. These resources include the availability of financial, human, and administrative resources. Effective utilisation of these resources is essential to achieve a competitive advantage. Resource availability and capabilities can be defined at individual, firm and interfirm levels.

At the individual level, the resources refer to the norms and values of decision-makers; at the institutional level or firm level, the resource-based refers to organisational culture and politics. The entrepreneurship view comprises three phases opportunity refinement, leveraging and championing. Opportunity refinement includes creating awareness of opportunities, leveraging, sourcing, acquiring resources, mobilising combined resources and advocating. In the case of microfinancing, the formal financial institutions are unwilling to lend to the micro borrowers due to a lack of collateral. Self-help groups under the self-help group linkage programme by NABARD aims to provide access to finance for the people at the bottom of the pyramid. These organisations can access finance through loans from a formal financial institution under the self-help group linkage programme through social capital. Social capital is a unique phenomenon that helps to replace physical collateral with social collateral in a group scenario and facilitates access to finance.

Community

Community refers to a specific geographic area with defined boundaries and comprises people with homogenous interests and activities. These organisations are the entity that comes together to serve the common good. It refers to the mechanism through which the community recognises the organisation's objectives and resources and leverages them to achieve the goal. These community organisations referred to achieving the objectives through the effective utilisation of resources and shared norms and values. Microfinance is a challenge for the people at the bottom of the pyramid due to the lack of collateral. Collective organisations provide a substitute for physical capital in the form of social capital and enable financial inclusion for micro borrowers. The key to financialisation is learning with the people, creating a new knowledge database, and creating institutional capacity. Community organisations enable collaboration and empowerment. Community organisations refer to the process through which the community's resources are diverted towards the welfare of society. Community organisations are defined as a set of 14 principles comprising effective organisation balance, planning as complex value-based, knowing the basic decision-making structure, opposition to change, making the change from inside, record-keeping and note-taking, media are unpredictable, and effective organisation balances product and processes. Microfinance-based (SHG Bank linkage) model emphasises that both the bank and MFI model drive their advantage over the population's competition and homogeneity. SHG Bank linkage programme increased the women's participation in group savings.

As mentioned in Fig. 7, social capital builds a relationship that helps people and community-based organisations access the necessary resources. Social capital

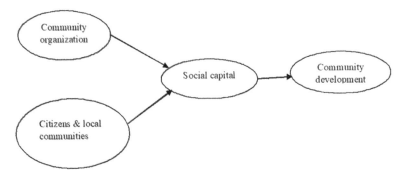

Fig. 7.   Impact of Community Organisation on Development
Through Social Capital.

is defined as a linkage that comprises (1) networks, (2) trust and (3) access to resources.

Social Capital

Social capital is the aggregate of resources obtained by a person or a group by possessing an enduring network of more or less formalised ties of mutual acquaintance and recognition. The social organisation aims to achieve its objective using its resources. Social capital refers to comradeship, collective efficacy, connectivity in network and structural equivalence, or uniformity of nodes across structures. Through the theoretical lens of the RBV, social capital in a community setup provides members of the network with the benefit from collectively owned capital. A hierarchal network resource comprises positions, authority, rules and agents connected to the source. Social capital refers to the investment in external relations by the members, by which they gain access to valuable contacts and information. And by investing in internal linkages, the members can exercise effective governance.

Social capital includes structural and cognitive components. Coleman & Roker (1998) refers to the network-based interpretation of social capital. The Social capital is located in the network structure. And situated in a network facilitated by closure and multiplex ties, it leads to the emergence of cognitive capital as norms, attitudes, trusts, and sanctions. Norms, values, attitudes and beliefs that produce and perpetuate positive interdependence of utility functions are called cognitive and social capital. Rules, processes, precedents and networks are examples of structural social capital that help people work together for mutual benefit. Social capital comprises norms, exchange reciprocity, group membership and social engagement.

There is no consensus on the definition of social capital, and different authors have given different meanings. As per the extant literature, the colonial capital has been designed as (1) the relations an actor maintains with other actors, (2) the structure of relations among actors within a collectively or (3) both types of linkages. As per the relations that an actor maintains, social capital is defined as a resource that allows a focused actor to take action on behalf of another actor. And thus, membership in a social network facilitates actor action through direct and indirect ties. As an outcome of relations, an actor maintains with other actors; social capital is defined as the ability of the people to work together by informal values or shared norms. Social capital has further been described as a culture of trust in which networks emerge. Social capital is organisation features such as norms, networks, and social trust that lead to cooperation and coordination. Emphasising the web of cooperative relationships, define social capital as means to resolve the collective action problem. From the perspective of social structure, social capital has been described as a social structure that facilitates specific actions of individuals within the structure. It has been defined as a resource that actors derive from specific social structures and pursue interests. From the dual perspective of relations between the actor and structure of relations, the colonial capital has been referred to as the sum of actual and potential resources embedded within and derived through a Network of relationships possessed by an individual or social structure. Hence to summarise, the set of resources made accessible to a group through group members' social relationships within the group's social structure, as well as in the broader formal and informal structure of the organisation, is referred to as social capital.

Community Organisations

Community refers to a specific geographic area with defined boundaries and comprises people with homogenous interests and activities. These organisations are the entity that comes together to serve the common interest. Community organisation refers to the mechanism through which the community recognises the objectives and resources of organisation (Internal/External) and leverages these resources to achieve the goal. These community organisations referred to the achievement of the objectives through the effective utilisation of resources and shared norms and values. Microfinance is a challenge for the people at the bottom of the pyramid due to the lack of collateral. Collective organisations provide a substitute for physical capital in the form of social capital and enable financial inclusion for micro borrowers. The key to financialisation is learning with the people, creating a new knowledge database, and creating institutional capacity. Community organisations enable the achievement of collaboration and empowerment. Community organisations refer to the process through which the community's resources are diverted towards the welfare of society.

Principles of Community Organisations

Community organisations comprise 14 principles:

(1) Effective Organizing Balances Process and Product
(2) Planning Is a Complex Value-based, Socio-political and Technical Process
(3) There Is No Such Thing as "Rational" and "Irrational" from the Perspective of How Problems Are Defined or Resources Are Allocated
(4) Know and Make Your Case; Principle
(5) The "Community" Is Not Monolithic;
(6) Know the Decision-Making Structures of the Target System: who holds The Formal power (Authority) as critical actors and who holds Informal power (Influence) as facilitating actors
(7) Do Not Assume that the target You Want to Influence Is a Unified, Monolithic System
(8) Assume Nobody Knows Anything, Anytime;
(9) Assume Goodwill and Common Cause on the Part of Those Who control and operate the System
(10) Assume the Principle of Least Contest. Escalate the Process Only as Needed
(11) There Will Always Be Opposition to Change at Some Level, Be it Active or Passive Resistance
(12) Making Change from the Inside, Assess Risks Realistically–Identify and Weigh Costs against Gains
(13) Recordkeeping and Notetaking are Political, not Clerical Functions;
(14) The Media Are Unpredictable and A-moral. Proceed with Caution.

Media are unpredictable, and effective organisation balances products and processes. Microfinance based (SHG Bank linkage) model emphasises both the bank and MFI model to drive their advantage over the competition and homogeneity within the population. Various studies have highlighted that exposure to the SHG Bprogramge programme increased women's participation in group savings.

Case Study: MAC Society (Mutually Aided Cooperative Society)

Each MAC society has one member, one family and one membership. They are from the nearby and same village. In each community, approximately 350 families take membership. Based on the cluster approach, they are located near each other. SHGs are unregistered and open a joint account in the name of a self-help group. But the MAC bodies are registered bodies and maintain a proper book of accounts, and an audit is conducted annually. The audit reports and books of accounts are submitted for renewal. In Self-help groups. SHG is a small group of 10–12 people. SHGs formation is not homogenous and non-activity based. Guidelines allow the coverage of houses on the same lane.

Some houses are doing pottery, some are doing weaving, and the next household is doing petty businesses. These non-homogenous take loans under the SHGBLP.

One member utilises the loan for pottery, and one uses it for weaving. This leads to non-repayment of loans. In an SHG which is homogenous, members can monitor each other. Under SBLP, members have different skillset; some are good at baking, firing, etc. In a MAC society as well, people have diversified skill sets. There are two kinds of loans. A loan is in the society's name for the purchase of raw materials, and another kind of loan is a loan on working capital for the construction of assets. In SHG, members are not able to prepare the books of accounts. The Government societies form SHG and have one structure, Sangh Mitra, under which 10–15 SHG are formed into federations or village organisations. At the group or taluk level, a three-tier system is followed at the village system, taluk level. The Government agencies like DRDA form the Self-help group. They have one kind of structure, which is called Sangh Mitra. 10 to 15 SHGs are assembled into a village organisation or federation at the taluk level into Mandal Samkhya and district level one federation.

In NRLM, self-help groups are responsible for maintaining the books of accounts. The member participation in the self-help group is significantly less due to Sangh Mitra, as she is responsible for maintaining the books of accounts. Under NRLM, a few SHGs, where the group leaders are active, can keep the books of accounts. Lack of financial literacy is the main reason for the non-maintenance of the books of account. Book account maintenance is not easy, and minimum education is required to maintain the books of account. Digital literacy is extremely important for the people at the bottom of the pyramid. The members can monitor each other, as these SHGs are located in area-specific clusters.

Each unit is responsible for utilising loans and providing loans for setting up the showrooms. These showrooms take responsibility for the payment of loans. Joint Liability Groups are not registered groups, but the group head can take responsibility for paying loans. If any member is not paying on time, the Joint Liability Group monitors only the group leader. In the cluster, 10–15 members are operational. Masters' artisans are responsible for monitoring the craftsmanship. All the master artisans are formed into apex bodies, and the master artisans can exercise pressure on him and the other groups. This craftsman is responsible for covering all the groups, and the artisans are brought from all over the world, including Benaras and West Bengal. MAC society and MSME have many benefits as they can be registered under the company's act. Schedule banks can provide loans to the banks, and MAC members know the banks. The self-help group model is complicated, and SHPI is outstanding and it allows the members to pursue various kinds of art, including pottery making, weavers and terracotta. Skill-building and hand-holding support are extremely important. Financial literacy is extremely important for promoting the Karigari among the group members.

Thus, in a community structure where members are related to each other and where the members can monitor each other, the network relations between the members lead to social capital. This social capital leads to access to financial services by substituting physical capital.

Case Study – A Self-Help Group

In our village, we have a service area, and we discuss with the artists out of those who have a basic idea of the art form; we select the people and then give them the SHG form. We individually visited the village and collected the data. After that, we conduct 2 group meetings, explain the benefits from the Government and us, and then form the groups. In rural areas, most people work banyan bait, making mats and weaving, which is in great demand. They also make coral mats and other items, such as handicrafts and hand embroidery. We also develop them, and this art is family art. We initially provided them with a loan, and after their development, they took a loan from the banks. Nowadays, groups are undertaking group meetings and discussing matters in the group. They maintain the attendance registers, financial registers, and passbooks. Only after the first period of performance do they get the loan. Initially, they get a loan of Rs. 10,000. Sometimes, the member cannot pay, the group members pay back the loan, and after two to three days, they collect the loan. This kind of problem is coming of strategic default in one or two groups, but these days we are closely interacting with the groups and taking drastic steps. CRP (Community resource person) is doing a social audit, and banks are grading the SHG performance. Bank officers do not visit generally. Only in case of loan default is the bank officer visiting the SHG, and we help them. We are NGO Committee, select the officers for field visits and train them; we do the audit, give them training, and provide them with training.

NGO is not offering individual loans, which are given to the SHG. Insurance is also provided, and we weekly visit the SHG. And in case of any problem, we visit them and solve it. These days SHG members are given digital literacy, especially the leader. They are proficient at using WhatsApp and mobile. We conducted digital and financial literacy training for the members. They become independent after some time, and then we leave them. Their families have been reaping the benefits of these initiatives. The government is providing them support to visit and attend marketing events. They provide funds to these people, and NABARD is also supporting them. We are providing them the training regarding the colour and designs. At the time of joining, they are brainwashed and trained them. They come to the bank when we tell them and are influenced by 2 and 3. This programme has become technologically and financially sustainable through training the women members and them. NABARD is supporting our organisation and creating a lot of awareness for the financial literacy programme. Hence, a lot of members receive financial literacy.

Conclusion

Microfinance plays an extremely important role in the eradication of poverty by providing capital to the poor. Despite being a necessity, the micro-poors are devoid of access to capital in the form of credit. This is due to the lack of physical collateral and lack of information about the creditworthiness of the poor. The unique self-help group bank linkage programme plays a vital role in providing credit options to the poor based on social capital. Social capital is embedded in the social contract that governs the functioning of self-help groups. Social capital enables the members of the poor community to get access to financial services. The social capital in the groups is structuralist and is derived from the existing cognitive factors such as rules, and norms and affective factors such as the beliefs, culture, and context of the group. Like any other form of capital, social capital has a transformative capacity derived from network relations. Social capital facilitates exchange among the members of the groups in the form of internal lending. This exchange is facilitated by the transfer of soft information derived from the existing personal relationships among the group members. The structure of the groups also enables access to external capital from the banks. The groups' hard information in the form of savings, credit, and income records facilitates access to credit services. Social capital is generated through the act of individuals and is constitutive. It provides a substitute for the physical collateral and enables the group members to access credit. It leads to trust, reciprocity, and collaboration and is operationalised through a social contract. Due to social capital, the cost of banking comes down dramatically. The banks are unwilling to monitor the members due to the high cost of screening, monitoring, and sanctions. But the social capital facilitates the group members to peer screen each other, peer select each other, and enforce the social contract to facilitate access to financial services and credit.

Summary

Poverty is a social problem, and globally, 1.4 billion people do not have access to financial resources. These people do not have any access to the physical collateral, and the formal institutions do not have any information about the creditworthiness of the poor. The joint liability group is an example of social capital through the social contract. In a group, the homogenous set of members come together to achieve access to financial resources. These members share a set of social relationships that enable the poor to achieve their social goals. Social capital can be either cognitive or affective or horizontal or vertical. The horizontal relationship refers to the relationship among the members, and the vertical relationships refer to the relationship between the bank and the members. Cognitive, social capital refers to the shared norms and beliefs and Affective social capital refers to the emotional relationships among the members of the community. Empowerment strategy refers to the relationships among the members in the form of closure or bonding. Closure refers to the relationship among the community members, and bridging refers to the relationship between the bank and the members. Social capital has a transformative ability, and it is nurtured through the relationship among the members of the group. Social capital is either structural or relational. The structural relationship is through networks and affiliations. Relational social capital is developed through social affiliations and networks. The source of social capital is either soft information or hard information. Through the lens of structuralist theory, the self-help group is a set of social rules and regulations institutionalised in the form of social relationships. The perfect example of social capital is the self-help group, formed on the basis of the social relationships among the members of the group. Due to the social relationships and social contract, the member's peer monitors each other to ensure the repayment of the group loans. The social contract is characterised by joint liability, where each member is responsible jointly for the liabilities of the group.

References

Adler, P. S., & Kwon, S. W. (2002). Social capital: Prospects for a new concept. *Academy of Management Review, 27*(1), 17–40.

Asian Development Bank. (2011). *Understanding poverty in India.* © Asian Development Bank. http://hdl.handle.net/11540/135. License: CC BY 3.0 IGO.

Beck, T., Demirgüç-Kunt, A., & Levine, R. (2000). New database on financial development and structure. *World Bank Economic Review.*

Bluhm, R., de Crombrugghe, D. P. I., & Szirmai, A. (2014). *Poor trends – The pace of poverty reduction after the Millennium Development Agenda.* (UNU-MERIT Working Papers; No. 006). UNU-MERIT.

Coleman, J., & Roker, D. (1998). Adolescence. *The Psychologist, 11*(12), 593–598.

Halpern, D. (2005). *Social capital.* Polity.

Inglehart, R. (1997). *Modernization and post-modernization: Cultural, economic and political change in 43 societies.* Princeton University Press.

Maclean, S. (2010). *The social work pocket guide to reflective practice* (pp. 8–106).

Mohan, G., & Mohan, J. (2002). Placing social capital. *Progress in Human Geography, 26*(2), 191–210.

Pretty, J., & Ward, H. (2001). Social capital and the environment. *World Development, 29*(2), 209–227.

Putnam, R. (1993). The prosperous community: Social capital and public life. *The American Prospect, 4*, 35–42.

Putnam, R. (2001). Social capital: Measurement and consequences. *Canadian Journal of Policy Research, 2*(1), 41–51.

Robison, L. J., Schmid, A. A., & Siles, M. E. (2002). Is social capital really capital? *Review of Social Economy, 60*(1), 1–21.

Van Bastelaer, T., & Leathers, H. (2006). Trust in lending: Social capital and joint liability seed loans in Southern Zambia. *World Development, 34*(10), 1788–1807.

Chapter 3

Inclusive Financial System in India

Digitisation of the Bombay Stock Exchange

Financial inclusion helps lift people out of poverty and can help speed economic development. It can draw more women into the mainstream of economic activity, harnessing their contribution to society.

Microfinance and Development in Emerging Economies, 47–67
Copyright © 2023 Nishi Malhotra
Published under exclusive licence by Emerald Publishing Limited
doi:10.1108/978-1-83753-826-320231003

Financial Perspective

One hundred forty-two years earlier, the stock exchange started under the banyan tree, and in 2017, the stock exchange issued its first equity shares through IPO (Initial Public Offering). It is the world's largest stock exchange (Lokeshwarri, 2022). *Due to the favourable investment environment, the trade volume on the equity markets has increased tremendously. BSE Limited is the first Indian stock exchange in Dalal Street, Bombay, India. It is the oldest stock exchange in India and the 10th largest stock exchange in the world. Several market reforms had taken place since 1986 when the BSE developed the Bombay Stock Exchange Index, which enables the members to measure their performance. This market has also introduced the derivatives segment of the market. In 1995, the Bombay Stock Exchange switched to electronic trading systems CMC Limited developed called BOLT* (Team Cafe mutual, 2015). *This system enables the users to switch to the digital mode of transactions and helps reduce the transaction cost and increase the volume of trade in this market. BSE has taken several steps to increase financial literacy among its members. With increased literacy levels, members can maximise their returns and utility.*

Introduction

In any economy, the financial system plays a significant institutional role in financial transformation. It is a vehicle for the economic transformation and development of an economy. Finance is considered the lifeblood of business, and the financial system is a conduit that ensures the circular flow of money in an economy by channelising the savings generated in the households in the form of investments, providing the development of a self-reliant economy. It helps to bridge the gap between the present state and the future of an economic system. The financial system also ensures the equitable distribution of resources among the various economic agents. There are various definitions of the financial system that various authors provide. As per Van Horne, 'Financial system is the purpose of the financial markets to allocate the savings efficiently in the economy to the ultimate users either for the investment in the real assets or for consumption' (Van Horne & Wachowicz, 2008). According to Robinson, the financial system is a bridge that works as a conduit between the savings generated in the economy and investments made to ensure wealth creation (Robinson, 2001). The main objective of the financial system in an economy is to mobilise savings and capital formation and wealth creation to boost the level of economic growth and development economics. In a financial economy, to manage the circular flow of savings and investments, several different institutions and financial players are integrated to ensure wealth creation and development. The efficiency of any financial system depends on how robust the economy's financial systems are. In a non-inclusive financial system, the members of society are devoid of participating in the financial process. Thus, the process of savings and investments involves the participation of various players, such as financial institutions, players, instruments and services. Because of the importance of this system, it is crucial to regulate and supervise the workings of the financial system. This chapter attempts to understand India's financial system and how it is set to become more inclusive with various policy initiatives.

Indian Financial Systems

The financial system comprises financial institutions, financial markets, financial instruments, insurance companies, investment companies and pension funds. The critical financial intermediation role is to frame rules and norms for the operation of the markets (Bhatt, 1991). The financial system comprises the financial environment, which includes the rules and regulations in the market. It comprises the relationships among the various financial entities and financial claims. Due to the complex nature of the financial markets, it is imperative to match financial services' supply and demand through contingent claims and synthetic financial products. The financial intermediation activities comprise (1) brokerage activities and (2) transformation of the quality of assets. The brokerage activities comprise transaction services, financial consultancy, loan granting, etc. And the transformation of quality assets comprises various intermediary activities such as monitoring activities, risk management, insurance activities and mitigating the market liquidity risk. The financial intermediary plays an essential role in the market by performing the following functions:

(1) The financial intermediary also reduces the *transaction costs* in an organisation
(2) The financial intermediary reduces the *liquidity risk* in the market, and it leads to debt renegotiation in the markets
(3) The financial intermediary provides a mechanism for pooling resources and transferring the resources in an economic system
(4) The financial intermediary helps in determining the prices for the commodities by taking into account the risk element
(5) The financial intermediary provides the necessary information that is required to mitigate the problem of adverse selection and moral hazard in the markets. Thus, it helps in the reduction of information asymmetry in the markets

(1) *Reduction in transaction costs* – Financial intermediaries enable the reduction in transaction costs. In a world with imperfect information about the creditworthiness of the borrowers, the reduction of transaction costs is not possible. This is the primary reason that the small borrowers, who do not have adequate collateral and about whom the banks do not have any information about the creditworthiness of the poor, cannot avail the loans from the markets. In this scenario, the adoption of contingent claims in the form of options and group lending plays a significant role. Group lending is often referred to as loan commitment. This loan commitment in the form of

joint liability plays a significant role in mitigating the problem of information asymmetry in the form of moral hazard and adverse selection.

(2) *Liquidity risk* – The financial players in an imperfect market face liquidity risk in terms of the borrowers' ability to meet the borrowers' liquidity needs. In this regard, the provision of the deposit insurance contract plays an essential role in reducing the risk of a bank run. The bank run is generally a phenomenon in which if one player withdraws money from one market, all the players withdraw the money from the markets.

(3) *Information asymmetry* – One of the significant factors impacting the debt markets is the lack of information that the borrowers have regarding their financial capability of the borrowers. In this regard, the information asymmetry on the part of borrowers leads to higher monitoring costs and free riding. This information asymmetry leads to the issue of moral hazard and adverse selection. Diversifying the portfolio can mitigate the risk of moral hazard and adverse selection.

(4) *Transformation through contingent claims and financial engineering* – The terms of debt can be renegotiated in the financial markets to mitigate the issue of information asymmetry in terms of moral hazard and adverse selection. Financial intermediaries provide a solution through the origination of financial claims or contingent claims in the form of derivatives.

In a free economy, financial growth and development depend on how the financial savings are channelled into the economy. These savings are then converted into an investment, called capital formation. This investment forms the backbone of manufacturing and production in the economy. The entire output produced in the economy is called the gross domestic product in the economy. The capital formation comprises three significant functions: savings, finance and investment. Through the circular flow in the economy, the funds flow from the financial institutions to the borrowers and the manufacturing organisations. Financial intermediaries play a significant role in financial intermediation to facilitate the circular flow of funds in the economy. This is called the functions of the financial system in a free economy. The circular flow of savings in the form of investment is described below (see Fig. 1).

The circular flow of the model shows the interaction between the various actors of the economy, namely the households and the businesses. The significant exchanges between the different actors occur in the economy through the flow of goods and services as the economic agents. The money moves from households to the financial markets in the form of savings and from financial markets to businesses in the form of investments. The financial markets act as financial intermediaries, including banks and financial institutions. The firms provide the payoffs to the households through wages, interest, rent and profits. The households provide the factors of production to the economy in the form of land, labour, capital and enterprise. The firms provide the factor payments to the households through wages, profits, rent and interest. The households make consumption expenditures on the goods and services provided by the households. The households also make payments of taxes to the Government, and the firms make the payment of net taxes to the Government. Firms purchase various goods and services from the Government, and the households provide the wages and salaries

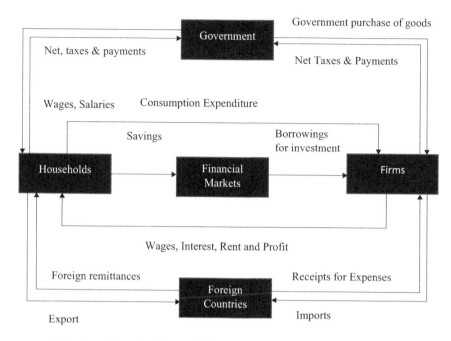

Fig. 1.   Circular Flow of Economy. *Source:* By the Authors.

to the Government. The households manufacture products and facilitate exports and receive remittances from foreign nations. And foreign nations facilitate imports from the firms and receipt for the expenses incurred. This is called a circular flow of money in the economy.

Stakeholders in a Financial System

The financial system in India is organised in the form of a structure comprising financial intermediaries, regulators and financial markets. Together these entities constitute the financial system of India. The financial system comprises financial intermediaries, financial markets and regulators that control and supervise the functioning of the financial systems. A brief description of the stakeholders in the financial system is given next:

Financial Intermediaries: Financial intermediaries refer to the institutional entities that act as a conduit between the savers and the investors. The main institutional entities in a financial system comprise banks, financial institutions, insurance, mutual funds and the major non-banking financial companies. These intermediaries help to convert the savings of the households into investments. The process of channelisation of savings to investors is called financial intermediation. Financial intermediaries facilitate the efficient allocation of resources across time and space. In the five-year planning system of India, financial intermediaries like banks have an important role in capital formation. The financial intermediaries play an important role in mitigating the friction in the allocation of resources by the markets. The Reserve Bank of India created financial institutions such as commercial banks, development institutions and financial institutions to promote the financial growth of the economy. The Narasimhan Committee, in 1990, was constituted to ensure the reformation of the financial systems. The committee highlighted that till the 1990s, the financial system was mainly a way to combat the deficits the government incurred. The committee recommended various measures such as deregulation of the interest rates in a phased manner and reduction in reserve requirement. The Narasimhan committee divulged the need for a stronger reformation of the financial intermediaries' role in allocating resources. This reformation of the financial system and an enhanced role for the financial intermediaries was mainly a result of the plan priorities. The plans envisaged an increased role for the competition and private sector in achieving economic growth. In the post-liberalisation period, an enhanced role was envisaged for the private sector. There were various regulatory and legal developments to reform the banking sector and make the allocation of financial resources through the capital markets much more efficient. During this period, the BIS (Basel International Settlement) norms related to Non-Performing Assets aimed to improve the banks' financial health. The planning posts in the 1990s were mainly aimed at market orientation and reformed the banking systems. It aimed to improve the bank balance sheet to meet prudential norms. With the current reforms, the share of the banking system in NPAs has reduced dramatically. Financial intermediaries play an essential role in overcoming the problem of information asymmetry, which comprises moral hazard and adverse selection. As per Diamond (1984), financial intermediaries play an essential role in screening and monitoring risky investments to ensure financial development and economic growth. The banks, security underwriters, rating agencies, etc. perform the role of financial intermediation. The banks provide the necessary capital to lubricate the manufacturing and production in the economy. Banks help to combat the deficiency of money supply in the economy, and the financial rating agencies provide the risk categorisation for the economy. The banking players also help establish product distribution channels and maintain customer relationships. Financial intermediation in any country is strongly correlated with economic growth. The nations with better regulatory systems and financial systems have better economic growth. This includes the regulations regarding the creditor's rights. Financial intermediation comprises borrowing and lending, which is based on financial contracts. The robustness of the financial systems depends on the debtor's and creditor's rights. Indian financial system and contracts still lack sufficient creditor rights. The efficiency of the financial system comprises acquiring information, exercising corporate control, risk management and mobilisation of savings. In order to implement financial reforms, there is a need for an efficient financial system. The financial system should be able to ensure efficient lending and borrowing. In the context of the Indian economy, borrowing and lending have been liberalised. Also, the regulatory system in the country has been liberalised. The role of the financial intermediaries can be described as (1) pricing the assets and (2) investing the cash flows in the available investment opportunities.

Role of Financial Intermediary in an Economy

As mentioned in the circular flow of income, the financial intermediaries help circulate the funds from the households in savings to the financial markets. These markets channel these savings in the form of investments. The financial intermediaries provide various combinations of return and risk to the investors. They bring together the buyer and seller in the economy. These intermediaries provide the economy with various risk and return combinations. Intermediaries help to pool the capital and to mitigate the risk by diversification. These intermediaries help to reduce liquidity and investment risk. Investment contracts refer to the financial intermediaries' securitisation, asset management, and underwriting function. Financial contracting plays an extremely important role in the efficient allocation of resources. These financial intermediaries play an important role in designing investment contracts. It also emphasises monitoring the performance of the borrowers or investors. If the financial contracting is not robust, or there is a lack of creditor's rights, then the lending by the banks will become unprofitable. Generally, the banks are supposed to perform the monitoring function in case of investment contracts. Financial intermediaries face another kind of major risk, which includes liquidity risk. The liquidity risk comprises the risk that the financial intermediary might suffer from a liquidity crunch. The financial intermediaries pool the resources of the various investors and thus help in the allocation of resources. Banks and financial intermediaries generally have better information about creditors and borrowers. In India, a sizeable number of borrowers are below the poverty line and do not have enough collateral and information about the creditworthiness of the poor. And the banks do not find them profitable to provide them the credit. They have to incur higher costs of financial intermediation in monitoring and screening. With financial development, the costs of financial intermediation have gone down dramatically. The financial intermediaries help to reduce the following risks: (1) liquidity risk, (2) informational risk (3) portfolio risk. The monitoring role of the banks has been highlighted in the form of the banks' potential to offer delegated monitoring. Diamond Dybvig (1983) pools the savings of the savers and provides sufficient liquidity to the creditors. The banks pool the savings of the investors and invest these savings in investment portfolios. Modern-day banking is fraught with many more challenges, such as digitising banking platforms. These digital platforms help supply the borrowers' funds to the suppliers.

With deregulation, liberalisation and internationalisation, the role of financial intermediaries is fast disappearing in the markets. In the 1990s, the needs will become fully liberalised. Contrary to the market-based approach, free markets determine the optimal allocation of resources. However, financial intermediation helps resolve moral hazard and adverse selection problems. The monitoring function is one of the malfunctions of the financial intermediaries, and in the digital era, the monitoring cost is dramatically reduced. Thus, according to the modern view, financial intermediation exists because of imperfections in the markets. With the reduction in imperfections in the markets, the role of financial intermediaries will be dramatically reduced.

Nature of the Markets and the Role of the Financial Intermediaries

In the case of a complete market, in an *Arrow Debreu* world, the role of the financial intermediaries is not relevant as financial engineering does not have much relevance. In a complete market, the price of the securities can be determined by replicating the prices for the existing securities. But in incomplete markets, the contingent claims can improve the efficiency of the markets as provided in (Ross, 1976).

Value Creation and the Role of Financial Intermediaries

Financial intermediaries play an important role in value creation through various banking services – payment services, asset transformation, risk management, information processing and borrower monitoring. The research indicates that modern banking plays a vital role in transforming assets, and traditional banking plays a critical role in reducing the cost of financial intermediation. In an imperfect financial market environment, multiple stars are missing in the world of the Moon. This implies that many borrowers will not be able to get a matching supply for the funds in the imperfect markets. This leads to a drastic increase in the rate of interest. Like a revolving universe that moves farther and farther away, due to the lack of financial innovations, there will always be an enhanced role for the financial intermediaries. To meet these requirements, the financial intermediaries have introduced several synthetic products, such as derivatives and options, to insure against the risk due to imperfections in a *non-Arrow Debreu* world. Another example is the determination of interest rates, deposit insurance, and access to financial services for the people at the bottom of the pyramid. In a primitive market homogenised in terms of the type of products, there are insufficient returns for the investment. In this scenario, the attempt is to de-homogenise the product markets. This is known as *value creation* in the markets, which is the rationale behind financial intermediation. Despite all the reforms and digitisation attempts, due to a lack of proper regulation regarding property rights and the availability of perfect information about the creditworthiness of the borrowers, the problems of moral hazard and adverse selection are perpetually present in the financial markets. Due to the presence of unknown uncertainty in the markets, the composition of interest rates remains an important question. The interest rates thus include the opportunity cost of capital and the riskiness in determining the interest rates.

Supply-Side Factors

Supply-factors play a vital role to perform the financial functions of financial intermediation. In the case of a financial intermediary, the supply-side factors comprise the determination of the reserve requirements, the determination of the interest rates and the supply of loans. Similarly, the demand for financial intermediation depends on the interest rates prevailing in the markets, inflation costs and the opportunity costs of capital. The level of nominal interest rates determines the opportunity costs of capital in the market. Various stakeholders in the financial markets are mentioned as follows:

Financial Markets: Financial markets are where the buyers and the sellers meet together to fulfil their demand and supply for finance. In the case of the Indian financial system, the market comprises the primary markets, where the lenders and the borrowers meet to meet their demand for financial instruments. The secondary market person comes to buy and sell the financial instruments. Similarly, money markets refer to the markets where the lending and borrowing of short-term money instruments take place. The financial markets comprise the money markets, capital markets, government securities markets, foreign exchange markets and credit markets.

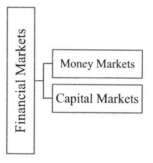

Fig. 2.   Type of Financial Markets.
Source: By the Authors.

a. *Money Markets* – The money market is a market for short-term funds, which are securities with a maturity period of less than one year. Money markets provide funds for credit instruments, which include bills of exchange, commercial papers, promissory notes, bonds, certificates of deposit etc. Money markets do not imply a physical marketplace. It is a network of buyers, the retail customers or institutional investors, and the lenders, who are the financial institutions dealing in money market instruments. The money market in India comprises the central bank, i.e., the Reserve Bank of India, the commercial banks, cooperative banks and other specialised financial institutions. These markets are highly liquid and meet the short-term borrowing needs of investors. The instruments traded in the money markets have a maturity of less than one year. A description of the money markets is given below:

b. *Treasury Bills:* The Government of India issues treasury bills for 14 days to 364 days. These are the most popular treasury instruments. These instruments are issued at a discount and repaid at par.

c. *Commercial Paper:* Commercial papers are money market instruments with a maturity of less than one year. The corporates issue these instruments to meet their short-term need for funds or working capital requirements. The maturity date for the commercial paper is 15 days to 1 year. The Reserve bank of India lays down the policies regarding the issue of commercial paper.

d. *Commercial Bills:* Commercial bills are the money market instruments issued by corporates to meet their short-term funds requirements. These instruments satisfy the short-term fund requirement of the corporate

e. *Certificate of Deposits:* Certificate of deposits refers to the negotiable deposit which the commercial banks accept. Generally, it is issued through promissory notes. The duration for the certificate of the deposit ranges between 3 months and one year. It can be given a maximum for period of 3 years.

f. *Call Money:* Financial institutions borrow money at extremely short notice to manage their cash flows. This is referred to as 'call money'. In the markets, the interest rates for call money are susceptible to demand and supply. It is an interest-paying instrument issued by one financial institution to another. It is a short-term financial loan that is payable immediately on demand. Brokerage houses use call money as a short-term source of funding. It is used to maintain the margin money for the customers who leverage their investments.

g. *CBLO (Collateralised Borrowing and Lending Obligation):* CBLO is a money market instrument that refers to an obligation between the borrower and lender regarding the terms and conditions of the loan. The instrument is like a bond for the lender. The lender issues the bond, and the borrower sells the money market instrument with interest. This instrument is meant for individuals who cannot participate in the interbank call money markets. The borrower must repay the loan at a future date, and the lender has the right to receive the money. The Credit Clearing Corporation of India developed this instrument to help financial and non-financial institutions meet their liquidity requirements. It is a collateralised instrument backed by Government securities, due to which the rates are lower than the interbank call money rates. Repurchase agreements are generally safe investments as the collateral securities are generally treasury bonds.

h. *Money Repo Rate* – A money repo rate instrument is a short-term borrowing for the dealers in government securities. The government securities dealers sell the securities to investors on short term basis and repurchase them on the following day. The repo rate is a slight difference between the buying and selling rates. The Reserve Bank of India has undertaken various reforms, such as the introduction of the Liquidity Adjustment Facility (LAF). LAF was introduced due to the recommendation made by the Narasimhan Committee in 1998. It helps the RBI borrow money through repurchase agreement or repos or make loans to RBI through reverse repo agreements. In 2004, the Liquidity Adjustment Facility was furthered by the issuance of the Market Stabilisation scheme to insulate the monetary conditions from the impact of large-scale capital flow.

Inclusive Money Markets in India

The money market in a nation is significant as it helps to implement the monetary policy in a country. Since the liberalisation in 1990, many efforts have been made to integrate all the parts of the financial markets. The money market is the most liquid in India, with securities having a maturity of one year or less than one year. The monetary policy in any nation is aimed at achieving stability and growth, and the central bank of India, i.e., the Reserve Bank of India, had to modify its monetary policy a number of times to achieve the objectives. There have been reforms to develop the money markets. Despite various measures taken in the 1980s, which included the setting up of the Discount and Finance House of India, the introduction of certificates of deposits, commercial papers, interbank deposits and reforms of call money were unable to meet the goals and objectives of market development. In 1998, the Internal Working Committee formed under the aegis of the Narasimhan Committee made various recommendations, such as moving from a loan-based system to a cash credit system. In a deregulated and liberalised banking environment, the banks are given more autonomy to decide their distribution of the working capital loans as either the cash credit or the loan-based system. Similarly, for the Treasury Bills, an auction system has been introduced. The Reserve Bank of India has completely phased out the ad-hoc treasury bill system. Earlier to monetise the fiscal deficit now this instrument has been completely phased out, ending the fiscal deficit's automatic monetisation. Thus, the introduction of the CBLO (Collateralized Borrowing and Lending Obligation), Liquidity Adjustment Facility, and Market Stabilisation System is the key reforms being undertaken in the money markets.

(1) *Financial regulatory authority* – In the financial markets of India, the operations have been managed through regulations. Independent regulators regulate the functioning of the markets through the various regulatory bodies linked to the Ministry of Finance. The Ministry of Finance, Government of India, governs the functioning of the financial markets. The Reserve Bank of India (RBI) is the central bank that regulates the functioning of the financial markets in the economy. The capital markets in the economy are regulated by the SEBI (Securities and Exchange Board of India), and NSE (National Stock Exchange) regulates the secondary market activities in the economy. To regulate the capital markets, it is imperative to introduce competitive regulations, which comprise the Companies Act of 1956, the SEBI Act of 1992, the Securities and Contracts Regulations Act of 1956, the Depositories Act of 1956, and the Companies Act, 1956. These regulations are needed for the smooth functioning of the capital markets.

The SEBI Act, 1992: The SEBI Act, 1992, is promogulated to facilitate (1) the protection of the rights of the investors in the securities market, (2) promotion of the development of the securities market and (3) regulation of the securities market. This act provides the jurisdiction that extends to the companies for the issuance of securities. This act provides the market the power to regulate the intermediaries' functioning and penalise the violations. The SEBI Act provides autonomy to the financial markets.

The Securities Contracts Regulation Act, 1956: It regulates the functioning of the securities market to protect the rights and the interests of the investors, promotes the development of the securities market, and regulates the securities market. It has the authority to regulate the financial markets and to penalise the violations of the Securities Act of 1956.

The Depositories Act, 1996: The Depositories Act, 1996, aims to regulate the establishment of depositories to make the securities freely transferrable, dematerialisation the securities and maintenance of the order books. This Act is aimed at making the transfer of securities freely transferable.

The Companies Act, 1956: The Companies Act, 1956, aims to strengthen the existing regulatory framework. This Act aims to provide for the allotment and transfer of securities. It facilitates the efficient management of the companies, disclosure of the issues that arise in the capital and provides information about the functioning of the companies.

SEBI has established many reforms in the capital markets to make the markets safer for investors. To modernise the capital markets, the SEBI has taken several initiatives which include control over the capital issue, establishment of the regulator, screen-based trading, risk management, promote investor and securities market awareness, debt listing agreement, grading of IPOs (Initial Public Offerings), control the corporate debt market and setting of the SME markets. The efficient financial systems are characterised by the following features such as low risk, convenience and efficient management. The financial systems ensure that the risk is inherent in the financial instruments and that the securities are diversified away. The diversification of the risks provides for balanced growth. It further provides convenience, in terms of leveraging the savings, so that the financialisation becomes affordable. Further, financial intermediation should provide for the efficient management of financial resources.

Major Financial Intermediaries in the Indian Financial System

The major financial intermediaries are given below:

(1) Commercial Banks
(2) Non-Banking Financial Companies
(3) Mutual Funds
(4) Insurance Companies
(5) Financial Markets
(6) Regulators

(1) *Commercial Banks:* Commercial banks are financial institutions that receive money from depositors in deposits and then lend it to the borrowers. From the borrowed funds, the banks create assets. In the year 1969, the banks were

nationalised, and these banks have subsequently become the vehicle of development in the economy. These banks are the instruments of economic growth and development. These institutions act as the vehicle for the government's funding activities.

(2) *Non-banking Financial Companies:* The non-banking financial companies are fund-based or advisory based. These non-banking financial companies provide microfinance to the micro borrowers at the bottom of the pyramid.

(3) *Mutual Funds:* Mutual funds are investment vehicles comprising the portfolio of securities. These mutual funds are managed by the trusts and the asset management companies to ensure adequate returns on investment.

(4) *Financial Markets:* The financial markets are the intermediaries that provide a platform for buying and selling securities. The financial markets are of two types: capital and securities. The capital markets help provide and raise loans from the financial markets and the money markets play an important role in raising short-term finance from the markets. The capital markets play an important role in raising long-term loans from the markets.

(5) *Insurance Companies:* Insurance companies are the financial players that provide security against the financial risks in the market. These players in the insurance sector play an important role in mitigating the risk.

(6) *Regulators:* Regulators in the financial markets play an important role in protecting investors against financial risks. In the financial markets, the regulators protect the participants in the markets.

Inclusive Financial System

There is conclusive proof that finance leads to growth. The literature highlights that financial development leads to economic growth. Renowned economist such as Joseph Schumpeter highlights that banks play an important role in economic growth. The literature highlights that developed financial markets can facilitate economic growth. The banking sector plays an important role in ensuring equitable growth and development. Inclusive growth in an economy plays a vital role in ensuring equitable growth. The basic premise of equitable growth is that all the sections of society, including the poor and the weaker sections of society, are included in the growth story. Equitable growth is based on the assumption that inclusive, equitable growth leads to the maximisation of economic opportunities and equal opportunities for all sections of society. One of the major imperatives for equitable growth is that all the members of society must be included in the growth story. Inclusive growth leads to a reduction in the level of society. Financial exclusion is defined as the ability of the members to access basic financial services. There are various reasons for financial exclusion, including conditions, self-exclusion and price exclusion. The primary reason for the exclusion among the members. With the advent of technology financial system has become highly inclusive. Through technology, access to financial services is made available to the members at the bottom of the pyramid. In India, the expansion of financial credit is constrained due to the high transaction costs and the lack of financial intermediation. As far as providing credit to the poor people at the bottom of the pyramids is concerned, the lack of financial collateral and information to the bankers regarding the creditworthiness of the poor. In this scenario, many banks are unwilling to provide credit to the poor people at the bottom of the pyramid. The banks are reluctant to provide microfinance to poor people. Due to this reason, poor people have to rely on money lenders and the informal channel of finance for availing of finance.

Financial Literacy and Financial Inclusion

Financial literacy is defined as the ability of an individual to understand financial concepts and information. Financial literacy is defined as (1) cognition and knowledge about financial terms, (2) the capability to understand financial terms and concepts, (3) the aptitude and the ability to manage funds, (4) the set of skills to understand the financial concepts and financial practices and (5) efficacy to manage the personal finances. Approximately 24% of the population in India is financially illiterate (Braunstein & Welch, 2002; Gupta, 2021). The formal teaching and social intermediation lead to crystallised intelligence, which lies dormant in the users' minds. Most of the social intermediation initiatives lead to knowledge that is not operationalised and lies dormant in the minds of consumers. The emphasis is to bring about behavioural changes to promote the financial inclusion of the poor. In India, various financial institutions such as the Central Bank of India Reserve Bank of India and NABARD undertake various financial literacy campaigns to educate users of financial information. Though 80% of the population is financially literate, only 24% are financially literate. Since 2013, there has been 15% financial literacy 2013, and a lot of efforts are needed to achieve the milestones in higher literacy. Approximately 75% of the population still has to learn to plan how to spend, borrow and earn money. Financial literacy is extremely important for an individual, whether a man or a woman. And financial literacy levels ensure the well-being of households as there is a need for knowledge about various financial concepts to ensure financial well-being (Chen & Volpe, 1998; Hilgert et al., 2003; Lusardi, 2019; Mandell, 1998; Mishkin, 2018; Pejic Bach et al., 2019; Tennyson & Nguyen, 2001; Yan, 2023). Financially literate adults are able to make better financial decisions, increasing financial security. In India, the National Centre for Financial Education undertakes various financial literacy programmes in collaboration with SEBI, NISM and the Reserve Bank of India. The Government of India has undertaken various initiatives, including designing the pedagogy for financial education and capacity building in the NGOs and educational institutions through the train the trainer programme.

Further banks and financial institutions have a role in financial literacy. It also involves the adoption of schools by banks and financial institutions. Virtual classrooms and smart classrooms with ICT (Information Communication Technology) are being designed to impart financial knowledge to the people at the bottom of the pyramid. Financial literacy can be promoted to bring the weaker sections of society into the ambit of the institutional financial literacy framework. Indian Government has adopted an integrated approach to promoting financial literacy in rural regions of India.

UN Sustainable Development Goals and Role of the Indian Government

The UN Sustainable Development Goal of poverty reduction is aimed at ensuring reducing the level of poverty. To achieve this goal by 2030, the United Nations seeks to transform the lives of poor people through financial inclusion. The Government of India envisages promoting financial literacy to provide low-income households with access to affordable and convenient tools to access economic opportunities. Financial inclusion enables individuals to save money, cope with shocks and protect their assets against the. Financial literacy also enables the individual to take advantage of economic opportunities to ensure access to transfer payments and government services. Financial literacy per se enables the people at the bottom of the pyramid to access economic opportunities and take advantage of government schemes, including government transfers in the form of wages and transfer payments. The lack of financial inclusion is an important problem, particularly for the financial farmers. A lack of financial services makes it harder for farmers to manage their financial risks. Formal finance meets less than the $200 billion requirement of the farmers. The Government of India has introduced various schemes such as agricultural services such as microinsurance and subsidised credit needs to improve the financial resilience of the poor at the bottom of the pyramid. In this regard, financial literacy plays an extremely important role in ensuring that poor people and farmers gain information about the financial services the Government of India provides. For households, financial literacy provides the means and avenues to access financial and digital services. Financial literacy plays an important role in enabling people to access financial services. Despite all the efforts, financial literacy programmes and training do not reap any benefits. This is due to the lack of financial attitude that despite social intermediation, the investors cannot avail the financial services. As per the research by OECD, financial literacy comprises financial knowledge, financial attitude and financial behaviour. People with lower levels of financial literacy cannot understand financial concepts and terms. They cannot adopt positive financial behaviour despite their lack of financial literacy.

Outreach and Usage

Savings and investments are important for the economic growth of the Indian economy. But the lackadaisical growth of savings and investment is attributable to either the high level of expenditure or the lack of financial literacy. The poor members are not financially literate, so the poor members of the community cannot access financial services. Most of the members of the Indian rural community are unable to access financial services. More than 1/3rd of the Indian poor are financially illiterate. They lack access to bank services or microfinance. Due to this, the members of the rural community are exposed to the risk of lending from informal institutions such as money lenders, loan sharks, and other informal financial institutions. The Government of India has undertaken various financial inclusion initiatives such as Pradhan Mantri Jan Dhan Yojana (PMJDY) and direct benefit transfer under various schemes. However, due to the lack of financial literacy, the outreach of financial services is extremely limited (Fig. 3).

In a financially excluded system, the members of the people at the bottom of the pyramid do not have access to financial services. Through financial inclusion, the members are able to get access to financial services. Financial inclusion increases the outreach to financial services. Financial literacy promotes the financial inclusion of the poor. Despite this, access to financial services might not be propagated among the community members at the bottom of the pyramid due to the lack of financial literacy. A system in which the members have access to financial services and an adequate financial literacy is called an inclusive financial system.

Financial literacy enables an individual to improve outreach by providing financial services to the people at the bottom of the pyramid. It allows the people at the bottom of the pyramid to access financial services, through which the members learn to manage their money. Through access to financial knowledge, the women members of the community learn to access and avail of business opportunities. Financial literacy empowers the people at the bottom of the pyramid to access financial services and optimally manage their financial resources. With the foundational knowledge, the poor members of society can access financial services. Financial literacy improves the usage of financial services.

Digital and Financial Inclusive System

In India, the NeGP (National e-Governance Plan) has led to financial inclusion through projects such as Aadhar and Financial Inclusion. The use of digital

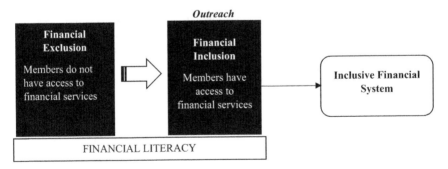

Fig. 3.   Role of Financial Literacy to Promote Inclusive Financial System. *Source:* By the Authors.

technology in the financial domain is transforming the way the financial system operates. The digitisation of the financial system facilitates the automation of payment services, borrowings, and investment services. The use of the digital mode of finance enables financial service providers to innovate how financial services are delivered to the people at the bottom of pyramids. National initiatives such as UID (Unique Identification Number). Financial inclusion helps the members of the community to avail of financial services. The central regulatory authority works together to ensure control and regulate the financial system. Digital financial inclusion refers to implementing digital technology to serve the people at the bottom of the pyramid. Digital financial inclusion aims to ensure the faster dissemination of information and equitable distribution of resources to the people at the bottom of the pyramid. This mode of financial inclusion is the means to provide financial services to the people at the bottom of the pyramid. This form of financial inclusion emphasises technology's important role in making financial services available to the people at the bottom of the pyramid. The radical innovation in the information communication technology (ICT) has an important role to play in the form of access to financial services for the people at the bottom of the pyramid. This form of financial inclusion is important to ensure access to services for the people at the bottom of the pyramid.

Factors that Impact the Financial Inclusion

There are two kinds of factors that impact digital financial inclusion in an economy. These two factors include (1) structural factors and (2) policy factors. The structural factors refer to the decisions regarding implementing digital and ICT to ensure access to financial services for the people at the bottom of the pyramid. The policy factors are essential in creating a policy environment to facilitate financial inclusion. Financial inclusion implies access to financial services for the people at the bottom of the pyramid. The various schemes that the Government of India has undertaken for the financial inclusion of the poor include (1) Pradhan Mantri Jan Dhan Yojana, (2) Atal Pension Yojana, (3) Stand Up India scheme, (4) Pradhan Mantri Mudra Yojana, (5) Sukanya Smridhi Scheme, (6) Jeevan Suraksha Bandhan Yojana, (7) Credit Enhancement Guarantee Scheme, (8) Venture Capital Fund and (9) Varishtha Pension Yojana. Digital financial inclusion initiatives include various schemes such as In the Indian context, the financial initiatives undertaken in the domain of financial inclusion are mentioned:

(1) *Structural factors* – The structural factors responsible for delivering financial services to the poor people at the bottom pyramid. It refers to the various digital initiatives that the Government of India launches to facilitate the financial inclusion of the poor. The government launched the e-governance initiative that comprises various digital initiatives such as e-Governance, mobile e-health and digital finance for financial inclusion, e-Wallets,

Aadhar, Digi locker, MyGOV, Bharat net, Smart Cities, Common services centre, Digitisation of post offices, Universal access to services, Public Wi-Fi hotspots, India stack, PMDISHA (Pradhan Mantri Gramin Digital Saksharta Abhiyaan), e-Health and the Government of India has introduced e-Education. India has also introduced the first rural internet service provider, n-Lounge, to provide financial services to the people at the bottom of the pyramid. Besides that, the Government has introduced the project Drishtee to provide e-Governance services to the people at the bottom of the pyramid.

(2) *Policy factors* – The Government of India has introduced various policies to combat financial exclusion in the economy. There is an expected increase in manufacturing to US$355 billion by 2025. The policy initiative includes various Acts and rules introduced by the Government of India to facilitate the financial inclusion of the poor. The Government of India will introduce the new Digital Act to facilitate the digital inclusion of the poor. The Government of India also aims to introduce the new data security act to protect the data. The Government has introduced the CSC (Common Services Centre) in order to ensure the delivery of e-Governance services to people at the bottom of the pyramid. Besides that, to provide seamless connectivity to internet connectivity till the last mile, the Government of India has introduced the SWAN (State Wide Area Network) and SSDG (State Service Delivery Gateway) to ensure the delivery of services to the poor. This policy initiative aims to provide the delivery of financial services for the poor. The Government of India has envisaged the infrastructure of Digital India, comprising nine central pillars that include Broadband highways, e-Governance (Reforming through the Government technology), e Kranti (Electronic delivery of service), public internet access programme, universal access to phones name a few. The broadband highways comprise broadband for all rural citizens, national information infrastructure, and broadband for all urban citizens. The primary objective of the digital inclusion programme is to provide universal access to mobile connectivity in India. Besides, the Government of India has introduced the Common Services Centre. Under the e Kranti movement of India, the Government has introduced various programmes such as technology for education, technology for health, technology for planning, technology for the farmers, technology for security, technology for financial inclusion, technology for justice, and technology security. The Digital India programme is spear headed by the Department of Information Technology in India. Financial literacy is a critical policy decision that impacts the role of a highly inclusive society. Fig. 2 describes the inclusive digital system as integrating broadband highways, citizen-centric services, internet access and financial literacy (Fig. 4).

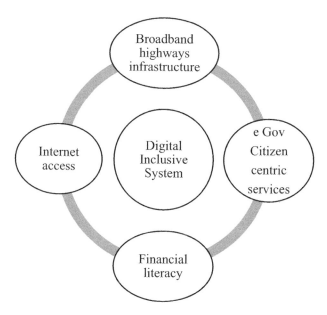

Fig. 4.   Financial Inclusive System in India.

Financial Intermediation and Social Intermediation

In the modern-day financial system, involving Non-Government Organisations (NGOs) and nonprofit institutions is imperative to ensure financial intermediation with social intermediation. The micro-poor at the bottom of the pyramid does not have access to financial services. Poverty in India is a problem of lack of physical collateral and information about the creditworthiness of the poor. Thus, poverty in India is a market failure. NGOs play an essential role in overcoming poverty's constraints through social capital, which includes network relations and relationships with the members of the community. This social capital further provides access to financial services to the poor at the bottom of the pyramid. Thus, social intermediation further leads to the generation of human capital. Moreover, the institutionalisation of relationships leads to the generation of social capital. This further leads to access to financial services for the people at the bottom of the pyramid. Thus, in an inclusive financial system, social intermediation plays a vital role in the generation of social capital. Thus, provides access to financial services to the members at the bottom of the pyramid. The digital financial infrastructure aims to ensure the timely and seamless delivery of financial services to people at the bottom of the pyramid. This digitisation has helped to reduce transaction costs drastically.

Conclusion

Financial systems in India are inclusive as it enables poor community members to access financial services based on social capital. Digitisation of the financial services at the bottom of the pyramid has facilitated the poor members of the community to access finance. Digital technology enables the people at the bottom of the pyramid to access financial services at the bottom of the pyramid. Till the 1980s, the financial system was mainly donor or subsidy based. However, in the 1990s, with the liberalisation of the economy and the opening of the financial system, developing economies worldwide aimed to achieve sustainable growth and development by 2030. Poverty reduction has been adopted as one of the primary sustainable development goals. In this regard, the Government of India has laid down a road map to ensure access to financial services for the people at the bottom of the pyramid.

Summary

Financial systems comprise different entities such as a commercial banks, non-banking finance companies, brokerage and insurance companies that help bring together the buyers and the sellers. The financial system comprises financial intermediaries, which refer to the indirect market, and the direct market, which comprises financial markets. The financial markets refer to the money markets and the capital markets. The indirect market or financial intermediation is vital in reducing transaction costs, liquidity risk, information asymmetry and transformation through contingent claims and financial reengineering. A healthy financial system establishes the circular flow of income in an economy. The financial system comprises commercial banks, non-banking financial companies, insurance and brokerage firms. An inclusive financial system leads to equitable growth. Financial literacy plays another important role in promoting the inclusion of the marginalised. There is a need to change the attitude of the marginalised poor. The financial exclusion can be mitigated by improving the outreach of financial services to the poor. Various structural and policy factors impact the financial inclusion of the poor through the creation of an ecosystem and social intermediation of the poor.

References

Bhatt, V. V. (1991). On improving effectiveness and efficiency of financial system in India. *Economic and Political Weekly, 26*(41), 2367–2372. http://www.jstor.org/stable/4398155

Braunstein, S., & Welch, C. (2002, November). Financial literacy: An overview of practice, research and policy. *Federal Reserve Bulletin, 87*(11), 445–457.

Chen, H., & Volpe, R. P. (1998). An analysis of personal financial literacy among college students. *Financial Services Review, 7*, 107–128.

Diamond, D. W. (1984). Financial intermediation and delegated monitoring. *Review of Economic Studies, 51*, 393–414. https://doi.org/10.2307/2297430

Diamond, D., & Dybvig, P. (1983). Bank runs, deposit insurance and liquidity. *Journal of Political Economics, 91*, 401–419. http://doi.org/10.1086/261155

Gupta, U. (2021, January). Are we missing an important piece of the education puzzle? https://www.linkedin.com/pulse/we-missing-important-piece-education-puzzle-ullas-gupta/

Hilgert, M., Hogarth, J., & Beverly, S. (2003, July). *Household financial management: The connection between knowledge and behavior* (pp. 309–322). Federal Reserve Bulletin.

Lokeshwarri, S. (2022). Stock market: From banyan tree to the cloud. *Business Line.*

Lusardi, A. (2019). Financial literacy and the need for financial education: Evidence and implications. *Swiss J Economics Statistics, 155*, 1. https://doi.org/10.1186/s41937-019-0027-5

Mandell, L. (1998). *Our vulnerable youth: The financial literacy of American 12th graders.* Jumpstart Coalition.

Mishkin, F. S. (2018). *Economics of money, banking and financial markets* (12th ed.). Pearson.

Pejić Bach, M., Krstić, Ž., Seljan, S., & Turulja, L. (2019). Text mining for big data analysis in financial sector: A literature review. *Sustainability, 11*(5), 1277. https://doi.org/10.3390/su11051277

Robinson, M. S. (2001). *The microfinance revolution: Sustainable finance for the poor.* World Bank.

Ross, D. M., & Ross, S. A. (1976). *Hyperactivity: Research, theory, and action.* John Wiley & Sons.

Team Cafe mutual. (2015). Only 24% of Indians are financially literate: S&P survey. https://cafemutual.com/news/industry/10045-only-24-of-indians-are-financially-literate-sp-survey

Tennyson, S., & Nguyen, C. (2001). State curriculum mandates and student knowledge of personal finance. *The Journal of Consumer Affairs, 35*(2), 241–262.

Van Horne, J. C., & Wachowicz, J. M. (2008). *Fundamentals of financial management* (13th ed.). Financial Times/Prentice Hall.

Yan, L. (2023). India's financial system. *Nature Climate Change, 13*, 116. https://doi.org/10.1038/s41558-023-01611-w

Chapter 4

Digital Financial System

Ingreso Solidaro – Digital Inclusion

Social Perspective

During the COVID-19 pandemic, Colombia rolled out the famous Ingreso Solidaro programme. This unique programme was implemented in Public Private Partnership. It transferred the emergency relief funds to 2.5 million households, of which 60% are headed by women. 1 million households were reached using the app. It was

Microfinance and Development in Emerging Economies, 69–92

Copyright © 2023 Nishi Malhotra

Published under exclusive licence by Emerald Publishing Limited

doi:10.1108/978-1-83753-826-320231004

observed that the people who receive the Government transfer through traditional accounts are more likely to cash out and go bankrupt than mobile wallets. These mobile wallets were used to make deposits. This case study further highlights the potential of digital financial inclusion to promote financial inclusion.

Introduction

Financial inclusion implies providing access to financial services to people at the bottom of the pyramid. Financial inclusion helps to achieve development and economic growth by ensuring access to financial services through government intervention. Out of various sustainable development goals, the achievement of the sustainable development goal of poverty reduction, women empowerment depends on providing access to financial services to the poor. Digital financial inclusion refers to universal access to financial services with transformative technologies. These technologies include the use of ICT – information communication technology) to deliver financial services to poor people at their doorsteps. Digital financial inclusion involves the deployment of technology and has far-reaching ramifications regarding poverty reduction. In developing nations, borrowers cannot access finance due to the lack of physical collateral and the lack of information about the creditworthiness of the poor. Technology implementation has reduced transaction costs and improved access to financial services for the poor people at the bottom of the pyramid. When the respondents cannot access financial services, they fall into the trap of borrowing from money lenders and money sharks at a higher interest rate. This leads to poverty. Thus, poverty is an outcome of the financial exclusion of the poor. Digital inclusion also helps to reduce the disparities between urban and rural households. It also helps to reduce gender disparities.

The sustainable development goal of financial inclusion has been adopted under the *Maya declaration by the alliance for financial inclusion.* This declaration commits to creating an enabling environment to harness new technology; this increases access and lowers the cost of transactions. Besides, it integrates consumer protection. By adopting the Maya declaration, India has established a regulatory framework to ensure the financial inclusion of the poor. Then at G20 Summit in 2010, nations from all over the globe adopted the goal of financial inclusion. The sustainable development goals of the United Nations highlight the importance of adopting the goal of poverty reduction, women empowerment and zero hunger through the financial inclusion process. Various communities, international bodies and affiliations have set 2030 as the milestone year to achieve financial inclusion. The challenge to achieving this goal is the high amount of financial commitment needed to implement this goal.

Policy Framework for Digital Inclusion

Indian Government has thrust on rapid digitisation of the Indian economy in the wake of a pandemic like COVID-19. Digital technology enables the members at the bottom of the pyramid to access financial services at a reduced cost and with the lowest maintenance costs. India has leaped to adopt digital technologies and emerged as a leader in digital innovation. With the setting up of NPCI (National Payment Corporation of India), and UPI (Unified Payment Interface), the Government has already set the pace for financial inclusion. The proposal to establish the neo banks or the digital banks is akin to providing stars to the missing moon. The Nachiket Mor Committee report, 2014 recommended promoting financial inclusion in the mission mode. In 2014, the RBI (Reserve Bank of India) gave the licences for the setting up of payment banks and small finance banks.

The payment banks serve as narrow banks providing various services such as offering and accepting deposits and payment services without credit services. Various small finance banks are full-fledged banks that offer comprehensive banking services. Digital Banks are defined under the banking regulation act of 1949. These banks provide multiple services, such as issuing deposits, making loans, and providing the full range of services to the poor. These digital banks will be subject to the same liquidity norms as other commercial banks. However, digital banks will be different from digital banking units. During the budget session of FY 2023, the finance minister floated the proposal to set up digital banking units for 75 Commercial bank units. Digital banking units do not have a legal entity, but digital banks have a legal entity. Digital banks, compared to commercial banks, will be highly efficient and provide a meagre transaction cost.

Thus, neo-banking has emerged as a solution to the problem of financial exclusion of the poor members in the hinterland. The Government in India is looking to set up a full-fledged digital bank. Digital banking will be disruptive in the age of financial inclusion and will serve as the bedrock of financial inclusion. The Digital revolution started in India with the adoption of various initiatives such as PMJDY (Pradhan Mantri Jan Dhan Yojana), e-KYC (Know your customer), and UPI (Unified Payment Interface). These initiatives served as the bedrock of development. In imperfect credit markets, where the demand and supply of credit is not matching, technology came to play the role of an enabler. Digital banks will be set up under the Banking Regulation Act. Thus, with the India stack of banks, Aadhar, UPI, and NPCI, India is set to outdo the local players in providing banking services at the doorstep of the citizens of the country.

Existing Rift Between Digital Policies and Objective of Banking

The existing policy frameworks for digital banking are being challenged. Because of the lack of financial literacy among the poor members of society, the impact of digital banking will be lackadaisical. The adoption of digital technology or digital capital is very context-dependent. It depends on the existence of the technological infrastructure. Moreover, digitisation is not only about ensuring access to technology through outreach and expanding digital technology. But it depends on the number of skills imbibed within an individual. Moreover, the use of digital capital is impacted by various other cultural and social factors. These social factors include the status of the individual in the market. In today's scenario, technology is constantly evolving, and this fast change and obsolescence make the existing skill sets redundant. Digital engagement through the normative and compulsory mandate of the Government of India to adopt technology is not enough to adopt the technology. There is a need to sanitise the players. To leverage the digital capital that has the transformative capability to transform inputs into outputs, social intermediation, and training are needed to ensure access to banks at the doorsteps. To implement digital technology, the steps need to be taken in three dimensions – (1) Pre-condition – The precondition involves the existing levels of financial exclusion, which includes price exclusion, self-exclusion, and access exclusion. For digital engagement, the thrust has been laid on improving the experience from the use of digital technology. Regarding the pre-conditions, the Government has to take steps to implement the ICT (Information Communication Technology), including setting up the Information Technology infrastructure, which includes seamless connectivity to the internet, broadband highways, and continuous access to financial services. The major objective of this digital transformation project is to achieve social equality, reinforce existing social equality and generate a new digital class. Thus, in order to adopt digital technology, three major factors have been identified, which include (1) social support and the social factors to create a conducive social environment, (2) the use of social networks (3) digital literacy. Fig. 1 defines in detail the impact of various factors that impact digital inclusion. There are various social factors that impact the level of digital inclusion in an economy. These factors are mainly (1) Social environment –

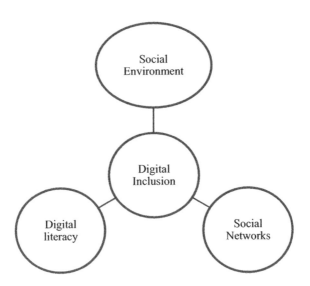

Fig. 1.   Factors Impacting the Adoption of Digital Inclusion. *Source: By the Author.*

The social environment that comprises the various social factors such as the family, and the support of the neighbourhood impacts the adoption of technology (2) Digital literacy – The level of digital literacy also impacts the level of digital inclusion in the economy. (3) Social networks – The existing social networks and relations in an economy also impact the level of digital inclusion in the economy.

Technological Identity – The Role of Social Factors in the Adoption of Technology

Within an organisation, technology adoption is determined by various social factors. These social factors include the impact of cultural factors, such as religion, social norms, beliefs, and attitudes, on adopting technology. Besides, that other social factors that impact the adoption of technology include social network relations and peer influence by the other community members on the adoption of the technology. Peer influence refers to the impact of the social actors on adopting the desired disposition. In India, approximately 64% of the members live in the hinterlands and rural India, (Annual Report, 2014–2015). These members are socially linked to each other through social networks. The adoption of standard technology in a particular social network is referred to as technological identity. This technological identity leads to digital inclusion in an economy. Besides, the level of digital literacy also determines digital inclusion in an economy. Digital literacy in an economy refers to knowledge about using technology and IT (Information Technology) to conduct business and exchange information. Despite all the forms of social intermediation, digital inclusion in the economy remains low. There is a need to bring about a change in the attitude of the members of the community through required social intermediation to facilitate digital inclusion.

Difference Between Technology Users and Non-Users

To facilitate technology usage and ensure digital inclusion, it is important to identify the individual differences between the different types of users. Various research studies highlight that those who use technology and those who do not use technology are different in terms of demographics, cultural, and social factors. It's essential to identify the difference between the individuals on the basis of these factors and then devise a strategy for achieving the strategic goals. Many studies establish a stark difference between those who use technology and those who do not use technology based on socioeconomic factors. Generally, higher socio-economic class members are more likely to use the technology. Thus, there is a need to identify the significant factors that lead to technology adoption. Digital capital comprises various components, and one of the major components is the socio-economic status of the user. Individual characteristics such as self-efficacy and personal factors impact the adoption of technology. Thus, the digital readiness of the users and techno capital in the ecosystem and the digital literacy levels determine the adoption of technology in an economy. Further,

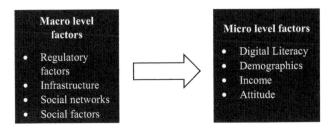

Fig. 2.   Factors Impacting the Adoption of Technology. *Source:* By
the Authors.

besides the macro factors, the individual-level factors also impact the adoption of
the level of technology (Fig. 2).

In the description of the various factors impacting the adoption of technology,
various macro-level and micro-level factors impact the adoption of technology.
Macro-level factors refer to regulatory factors, infrastructure, social networks, and
social factors. In the micro level factors, the level of digital literacy, demographics,
income, and attitude impact the digital inclusion and adoption of technology.

Progress of Digital Financial Inclusion in India

In 2014, the Finance Ministry in India laid down the foundation of the Financial
Inclusion programme in India. Emphasising the need to provide access to finance
to all the citizens at their doorsteps, the Finance Ministry laid down the Financial
Inclusion plan, which included the vital Aadhar scheme and specific reforms for
the financial sector. Under the aegis of the Pradhan Mantri Jan Dhan Yojana, in
2014, the Government of India started an ambitious plan to provide Banking
Accounts to all the people in India. In 2015–2016, the Government of India
introduced the Pradhan Mantri Jeevan Jyoti Yojana and Atal Pension Yojana.

Demonetisation and Financial Inclusion: Demonetisation that the Government
of India carried out in 2016–2017 gave a push to the Financial Inclusion programme. As a result of the Financial Inclusion programme, the usage of ICT
technology, in the form of Digital Cards and ICT platforms such as Mobile
Banking and Mobile Wallets, increased drastically (Fig. 3).

Due to the increased focus of the Indian Government, the PPI Instruments-led
Financial Inclusion got a significant push. The number of people having Mobile
Banking and PPI Instruments was a major inspiration. The upward trend in the
number of people doing Mobile Banking and Using PPI Cards became visible
from 2014–2015 (Fig. 4).

As the Government of India unveiled the PMJDY (Pradhan Mantri Jan Dhan
Yojana) in 2014-15, the usage of Credit Cards in India got a push. Notably, after
the Demonetisation wave in the year 2016, Credit Card Usage in India drastically
increased (Table 3) (Fig. 5).

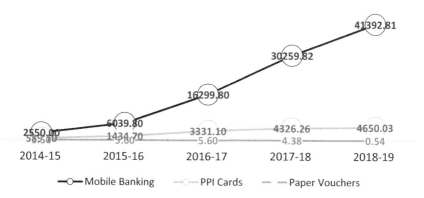

Fig. 3. Use of PPI Instruments and Financial Inclusion. *Source:* By the Author.

Electronic Payment Systems

In the year 2016, to give a push to the Trinity of reforms, including Aadhar, Jan Dhan Yojana, and Mobile Banking, the Government of India started the reforms and launched the Digital India platform. Various citizen-centric services offered under this programme were Real Time Gross Settlements (RTGS) services, Net Banking, PoS (Point of Sales) Terminal through Debit and Credit Cards, and Mobile Apps including (NEFT, RTGS, Net Banking) services (Table 4) (Fig. 6).

Real Time Gross Settlements

The Real Time Gross Settlements increased drastically because of the National e Governance Plan and Demonetisation in the year 2014-15. RTGS and prompt banking transactions showed an upward trend (Fig. 7).

Pradhan Mantri Jan Dhan Yojana

Pradhan Mantri Jan Dhan Yojana is a financial inclusion programme by the Government of India to provide Zero Balance Accounts to the general masses in

Table 1. Use of PPI Instruments and Financial Inclusion.

(In Lakhs)	2014–2015	2015–2016	2016–2017	2017–2018	2018–2019
M- Wallets	2,550.00	6,039.80	16,299.80	30,259.82	41,392.81
PPI Cards	589.10	1,434.70	3,331.10	4,326.26	4,650.03
Paper Vouchers	5.50	5.60	5.60	4.38	0.54

Source: By the Author.

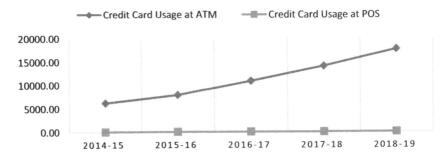

Fig. 4.   Credit Card Usage and Financial Institution. *Source:* By the Author.

India. This service is aimed at providing various financial services, including banking services, deposit services and remittances service to people at large. Financial inclusion aims to provide basic banking services at the doorstep of the citizens of India. Under this scheme, the number of accounts has increased dramatically after the demonetisation (Tables 6 and 7).

Digital Shift and Organizational Agility – Carving Nature at Joints

Businesses make efforts to integrate with the businesses to achieve profit maximisation objectives. Successful business transformation can be achieved by exploiting and exploring the dynamic capabilities to achieve the objective of competitive advantage and organisational agility. It is like carving nature at its joints. The ability to recognise the change in the internal and external environment as well as the ability to adapt effectively and efficiently in a cost-effective manner are two components of organisational capability (Seo & La Paz, 2008). Organisational agility is defined in the literature as a combination of sensing and responding capabilities (Tallon, 2019). To survive and succeed, the literature

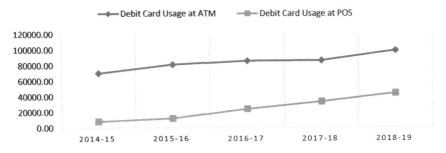

Fig. 5.   Debit Card Usage at ATM and POS.

Table 2. Credit Card Usage and Financial Inclusion.

(In Lacs)	2014–2015	2015–2016	2016–2017	2017–2018	2018–2019
Credit Card Usage at ATM	6,194.10	7,916.70	10,935.00	14,129.71	17,723.61
Credit Card Usage at POS	42.90	60.00	63.70	78.11	97.71

Source: By the Author.

emphasises the important role of being able to detect and respond to risks and opportunities (Lucas, 2012). Research studies highlight the importance of agile organisations and promote the idea that they must constantly be undergoing significant transformations (Teece, 2016). This involves implementing new IT changes and restructuring the organisational structure (IT) (Conboy & Fitzgerald, 2004). Their research study discussed organisational agility as the continual readiness of the entity to change rapidly. Lyytinen (2006) defines organisational agility as how and why the organisations sense and respond swiftly to change (March, 1991). Their study highlighted the importance of organisational agility in exploring new possibilities and exploiting old certainties. The literature emphasises the importance of exploration in terms of invention, discovery, experimentation, risk-taking, play, flexibility and exploitation. Their study work (March, 1981) discusses organisational change as the adaptive quest for new technologies as a means of adaptation. The author argues that technological change is implemented through refinement and innovation. It highlights the importance of experience in promoting organisational change. March (1963) in their research paper have discussed the importance of organisational change. Simon (1958) in his book asserts that organisations are a system of interrelated behaviours. The study highlights that organisational behaviour can be changed through learning

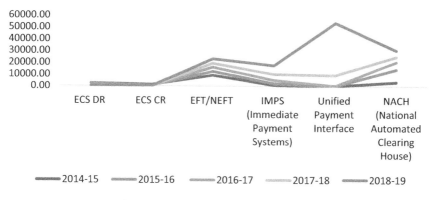

Fig. 6.   Electronic Payment System.

Table 3. Debit Card Usage at ATM and POS.

(In Lacs)	2014–2015	2015–2016	2016–2017	2017–2018	2018–2019
Debit Card Usage at ATM	69,964.80	80,733.90	85,630.60	86,022.56	98,596.15
Debit Card Usage at POS	8,080.90	11,736.10	23,993.00	33,433.93	44,142.81

or memory. Ashby's (1960) research study argues that the organisation is a dynamic system that responds to changes. Lee and Xia (2010) in their research study has defined organisational agility as the ability of an organisation to respond to changes in the external and internal environment. Sambamurthy et al. (2003) in their research study highlight that organisations can sense the environment and capitalise on their resources to leverage the opportunities. Davis (1989) in his research study highlights that seamless technology integration through interface leads to a helpful attitude towards technology. Venkatesh et al.'s (2003) research study highlights the importance of locational independence, habitual technology use, characteristics of an organisation, perceived job performance on organisational agility and organisational performance. Cyr et al.'s (2006) research study highlights the importance of design aesthetics to promote organisational agility. According to the author, task characteristics are significant for successful operations and organisational agility. Task characteristics refer to the perceived easiness and difficulty of the job. Eisenstat's (2000) research study highlights the importance of leadership commitment and

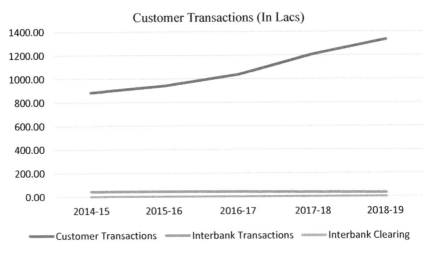

Fig. 7.   Real Time Gross Settlement.

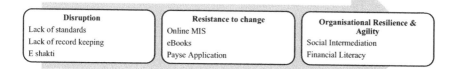

Fig. 8.   Technology Acceptance Model for Self-Help Groups Within
the Framework of Dynamic Punctuated Equilibrium.

involvement in ensuring organisational change. The study discusses six barriers to strategy implementation and learning in an organisation. The authors argue that ineffective senior leadership, conflicting priorities, poor vertical communication and coordination across businesses are the main obstacles to the functioning of an organisation. Gersick's (1991) research study highlights that system orientation works by adapting to organisational changes as the organisation moves from the equilibrium to the revolutionary change stage. The author has discussed three components of punctuated equilibrium: deep structure, equilibrium and revolutionary periods. The equilibrium period is defined as the set of organisational systems and processes that remain the same. The literature also mentions the various barriers to change, such as the pain of loss, uncertainty and the fear of failure in an organisation. The study highlights the revolutionary changes as the period during which the deep structures were dismantled, leaving the system

Table 4. Electronic Payment System.

Electronic Payment Systems (In Lacs)	2014–2015	2015–2016	2016–2017	2017–2018	2018–2019
ECS DR	2,260.10	2,247.50	87.60	15.40	9.26
ECS CR	1,153.50	390.00	101.00	61.36	53.57
EFT/NEFT	9,275.50	12,528.80	16,221.00	19,463.57	23,188.87
IMPS (Immediate Payment Systems)	783.70	2,208.10	5,067.30	10,097.98	17,529.09
Unified Payment Interface	–	–	179.00	9,152.00	53,534.03
NACH (National Automated Clearing House)	3,401.70	14,040.80	20,572.70	25,034.62	30,351.71

Table 5. Real-Time Gross Settlement.

RTGS (Real Time Gross Settlements)

RTGS (In Lacs)	2014–2015	2015–2016	2016–2017	2017–2018	2018–2019
Customer Transactions	883.90	939.50	1,036.60	1,207.12	1,333.00
Interbank Transactions	43.80	43.70	41.70	37.21	33.07
Interbank Clearing	0.10	0.20	0.20	0.24	0.27

disorganised. Considering these factors, we have deployed the Technology acceptance model in the context of our case study – self-help groups in Fatehabad, Haryana, India, and its impact on organisational agility. Self-help groups in Haryana, Fatehabad, have adopted a personalised web application by PaySe for collecting savings, depositing money into accounts and record keeping. Table 1 provides an overview of how the groups ensure enterprise agility through the technology acceptance model. In the aftermath of COVID-19, the groups sense change using the *Analyser* strategy to estimate the perceived usefulness and entrepreneurial orientation among the members of self-help groups. The literature highlights the ease of use of technology to build an attitude towards technology adoption. This was followed by a response to changes in social intermediation and technology adoption. Our model within the findings confirmed our assumptions within the interpretive TAM framework (Azjen & Fishbein, 1980) that technology change needs attitude building. The adoption of PaySe has led to improvement in financial outcomes for the members of the self-help groups in Fatehabad, Haryana, India. The success of organisational agility in a turbulent environment includes dynamic capabilities (Teece et al., 1997) to integrate, build and reconfigure internal and external competencies, market orientation or intelligence regarding the market conditions and the absorptive capacities including the routines and processes by which firms acquire, assimilate and transform information. Porter Me (1987) also highlights the importance of strategic flexibility. So

Table 6. Pradhan Mantri Jan Dhan Yojana Account.

Year	PMJDY
2014–2015	62,348,872
2015–2016	121,039,913
2016–2017	159,609,882
2017–2018	181,156,759
2018–2019	199,166,328

Table 7. Pradhan Mantri Jan Dhan Yojana.

Accounts Under Pradhan Mantri Jan Dhan Yojana

overall, the Haryana state level mission that runs these self-help groups is highly agile to have adopted technology swiftly during crisis through social intermediation (Table 8).

Perspectives on Dynamic Punctuated Equilibrium Model

Every information technology project goes through phases: the definition stage, system design, physical design and implementation stage. Abernathy and Utterback's (1978) research paper through the theoretical lens of dynamic punctuated equilibrium has highlighted the importance of incremental innovations and change. The author argues that sudden business innovation leads to instability, highlighting the need for change. Romanelli (1985) describes in detail the organisation's evolution through the theoretical lens of dynamic punctuated equilibrium. The author highlights in the wake of disruptions or externalities in the form of the pandemic that there is a need for social intermediation to ensure radical innovations (Mokyr, 1990). Loch et al. (1997) in their research study argue that technology adoption depends on the rate of incremental improvement, organisational learning and the system's resistance to switching between the equilibrium. Robinson and Scott (2007). in their research paper highlighted the punctuated equilibrium problem using normal distribution. Table 2 provides a glimpse of strategies deployed by groups to manage change.

Through the lens of the dynamic punctuated equilibrium model, strategic management needs to respond to the challenges and ensure seamless integration and IT alignment during the revolutionary periods (Table 9).

Table 10 discusses the strategic alignment through the theoretical lens of dynamic punctuated equilibrium. Hirschheim and Klein (1989), in their research paper, have addressed the issue of strategic IS alignment using the theoretical lens of dynamic punctuated equilibrium. The author has analysed the alignment between the business and information systems using Snow & Miles typology.

Table 8. Organisational Agility and Impact on Behavioural Dispositions.

Enterprise Agility	Perceived Usefulness	Perceived Ease of Use	Attitude Towards Use	Attitude Towards Change	Behavioural Intention to Use	Use of Technology
Sensing Change	(1) Locational independence (2) Seamless integration with a centralised system (3) Transparency (4) Improve business processes (5) Improve competitive advantage (6) Facilitate Audit (7) Enable organisations to diversify, expand and implement various strategies (8) Effective means to gather feedback (9) Autonomous (10) Knowledge sharing	(1) Operational through personalised platforms such as Mobile (2) Operational through simple PaySe cards (3) No need for additional equipment's (4) Collective ownership of results	*Affective:* Emotions, predispositions and perceptions of an individual impact the use of technology *Cognitive:* Knowledge level, education and Learning of a person impacts use of technology *Behavioural:* Personal traits and characteristics of a person impacts the use of technology	(1) Predispositions of the users regarding change play an important role in technology adoption (2) Rigid opinions (3) Past habits and affiliations with manual methods might obstruct the use of technology	(1) Motivation Time Saving Efficient Effective (2) Perceived security (3) Perceived Cost Savings (4) Perceived ubiquity (5) Perceived reachability (6) Social Value (7) Perceived value (8) Perceived Self-Efficacy (9) Perceived compatibility (10) Subjective Norms (11) Innovation experience (12) Self-efficacy (13) Perceived Risk (14) Compatibility	(1) Adoption of technology (2) Task feedback (3) Task significance

(11) Ensures timeliness of information for the organisation				
Develops virtual community				
(1) Reduces organisation expenditure				
(2) Team learning				
(3) Flexibility				
(4) Cost				
(5) Design				
Responding Change / Digitisation	(1) Sensitisation (2) Awareness (3) Attention seeking (4) Developing Interest (5) Autonomous use	(1) Positive reinforcement (2) Leveraging Virtual communities (3) Virtual communities (4) Leadership (5) Promoting self-learning (6) Team learning	(1) Commitment to change (2) Communicating Change (3) Training (4) Adoption of Change (5) Change Management (6) Appointing Change Agents	(1) Actual Adoption of Technology (2) Sustainability	The technology used by the members

Source: By the Authors.

Table 9. Models of Punctuated Equilibrium.

	Exploitative	**Exploratory**
Punctuated Equilibrium	The long period of exploitative changes	The brief period of exploratory Radical changes
Ambidexterity	Simultaneous exploitative changes	Simultaneous exploratory changes

The author argues that organisations undergo evolutionary changes during long periods of relative stability. This phase is followed by brief periods of revolutionary changes during which the revolutionary changes occur. Business strategies differ according to the phase of organisational change. Sabherwaal et al. (2001) in their research paper argue that the business strategies can be classified as defenders, prospectors and analysers. These pertain to business strategy attributes such as defensiveness, risk aversion, aggressiveness, proactiveness, analysis and futurity. As per the existing text and knowledge, the defender strategy is suitable for defensive businesses, risk-averse and low on aggressiveness, proactiveness, analysis and futurity, and prospectors and Analyser strategies are ideal for players who are low to medium on defensiveness, risk aversion, and high to medium on aggressiveness, proactiveness, analysis and futurity. Gersick's (1988) research study highlighted that groups follow a punctuated equilibrium model of development by alternating between inertia and revolution. Thus, group development can be studied using the dynamic punctuated equilibrium. Uotila's (2017) research study has discussed how the task environment, which comprises complexity and turbulence, impacts organisational change. In turbulent and complex environments, punctuated equilibrium is replaced by a dynamic equilibrium of ambidextrous nature. Huberman (1997), in their research paper, have used the dynamic punctuated equilibrium approach to discuss the issue of technology diffusion. The author argues that organisations adopt new technology during incremental shifts and maintain the old one. The long period of gradual changes is characterised by business strategies that are more akin to innovators. Thus, this stage is marked by continuous business innovation.

Case Study – Digital Village

The case study pertains to the digitisation of the self-help groups covered under the self-help group bank linkage programme. India within the state of Haryana, India, the Haryana State Government has undertaken the Haryana State Rural Livelihood Mission to provide access to financial services at the doorstep of the citizens of the nation.

Table 10. Punctuated Equilibrium and Snow and Miles Typology for IS Alignment.

Environment	Snow and Miles Typology	Evolutionary	Revolutionary Periods
Internal Environment	Deep Structures	(1) Mechanistic and centralised structures	(1) Structure reconfigures and disassembles (2) Semi-structure hybrid forms (3) Decentralised
	Strategy	(1) Defender Strategy (2) Differentiation strategy	*Business Strategy* (1) Analyser Strategy (2) Prospector Strategy (3) Reactor strategy
	Processes	(1) Stable (2) Risk of not being able to adapt to changes (3) Product engineering (4) Communication and Awareness	*Adaptation* IS, IM, IT strategy (1) Innovation (2) Creative imitators (3) Efficiency (4) Planning (5) Non-centralised control (6) Lack of Experience curve
	Ideology	*Organisational Adaptation* (1) The short period of metamorphic changes (2) Highly durable order (3) Equilibrium for an extended period *Goal Alignment*	*Organisational Agility* (1) Rapid and Radical spurts in change (2) Change is incremental (3) Resistance to Change (4) The crisis that breaks the systemic inertia (5) Opportunity to learn (6) Development of new structures

Table 10. *(Continued)*

Environment	Snow and Miles Typology	Evolutionary	Revolutionary Periods
			(7) Incremental adaptations
			Transformational Leadership Innovation Strategic Alignment
External Environment	Environment Characteristics	Stable	Complex environment Turbulence in the task environment
	Strategy	Exploitation Incremental Exploration	Exploration Incremental exploitation is not sufficient

Source: By the Authors.

Social Innovation – SHG Bank Linkage Programme

Microfinance is a way to give the poorest of the poor access to finance. Until the 1980s, most self-help groups were subsidised. During the 1990s financial crisis, the government could not sustain the donor-based microfinance programme through self-help groups. NABARD and MYRADA launched the SHG Bank Linkage initiative in 1987. The Reserve Bank of India piloted the SHG Bank Linkage initiative in 1991 and 1992. The Government of India formed a Working Group in 1995 headed by Sh. SK. Kalia, Managing Director of NABARD. In addition, the Union Budget announced that NABARD would credit link 2 lakh self-help groups in five years. The Pradhan Mantri Jan Dhan Yojana encourages people to save money. In 2016, digital transactions got a considerable boost. The NABARD Financial Inclusion initiative promoted technology in Rural Cooperative Banks. Promoting financial literacy in rural India has become a priority. Table 5 depicts the many characteristics of technology acceptance and organisational agility as seen through the theoretical lens of dynamic punctuated equilibrium. This helped us achieve data theory alignment and theory model alignment. While generating the theory, care was taken that the theory is parsimonious (Warren, 1976). The emergent model was found to conform to the principles of interpretative research (Klein & Myers, 1999) (Table 11).

Fig. 8 describes the self-help group's technology acceptance model within the dynamic punctuated equilibrium framework. From the resource-based view (RBV) framework, the organisation has various functional capabilities, such as

Table 11. Organisational Agility Through IT Alignment Through the Theoretical Lens of the Dynamic Punctuated Equilibrium Model.

Paradigm	Task	Structure	Technology	Organisational Agility
Resource-Based View	*Group-specific* 1. Leader selection 2. Literacy 3. VRIF 4. Resource allocation	1. Semi-formal group 2. Social Cohesion 3. Collaborative 4. Organisational capabilities	1. Digital Proficiency 2. Technological capabilities	Competitive Advantage
Resources ⟶	Capabilities ⟶		Competitive Advantage	
	"*Dynamic alignment of Business and Information Systems in a complex and ever-changing business environment to ensure appropriate leveraging of the resource capabilities in an organization. It leads to the emergence of the Dynamic Capabilities.*"			
Dynamic Alignment	**Business** 1. eBooks 2. Transactional data 3. Grading 4. Reports 5. MIS	**Structure** 1. Business Process Reengineering 2. IS Alignment 3. IM Alignment 4. IT Alignment **IT Capabilities** **Business Capabilities**	**Technology** 1. Web-based technologies 2. MIS 3. IT-based business ecosystem	Sensing ↓ Responding
Strategy Evolutionary ↓ Revolutionary	Prospector ↓ Analyzer Proactive ↓ Reactive	Mechanistic, Centralized	1. Low cost 2. Differentiation 3. Alliance 4. Innovation	

financial capabilities and technological capabilities, that are valuable, rare and cannot be imitated. Self-help groups in Haryana with a well-honed sensing capability responded by implementing PaySe Web applications. Technological capabilities lead to organisational agility. Dynamic alignment through the lens of punctuated equilibrium refers to a proactive approach to technology adoption during a crisis.

Issues and Challenges to the Financial System in India

Microfinance in India faces various challenges, such as high-interest rates, over-indebtedness, over-reliance on commercial banks, lack of financial literacy and awareness, regulatory concerns and legal challenges and higher costs of outreach. Various studies highlight that microfinance is needed by poor borrowers who lack the physical collateral and about whom the members do not have enough information. In this regard, microfinance is given the mandate to lend money to the people at the bottom of the pyramid. These members generally ask for a higher interest rate to cover the higher monitoring and screening costs. This high cost of microfinance is one of the significant weaknesses of the financial system in India. Microfinancing requires small borrowers to pay an extremely high rate of interest. In India, most of the small borrowers have taken the loan, and this leads to a very high level of indebtedness. The rural poor depend on the moneylenders and the informal borrowers, leading to a higher level of a tornado.

Moreover, the borrowers have excessive reliance on commercial banks. The heavily indebted rural borrowers lack financial understanding and access to formal loans, leading to a vicious cycle of poverty. In this institutional framework, adherence to debt laws and regulations is a deep concern. Because of these constraints, the cost of outreach is extremely high. Microfinance institutions (MFIs) in India face a trade-off between outreach and financial sustainability. With the increasing thrust on profitability and return on investment (ROI), the MFIs in India do not find it viable to lend to rural borrowers. MFIs face many limitations in terms of financial sustainability. The government should undertake social intermediation initiatives to ensure equitable distribution of resources and preferable lending to the people at the bottom of the pyramid. The other major obstacle the microentrepreneurs faces is the discrimination by the bankers in India and asymmetric information. Understanding the difficulties that have led to the denial of loan access to the poor is essential. From the study, it becomes apparent that digital capital can be a low-cost solution to materialise the goal of loan access for different sections of society.

Social Organisations

In an economy, social organisations are essentially part of informal groups and are not governed by society's institutions. These organisations also include those involved in social activities, such as the legal and social environments. The RBV and bricolage are the foundations of these organisations. The primary goal of most of these organisations is to achieve a competitive edge by utilising valuable, inimitable and rare organisational (VRIO) resources. These groups provide solidarity, allowing the organisation to participate in a democratic, participatory process. Social capital is the sum of norms, networks and social ties among community members. It refers to a collection of social networks that improve a community's social well-being (Putnam, 1993).

Moreover, literature bifurcates literature on social capital based on direct and indirect ties. Baker and Faulkner (2009) has defined 'social capital as a resource that actors derive from the specific structures and then use to pursue interests, changes in a relationship create it'. Bourdieu (1984) has defined social capital as 'the aggregate of the actual possession of potential resources which are linked to the possession of a durable network of more or less institutionalised relationships of mutual acquaintance or recognition'. From external ties, one definition describes social capital as a resource derived from structures. The other defines it as resources linked to relations. They all consist of a specific aspect of social structure and facilitate the action of individuals within that structure. Social capital has been defined as ability due to membership in a group (Brehm & Rahn, 1997; Portes, 1998). This definition highlights the internal ties of the members. Fukuyama (2000) defined 'Social capital refers to the belief system and the specific set of informal values or norms that exist in a system'. More researchers define social capital as a 'culture of trust, voluntary means, and processes, expectations for action within a collectively' (Inglehart, 1997; Portes & Sensenbrenner, 1993; Thomas, 1996). The size of a social organisation's network also affects its social capital. In community development, social capital has been defined as the norms, network and trust among the community members to facilitate cooperation among members of the community and to facilitate the achievement of community objectives (Coleman, 1988; Putnam, 2001). Complementary to both views, Nahapiet and Ghoshal (1998) defined social capital as the sum of the network and the assets mobilised through the network.

Conclusion

Digitisation has emerged as a strategic capability for the people living in rural regions in India. Digital capital provides a strategic competency and competitive advantage to the people at the bottom pyramid. Digital prowess provides externalities in the form of resources and organisational capabilities. Through the theoretical lens of the *Dynamic Punctuated Equilibrium* model, digital capital provides the core competency and competitiveness to individuals and organisations during a period of crisis. Adoption of digital capability leads to improvement in production capacity. This further leads to a reduction in transaction costs and helps to achieve a competitive advantage. Indian rural villages are suffering from a lack of digital financial literacy. Through digital literacy, the members of the rural community can optimise the use of technology to maximise returns.

Summary

Digital financial inclusion refers to access to financial services through technology. Digital inclusion leads to a reduction in transaction costs and helps to reduce the level of poverty in India. E-governance framework and setting up of NPCI as the digital financial intermediary leads to the financial inclusion of the poor. Given the social context, there is a rift between the digital policies and objectives of banking in India. This is due to the lack of digital financial literacy. Three major factors determining the success of digital inclusion include social support, the use of social networks and digital literacy, and creating a social environment. The existence of social networks determines the technological identity of an IT system or organisation. Various social and individual factors impact technology adoption. Various digital inclusion initiatives such as PMJDY (Pradhan Mantri Jan Dhan Yojana), debit and credit cards impact digital inclusion. To achieve organisational agility, organisations explore new opportunities and exploit competitive advantage. And there is a need for digital literacy to achieve organisational agility through perceived usefulness and ease of business use. Through the lens of the dynamic punctuated equilibrium model, there is a need to change the internal and external environment. There is a need to overcome resistance through social intermediation. The Indian financial system suffers from various challenges, such as regulatory changes, high-interest rates and the need to reform the institutional framework to bring about change.

References

Abernathy, W. J., & Utterback, J. (1978). Patterns of industrial innovation. *Technology Review.*

Annual Report. (2014–2015). *Ministry of rural development.* https://www.rural.nic.in

Ashby, W. R. (1960). *Design for the brain.* Wiley.

Azjen, & Fishbein. (1980). *Understanding attitudes and predicting social behavior.* Prentice-Hall.

Baker, W., & Faulkner, R. R. (2009). Social capital, double embeddedness, and mechanisms of stability and change. *American Behavioral Scientist, 52*(11), 1531–1555. https://doi.org/10.1177/0002764209331525

Brehm, J., & Rahn, W. (1997). Individual-level evidence for the causes and consequences of social capital. *American Journal of Political Science, 41*(3), 999–1023. https://doi.org/10.2307/2111684

Bourdieu, P. (1984). *Distinction: A social critique of the judgement of taste.* Routledge and Kagan Paul Ltd.

Coleman, J. S. (1988). Social Capital in the Creation of Human Capital, *American Journal of Sociology (Supplement), 94,* S95–S120.

Coleman, J. S. (1990). *Foundations of social theory.* Harvard University Press.

Conboy, & Fitzgerald. (2004). *Toward a conceptual framework of agile methods.* Springer.

Cyr, D., Hassanein, K., Head, M., & Ivanov, A. (2006). The role of social presence in establishing loyalty in e-Service environments, *Interacting with Computers, 19*(1), January 2007, 4356. https://doi.org/10.1016/j.intcom.2006.07.010

Davis, F. (1989). Perceived usefulness & perecived ease of use and user acceptance of information technology. *MIS Quarterly, 13,* 319.

Eisenstat, B. a. (2000). The silent killers of strategy implementation and learning. *Sloan Management Review.*

Fukuyama, F. (2000, April). *Social capital and civil society.* IMF Working Paper No. 00/74.

Gersick. (1988). Time and transition in work teams: Towards a new model of group development. *Academy of Management Journal, 31*(1), 9–41.

Gersick, C. J. (1991). Revolutionary change theories: A multilevel exploration of punctuated equilibrium. *Academy of Management Review.*

Hirschheim, R. A., & Klein, H. K. (1989). Four paradigms of information systems development. *Communications of the ACM, 9*(4), 1199–1217.

Huberman, L. (1997). A punctuated equlibrium model of technology diffusion. *Management Sciences.*

Inglehart, R. (1997). *Modernization and post modernization: Cultural, economic, and political change in 43 societies.* Princeton University Press.

Klein, H. K., & Myers, M. D. (1999). A set of principles for conducting and evaluating interpretive field studies in information systems. *MIS Quarterly, 23*(1), 67–88.

Lee, G., & Xia, W. (2010). Toward agile: An integrated analysis of qualitative and quantitative field data on software development. *MIS Quarterly, 34*(1), 87–114.

Lucas, H. (2012). *The search for survival: Lessons from disruptive technologies* (s.l.). Praeger.

Lyytinen, K. a. G. M. R. (2006). Information system development agility as organizational learning. *European Journal of Information Systems, 15,* 183–199.

March, C. (1963). *Behavioral theory of firms.* Prentice Hall.

March, J. G. (1991). Exploration and exploitataion in organizational learning. *Organization Sciences.*

Mokyr. (1990). *The lever of riches: Technological creativity and economic progress.* Oxford University Press.

Nahapiet, J., & Ghoshal, S. (1998). Social capital, intellectual capital, and the organizational advantage. *The Academy of Management Review, 23*(2), 242–266. https://doi.org/10.2307/259373

Porter, Me. (1987). From competitive advantage to corporate strategy. *Harvard Business Review, 65*(3), 43–59.

Portes, A. (1998). Social capital: Its origins and applications in modern sociology. *Annual Review of Sociology, 24,* 1–24.

Portes, A., & Sensenbrenner, J. (1993). Embeddedness and immigration: Notes on the social determinants of economic action. *American Journal of Sociology, 98,* 1320–1350.

Putnam, R. (1993). The prosperous community: Social capital and public life. *The American Prospect, 4,* 35–42.

Putnam, R. D. (2001). Social capital: Measurement and consequences. *Isuma: Canadian Journal of Policy Research, 2*(Spring).

Robinson, S. (2007). Puntcuated equilibrium model in organizational decision making. s.l.:s.n.

Romanelli, T. a. (1985). Organizational evolution: Metamorphosis model of convergence and reorientation. In *Research in organizational behavior.*

Sabherwaal, et al. (2001). Alignment between business and IS startegies: A study of prospectors, analyzers & Defenders. *Information Systems Research, 12*(1), 11–33.

Sambamurthy, V., Bharadwaj, A., & Grover, V. (2003). Shaping agility through digital options: Reconceptualizing the role of information technology in contemporary firms. *MIS Quarterly, 27*, 237–263.

Seo, D., & La Paz, A. I. (2008). Exploring the dark side of IS in achieving organizational agility. *Communications of the ACM, 51*(11), 136–139.

Simon, J. G. M. a. H. (1958). *Organization*. John Wiley and Sons.

Tallon, Q. C. a. S. (2019). Information technology and the search for organizational agility: A systematic review with future research. *The Journal of Strategic Information Systems, 17*(28), 218–237.

Teece, D. P. M. L. S. (2016). Dynamic capabilities and organizational Agility: Risk, uncertainty. *California Management Review*.

Teece, D. J., Pisano, G., & Shuen, A. (1997). Dynamic capabilities and strategic management. *Strategic Management Journal, 18*(7), 509–533. http://doi.org/10.1002/(SICI)1097-0266(199708)18:73.0.CO;2-Z

Uotila, J. (2017). Punctuated equlibrium or ambidexterity: Dynamics of incremental and radical organizational change over time. *Industrial and Corporate Change 27*(1).

Venkatesh, V., Morris, M., Davis, G., & Davis, F. (2003). User acceptance information technology towards a unified view. *MIS Quarterly, 25*, 425–478. https://doi.org/10.2307/3003654

Warren, T. (1976). "In general" vs. "it depends": Some comments of the Gergen-Schlenker debate. *Personality and Social Psychology Bulletin*, 404–410.

Chapter 5

Cashless Financial Systems

The Cashless Economy of India

Social Perspective

India is set to become a cashless economy and transform India into a digitally empowered society. Through digital money, the relationship with money is constantly changing. NPCI in India introduced the digital ecosystem, and the National Finance Switch is the backbone of the digital financial system. They have introduced several integrated interfaces, including the BHIM App and UPI Application. These applications facilitate the easy transfer of money, and it has increased the usage of digital mode by citizens across the globe. With the development of an integrated financial network for digital transactions, including National Financial Switch (NFS), NACH (National Automated Clearing Systems), and AePS (Aadhar-enabled Payment Systems), the financial ecosystem has become highly user-friendly. NPCI has revolutionised the digital financial ecosystem by integrating financial switches, clearing systems and merchant banks. This has led to digital financial inclusion through a reduction in the cost of banking,

Microfinance and Development in Emerging Economies, 93–118
Copyright © 2023 Nishi Malhotra
Published under exclusive licence by Emerald Publishing Limited
doi:10.1108/978-1-83753-826-320231005

and increased access and reach, leading to last-mile connectivity. Mobile banking has become universal through UPI, with just one UPI identification. Citizens can connect to any commercial, cooperative or regional bank using an interface by a private vendor or BHIM. Access to financial services has become highly convenient and affordable.

Introduction

Before the introduction of money and cash, people used to transact and do commerce based on a barter system. For the first time, 5,000 years ago, the Mesopotamian people introduced the *shekel*. The gold coins were issued for the first time in 600–650 BC. Money acts as a medium of exchange and a store of value. Money is a commodity of trust that all have accepted. Earlier, cowrie shells, cigarettes, stones, gold and coins were used to represent money. Now hard coins can be used for the purpose of exchange. The currency now is being increasingly exchanged with digital money. Money has been at the heart of most human relationships, and the loss in the value of money can often lead to armed conflicts and aggression. Within the last few years, technology has taken the world by storm with the emergence of cryptocurrencies and digital currency. Digital currencies and platforms are changing the landscape of commerce in India. King Alyattes created the first documented currency in Lydia, which is now part of modern-day Turkey. The first currency minted had a symbol of a roaring lion face. The history of currency dates back to the twelfth and thirteenth centuries, as described in the book by Marco Polo.

After this period, stamped coins were introduced to promote exchange and commerce in the nation. The Mesopotamians introduced the concept of bartering for the first type, approximately 6,000 BC. The old traders used various commodities to facilitate exchange. These commodities include salt, tea, weapons and food. Before the discovery of money, many other commodities were used in the Mediterranean and the Near East. The commodities that were used for exchange included barley and wheat. Cowrie shells, bronze and shells have been used for exchange. White bread made from clam shells was used as money and for exchange and commerce. The first bit of coin was introduced millions of years ago in China in bronze and copper coins. These coins were introduced somewhere in 1000 BC in China. The first bit of proper money was the gold and silver. The first coin of gold and silver were introduced by the Greeks in Ionia, in Western part of modern Turkey. Midas and Croesus were extremely famous for gold and riches. The coins were manufactured in (742–814) by Charlemagne in Germany. The denier coins were introduced and used until the 1970s. Initially, the function of money was performed by various commodities and agricultural produce. The coins were minted by the kings to be used for themselves.

Further, the banks have created money to facilitate exchange, and the power of the money issued by the rulers depends on whether the citizens of a nation use the money issued by the ruler. For the first time, in the thirteenth century, King Louis IX of France (St Louis) directed that the coin be used for commerce. The existing rulers profited by selling the coins for a value higher than the production cost. To add to the trade of money and to increase the amount of profit generated, the rulers started to reduce the content of gold and silver, thus debasing the coin. Money can be defined as a network of changing numbers. In the sixteenth and seventeenth centuries, the scientific revolution led to the improvement in the way human beings measure things. Benjamin Franklin propagated many years ago that time is money. Aristotle propagated that the purpose of money is to facilitate the exchange. The Christian teachings about money changed after the Middle Ages when the Protestants propagated that making money is a service to god. Capitalism was born from the struggles of the Protestants.

These coins were manufactured using bronze and copper. In 500 BC, the first bit of coins were created with the emperor's and gods insignia. In 800 AD, the first silver coin was issued by Charlemagne and was accepted as a standard coin in Western Europe from 794 AD to 1200 AD. The shilling and pound became widely usable in the thirteenth century. Paper currency was created in China for the first time in 700 AD to 800 AD. In 1295, Marco Polo described how Kublai Khan Government issued a paper currency in his book. This currency was used as the currency, and who so ever counterfeited it was sentenced to death. The book by Marco Polo propagated the use of paper currency in Europe.

The bills of exchange were introduced in the thirteenth century. The Chinese paper currency was stopped from usage, and during the fifteenth century, the coins became popular worldwide. Government payments are vital in promoting transparency and ensuring freedom from consumption. Technology is vital in generating and propagating innovation among community members. Internet and digital technology are the enablers of change and innovation. This has also changed how technology has enabled businesses, the government, and other stakeholders to innovate and interact with the citizens. The banknotes were published for the first time in 1661, and credit cards were introduced in 1946. The industrial revolution made Britain the most powerful nation in the world. Many big banks and enterprises, such as Barclays and Lloyds, emerged as the most prominent multinational bank. The international trade in Britain gave rise to international trade. This international trade led to the development of ports and the international trade centre. Barrings and Rothchild were the two significant families that led to the setting up of the banks in London. In the eighteenth century, the British empire prevented the American colonies from having their currency. This dispute with Britain led to the independence of America. Aspiring for money and freedom, the Americans fought for their independence. The American veterans Robert Barron created a considerable fortune, and John D Rockefeller became a tycoon.

From 1837 to 1913, the famous banker John Pierpont Morgan became the most prominent banker. After the beginning of the First World War (1914–1918), the USA replaced India as the largest superpower. In the 1920s, runaway inflation led to a decline in the value of money. In the 1920s, nations across the globe faced the problem of the gold standard. The gold bar was dropped in 1914–1918, and paper money came into circulation. The world's nations adopted the Gold standard in the 1920s. It was once again suspended in the 1930s. Keynesian economics influenced government policies in the new era during the Second World War. A great deal of government spending ended the economic slowdown in the 1930s. In 1944, the Bretton Woods collapsed and led to the setting up of the International Monetary Funds (IMF), World Bank and WTO (World Trade Organization). A link was maintained between the world's money and gold to facilitate the working of the world economy. Till 1971, most nations used to ask the USA to pay for their currencies in terms of gold. In 1971, the remaining link between gold and the world bank was scrapped. And the national currencies of other nations are made to float against each other.

Digital Money

Digital technologies enable the Government to adopt the changes efficiently and effectively (David-West, 2016). These technologies allow the government to collaborate, co-create and innovate. Information communication technology (ICT) and innovation enable transformation and diminish the instances of fraud and corruption in the economy. The use of electronic payment systems enables to creation of an efficient and effective economic ecosystem (Barik & Sharma, 2019). Digitisation has emerged as an essential strategic policy tool to overcome the constraints of higher transaction costs and access to financial services. Modernisation and digitisation of the national payment systems and financial inclusion have further led to a higher level of efficiency and reduction in fraud and corruption in the system. The digitisation of the economy can lead to a higher rate of growth and productivity in the system. Digital payment is a renowned payment technology that empowers citizens to transform India into a transformed economy. In the wake of demonetisation, digitisation to achieve a cashless society has reached the utmost importance for a developing economy like India. The new form of electronic payments leads to a higher level of convenience and makes transactions easy and affordable. India was the first nation to have adopted the digital mode of payment and commerce during the crisis.

Technology adoption depends on the level of reach, availability and awareness. Money has developed out of the features of the earlier society. Money was often used to compensate the man and women. It was also used for offerings to the gods and goddesses and to pay tribute to kings in Babylon and Pharaohs in Egypt. The practice of writing the accounts emerged from the need to maintain grain accounts in temples and royal palaces. The practice of using clay tablets emerged earlier than 3000 BC. Policymakers throughout the world are promoting the idea of eliminating cash. The elimination of cash is aimed at removing illegal activity.

Cashless Economy

Digital India is a flagship programme being run by the state of India. This programme started with a vision to transform India into a digitally altered society.

It is a way forward to create an empowered community. Digital India aims to create a faceless, paperless and cashless economy. The users will not have to carry hard cash in a cashless economy. Instead, users can use a debit cards, credit cards, and payment banks to make the payment. In such an economy, the use of cash is not eliminated, but the use of cash is reduced to as much of an extent as possible. Many European nations have gone completely cashless. This includes the economy of Sweden and Denmark. Now, the Indian economy is on its way to being cashless. With the advent of various online applications such as BHIM Application, UPI, Digital India, Digital, Common Services Centre, Aadhar, NEFT, Digi Vyapar, electronic payments, and the digital economy has become a reality. At an individual level, to create a cashless society, the government has introduced various instruments such as banking cards, USSD (Unstructured Supplementary Service Data), AEPS (Aadhar Enabled Payment System), UPI (Unique Payment Identification), Mobile Wallets, Bank prepaid cards, Point of Sale, Internet Banking, Mobile Banking and Micro ATMs.

Digital India

Digital India is a programme to prepare India for the future. This programme has put technology at the centre. This programme integrates many ideas and practices into a universal, so that everything converges towards achieving a single goal. This programme is integrated by DeiTY (Department of Electronics and Information Technology) and is implemented by the state government. This programme pulls together many schemes and is implemented in a synchronised manner. It aims to deliver services to India's citizens and businesses at their doorsteps.

Vision of Digital India

India is a land of paradoxes and diversities. The phrase *Kos kos par badle paani, chaar kos par baani.* In India, people speak more than 1,599 languages. India is a diverse nation with many languages, races, creeds, castes, religions, and languages. There are multiple sects with different dances and music, and languages, and each state has cultural diversity. In India, on the one hand, we have the poorest of the poor; on the other hand, we have the richest of the world. It is an ancient civilisation that is more than 6,000 years old and aims to come to terms with the implementation of technology in a modern environment. In India, bullock carts co-exist with modern cars and private jets. In India, where marginalised Indians work hard to realise their dreams through hard work and education, the rich and powerful exert their right to rule the state. This is a land of paradoxes and diversity; on the one hand, millions of people live on the streets, millions of orphans live in orphanages, and wealthy millionaires ride plush cars and live the lives of millionaires. This nation has a vast divide between the rich and poor. Millions of Indians are living on the streets and have led their way to riches by following their passion. However, India is one of the most unequal nations in the world. There is a vast divide between the rich and poor in this nation regarding gender, income levels, and opportunities for employment and education. In a nation with unequal opportunities, the market forces of demand and supply are insufficient to ensure resource allocation. The neo-liberal policies have failed in the given scenario. In this nation, due to the failure of the market forces, there is very little sensitivity to the rights of the poor and vulnerable. In India, hunger is rampant, and there is abject poverty in the interiors of villages.

Contract Theory and Need for a Governance Structure

India is known for its rich diversity, culture and natural environments. It has diverse flora, fauna, castes, cultures and religions with different languages, traditions, dress, foods, languages and literature. The sustainability of such a diverse system depends on how far the existing governance systems can propose innovative solutions. To enable such change, the system members must be willing to accept such changes. The description of the need for governance structure as a way to achieve innovation is given below in Fig. 1. Thus, the governance structure that provides innovative solutions is the way to accommodate the diversity in the nation.

In the context of the Indian growth story, the contract theory propagates that the greater the amount of time that people from diverse cultures and sections spend with each other, the amount of understanding between the people of different groups. It manifests in the form of diversity and diverse cultures and practices. To manage this kind of various system, there is a need for a rich governance system that can direct the institutional framework to take into account the perspectives existing in different forms and provide various innovative solutions that lead to prosperity.

e-Governance in India

The electronic governance (e-Governance) in India is associated with implementing ICT to achieve the results of good governance (Sangita & Dash, 2005).

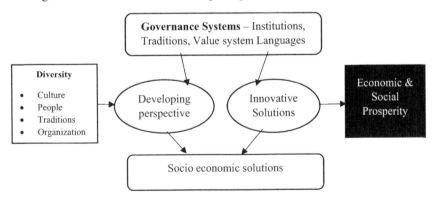

Fig. 1.   Vision of Digital India. *Source:* By the Authors.

ICT aims to ensure the electronic storage of information, transmission of information, processing of information, faster processing of information and speeding up the delivery of government services. E-Governance is aimed at ensuring the fast delivery of services. It also aims to promote transparency in the functioning of the Governments. It aims to promote the reach of government services at the doorsteps. E-Governance services are aimed at providing the reach to the services at the doorsteps of the Government of India. NeGP aims to transform the delivery of government services, improve the portfolio of government services, ensure optimum utilisation of core infrastructure, and leverage emerging technologies. It is aimed at integrating business and citizen-centric services to ensure the delivery of Government services at the doorstep of the citizens of India.

Pillars of Digital India

The vision of India is centred on three main pillars mainly (1) digital infrastructure, (2) governance of service and (3) digital empowerment.

(1) *Digital infrastructure as a utility for a citizen of India* – Digital India aims to put in place infrastructure as a utility for each citizen of India. This infrastructure includes the high-speed internet as the core utility, cradle to given identity, providing unique, identifiable and lifelong identity services. The use of the mobile account and bank account to enable participation in digital and financial space. It aims to provide access to citizen-centric services through the Common services centre. It aims to create a private space on the public cloud and a safe and secure cyberspace.

(2) *Governance and services on demand* – This digital programme aspect aims to integrate the departments across the jurisdiction seamlessly. It aims to provide services in real-time from online and mobile platforms. It aims to provide all the citizen entitlements on the cloud. It aims to transform service delivery to improve the ease of business digitally. It will also include digitising all financial transactions to make them electronic and cashless.

(3) *Digital Empowerment of Citizens* – To empower the citizens of India, digital India aims to make digital literacy universal. It aims to enable access to financial services through digital resources. It aims to provide all the digital certificates available on the cloud. It aims to create a collaborative platform to ensure democratic and participative governance. It also aims to provide portability of all entitlements through the cloud.

Nine Pillars of Digital India

Digital India has propagated nine different pillars of the digital India programme, which include (1) Broadway Highways, (2) E-Governance, (3) Electronics manufacturing, (4) Universal access to phones, (5) e Kranti, (6) IT for jobs,

(7) Public internet access for programmes, (8) Information for all (9) Early harvest to programmes.

This programme aims to provide broadband connectivity to the urban and rural regions. It also aims to put in place a National information infrastructure. The broadband for the rural regions is to be provided by the Department of India, with coverage of 250,000 GP. And in urban areas, the virtual network operators will provide broadband network services with a mandate for communication services in new infrastructure development buildings. The National Infrastructure network is integrating the SWAN, NKN and NOFN to be implemented in two years. This programme also aims to provide digital connectivity to the villages in India through the ongoing programmes driven by the Common Services Centre and the post offices. It also aims to create workflow automation to facilitate the electronic storage of information and a public grievance redressal system. The electronic service delivery system e Kranti comprises various citizen-centric services, which include technology for farmers, technology for education, technology for health, technology for planning, technology for justice, technology for financial inclusion, and technology for security. The information for all programmes aims to provide online messages and information to the citizens of India. It also aims to upload all the documents and certificates online. As part of the technology for electronic manufacturing programme, it aims to target zero imports. This includes improvising various programmes that include taxation incentives, export and import incentives, economies of scale, and focussing on various programmes. Digital India programme aims to propagate the training for the people in the Indian villages, providing the IT and ITES (Information technology and information technology-enabled services) and training the delivery agents. The early harvest programme aims to create public Wi-Fi hotspots, impart SMS-based weather services for the benefit of the Indian farmers, and provide biometric attendance for all the farmers. Besides, the Harvest in India programme also aims to provide various services for the benefit of the children in the villages of India. These services include online eBooks and a national portal for lost and found children. The digital India programme's institutional mechanism comprises the Monitoring Committee on Digital India, the Digital India Advisory Committee, and Apex Committee. These committees are managed by DeiTY and Line Ministers. The Monitoring Committee for managing the Digital India programme is to be headed by the Prime Minister of India, the Finance Minister, the Minister of Communication and Information technology, the Ministry of Research and Development, the Ministry of Human Resource Development, and the Ministry of Health. The Digital India programme's overall cost is approximate Rs. 100,000 crores. The digital India programme has provided broadband in 2.5 lakh schools and universities and aims to provide universal phone connectivity. It targets zero imports and 400,000 public internet access points, Wi-Fi in 2.5 lakh schools and universities, public Wi-Fi hotspots for citizens, digital inclusion for 1.7 crore trainers, and provision of e-Services across the Government. India aims to be a leader in providing IT services in health, education, and banking. It aims to empower citizens through the public cloud and internet access digitally. The e-Governance programme aims to reform the government through the use of technology. It includes digitising all the transactions across the departments using Information technology. It aims to provide for the electronic storage of information and workflow automation. The Government of India has also launched a programme for hosting government data on the cloud through the service called Meghraj. The Government of India has automated the public grievance redressal system. Within the ambit of the e-Kranti programme, the Government of India aims to expand the mission mode project, revamp the existing Mission Mode Projects and provide technology for education. Within the ambit of the digital literacy programme, the Government of India aims to ensure the digital inclusion of the poor and citizens of India. The government has also achieved the vision of digitisation of medical records. Digital services provided to the farmers include digitising all the information needed by the farmers. This includes providing all the information about the prices of agricultural commodities, cash loans and relief payments with online banking. To ensure the delivery of services, the digital infrastructure comprises providing the technology for security in the form of mobile and technology alerts. It also includes technology for financial inclusion, which includes providing services to people at the bottom of the pyramid. It also includes automating all the services related to court activities. It includes digitisation of the courts in the form of e-Courts. It also provides the technology for better planning, including GIS-based services for decision-making, social media, data analytics and National GIS Mission mode projects. It also includes providing technology security in the National Cyber Security Coordination Centre. The electronics manufacturing programme by the Government of India comprises M-SIPS, putting in place a cluster for promoting manufacturing in India. The national e-Governance plan aims to provide various citizen-centric services at the doorstep of the citizens of India. These services are to be provided in land records, commercial taxes, health, education, employment exchanges, Gram Panchayats, Police, Public Distribution Systems, Treasuries, e-District, Agriculture, Municipalities, etc. The main services provided in this domain include the e-Office, which includes the digitisation of all the official records; MCA21, which includes the digitisation of the Ministry of Corporate Affairs; digitisation of the income tax department; online VISA services; digitisation of the passport services, digitisation of the banking services, e Posts or digitisation of the postal services, Aadhar enabled digitisation of the services, digitisation of the central excise duty digitisation of insurance services. Besides, other digitised services include e-Courts, e-Processing, Common Services Centres and e-Business.

Indian Stack

Indian stack is a digital infrastructure enabling technology users to transact without obstacles. This infrastructure has given unique identification to the users. Indian stack has two major components: the unique identifier for each user and the digital payment infrastructure. This infrastructure is built by NPCI (National Payment Corporation of India). It is a pack of payment and transaction interfaces and public digital platforms that include Aadhar. This stack brings together the private and the public entities. The other example of the Indian stack is the consent layer, which comprises the DigiLocker, which ensures the storage of digital documents. It works with the help of digital signatures. And the UPI is the cashless layer that integrates the various applications in one place to facilitate interoperability. The financial stack creates a quick link between the individual users and the financial ecosystem. QR codes have been introduced to facilitate funds transfer from one individual to another to further inclusivity. It is an integrated attempt to converge the technology, regulations, and framework for governance. Indian stack is a set of Application Programing Interfaces (APIs) that allows businesses and start-ups to leverage the digital infrastructure to promote the use of digital technology to ensure the delivery of cashless and paperless transactions and services. The fiduciaries can also use API. Thus, the financial stack is soon emerging as a tool for data interoperability. The success of the financial inclusion programme in India depends on three major factors: a National Identification Number, the Bulk Payment system and the interoperable seamless system. The seamless, interoperable system promotes the seamless connectivity and delivery of financial services to the poor. UPI as functionality has been developed by the NPCI (National Payment Corporation of India).

NPCI also operates other functionalities, which include the RuPAY payment structure that works at a lower cost using the VISA and Mastercard. NPCI aims to integrate various payment systems and create a standardised process for conducting business. UPI provides a unique digital identifier for each bank or financial institution to facilitate the transfer of funds across the users. Thus, UPI provides an interoperable system that ensures the integration of all the players in the payment ecosystem. For the use of the government functionalities such as PMJDY (Pradhan Mantri Jan Dhan Yojana), the Aadhar biometric system is used for the validation of the identity of the user. For private payment banks, the identity of the customers is established using the secure payment environment comprising a unique PIN (Personal Identification Number). The digital value is taken into account by the bulk payments comprising the government payment systems, i.e., the government transfers.

Reforming E-Government Through Technology

The government is reformed through the use of technology (Nanda, 2022). The digitisation of governments aims to achieve inclusive growth, poverty reduction and ensure peace and law in society and integrity of the environment. The primary objective of e-Governance is to digitise all the working of all the ministries and government activities in India. It includes the digitisation of the government with the implementation of various technologies like online application tracking. The other aspect of digitisation of the Government is to make documentation easy and simple. The digitisation of government services through business process reengineering is aimed at making governance efficient and effective. It aims at digitising the online application filing and tracking, integrating the online services, putting in place an online identification programme through the use of Aadhar and Online ID identification programme and implementing the Mobile Seva programme. The primary objective of the e-Governance programme is to bring the citizens and the Government together through some digital platforms. It also aims to transform digital services through technology such as Aadhar, UPI, Digi Locker, UMANG and digital signature. It also aims to foster a spirit of research and development in the organisation, make India a global hub for innovation and emerging technology and foster responsibilities for emerging technologies such as artificial intelligence and machine learning.

National e-Governance Plan

In his *Grundlegung Zur Metaphysik de Sitton*, Immanuel Kant says, 'So act as to treat humanity, whether in their personal or in that of any other, in every case as an end withal, never as means only'. The famous proverb depicts that citizens are ending in themselves rather than as means to ends. In the post-independence era, the Government is the provider and coordinator of various services. Governments globally have realised the need for effective and efficient delivery of citizen-centric services. With the advent of technology, digitisation, and implementation of ICT are aimed at digitising significant citizen-centric services. This transformation of government services through the implementation of technology has the power to transform the lattice of relations between the Government, businesses, and citizens of India. This is often referred to as e-Governance in India. *E-Governance refers to the use of Information Communication Technology by the Government agencies (Wide Area Network, Internet, Mobile computing) to facilitate networking between the Government, Business, and Citizen centric services.* E-Governance has the means to reduce the level of corruption in the system and ensure more transparency in the functioning of the government departments. The digital governance model can potentially.

Stages in e-Governance

Since the 1990s, citizen-centric services in India have been computerised and digitised. E-Governance in India has various stages, which comprise (1) computerisation, (2) networking, (3) interface and (4) interconnectivity.

a. *Computerisation*: The first step in the implementation of the e-Governance programme is to provide computers in the various departments of the Government at the state and central level.
b. *Networking:* In this step, the various Government departments are linked and networked through technology.
c. *Interface:* In this face, an interface is created through the implementation of web-based service solutions to provide the interface between the government, businesses and citizens of India. Subsequently, the interfaces are linked through the use of technology.

Types of Interactions in e-Governance

E-Governance interactions between the various government agencies can be differentiated as (1) G2G (government to government), (2) G2C (government to citizens), (3) G2B (government to business).

Government to Government: The government departments are leveraging technology to restructure the business processes. This form of interaction is between the government agencies at the state, district or zonal level. Through this form of interaction, the dealings between the various forms of governments are digitalised.

Government to Citizens: The government provides various forms of services to the citizens of India. The goal of the national e-Governance plan is to ensure the delivery of various citizen-centric services to the citizens of India at their doorsteps.

Government to Business: The government provides various services to the business units. The digitisation of government services helps reduce the red tapeism and delay in delivering services.

Benefits of e-Governance

E-Governance provides various benefits, such as reduced costs, increased transparency and efficiency in delivering services to the poor.

(1) *Better access to information and services to citizens:* ICT ensures seamless access to citizen-centric services. It leads to a reduction in the cost of delivery. Based on the life cycle basis, e-Governance ensures access to information and services to the citizens of India.

(2) *Increased reach:* e-Governance ensures the reach of the various government services. Implementing area networks, mobile computing and internet helps to enhance the reach of government services for the citizens and the government department.

(3) *Improve accountability and transparency:* The ICT implementation enables Government to achieve clarity and accountability in the delivery of various citizen-centric and business-centric services.

Fig. 2 provides a snapshot of various benefits of e-Governance in India. The e-governance aims to provide seamless service delivery to businesses and citizens alike. The significant goals of e-Governance are to (1) improve service delivery, (2) create transparency and accountability, (3) empower people with technology, (4) enhance efficiency in the delivery of services, (5) offer better interface between government, business and citizens.

To facilitate comprehensive e-Governance, the thrust is on reforms in the domain of (1) process, (2) preparedness and (3) people. Before automating the services the government provides, there is a need to re-engineer the existing government processes.

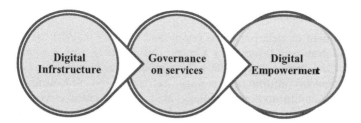

Fig. 2.   Vision of Digital India. *Source:* By the Authors.

Four Pillars of e-Governance

E-Governance has four significant pillars: (1) people, (2) process, (3) technology and (4) resources. To implement the agenda of e-Governance, leadership needs to be nurtured through improved commitment and change management. There is a need to promote leadership qualities through the required social intermediation and training. To transform the governance solutions, there is a need to reform the government processes.

There is a substantial digital divide between the rural and urban, poor and rich, and males and females in terms of technology implementation. There is a need for regulatory and supervision changes to ensure the adoption of technology.

Goals and Objectives of e-Governance

Since the adoption of the National e-Governance Plan, the objectives of digitisation have been mentioned as follows:

(1) To reduce red tape and bureaucratic delay in rendering government services to the citizens of India and businesses
(2) To ensure seamless transmission of information, processing of data, and speeding up of the governmental decision processes
(3) To promote transparency and accountability in the functioning of the government department
(4) To promote financial access and access to government services to the citizens of India at a low cost
(5) To promote transparency in the delivery of the citizen-centric services
(6) To reduce the digital divide in the country through intermediation and training.

E-Governance aims to ensure SMART (Simple, Moral, Accountable, Responsive, and Transparent) delivery of services to the citizen through Government agencies. It involves the use of information technology by government agencies to (1) ensure a faster exchange of information, (2) ensure a speedier delivery of government services, (3) promote efficient and effective delivery of services and (4) improve the administrative machinery and the quality of services.

E-Governance Initiatives in India

The department of electronics was established in India in 1970. In 1977, establishing the National Informatics Centric (NICS) 1977 was a significant step towards e-Governance. In the 1980s, the computer was brought into Government offices to ensure information storage, retrieval, and processing. With the improvement in information technology, many citizen-centric services were made online. However, a turning point in the history of e-Governance was the launching of NICNET in 1987. NICNET was a satellite-based computer network. In the domain of e-Governance services to citizens of India, various milestone projects such as the computerisation of Land records, Bhoomi project in Karnataka for online delivery of land records, Gyandoot in Madhya Pradesh, FRIENDS in Kerala and e-Seva in Andhra Pradesh were undertaken to improve the delivery of citizen-centric services efficiently and effectively. Similarly, financial inclusion initiative was conducted to computerise and digitise the banks and financial institutions.

Financial Inclusion in India

Financial inclusion aims to provide access to financial services to the citizens at their doorsteps (Ozili, 2021). In the 1990s, the Government of India undertook the famous Aadhar (Unique Identification) project to provide a unique identification number to all at their doorsteps. Within the ambit of this programme, the services provided by the banks and the payment service providers were digitised. The seamless connectivity was ensured through network connectivity and data management services. Rangarajan Committee provided the recommendation for financial inclusion. The Government of India recommends access to the banking system as the priority for poverty reduction and inclusive growth. The government has introduced various schemes such as *PMJDY (Pradhan Mantri Jan Dhan Yojana)* to provide universal banking to the people at the bottom of the pyramid. Besides that, the government has also started offering various schemes to the people at the bottom of the pyramid. This includes the *Direct Benefit Transfer*. The Government of India is targeting large-scale digitisation, with universal internet coverage and mobile computing, to ensure financial access to the people at the bottom of the pyramid.

Further, the government has tried to link all the financial accounts to a unique identification number. The government is also targeting setting up a digital infrastructure that includes digital identification, payment and settlement system. The Government of India has developed a new scheme under which Mobile Service Operators and fintech companies can provide banking services through a payment bank. Demonetisation gave a further push to cashless and digital banking in India.

Use of Technology by the Financial Institutions

Implementing technology in the banking sector has revolutionised the back office and front office as well as the processing of data. This has reduced costs and improved the quality and variety of services being provided to banking customers. The electronic payment system has completely replaced the manual payment system. With the advent of complex derivative products, banks have also acquired the technology for risk management. This risk management technology is helping the banks to mitigate the credit risk faced by the banks. The banks are increasingly using value risk management technologies and risk measurement technologies, which assist the bankers in reducing the interest rate risk. Financial institutions globally are using various tools to screen and monitor the customers who apply for credit. Thus, technology has come to play a vital role. From the analysis of the banking sector, it becomes clear that digital technology plays a significant role in banking. There are various issues in the implementation of digital technology. The adoption of technology is limited due to the requirement for a human touch. The people in the interiors of India find technology highly impersonal and sometimes feel that the use of foreign languages makes the use of technology extremely difficult. In this scenario, the Government of India and the central bank of India, i.e., the Reserve Bank of India, should focus more on developing mobile and ICT interfaces that use the local language.

Moreover, the adoption of digital finance also depends on the users' aspirations and attitudes. In addition, users find it extremely difficult to use complex products, and they prefer simple products. Thus, to facilitate the adoption of technology, it is extremely important to change the users' attitudes. Many users still prefer cash and are wary of using the technology. There is a need for more research on linkages between digital payments and financial inclusion. The Government of India has launched the Digital India and Financial inclusion programme that aims to centralise access to various Government services using UID (Unique Identification Number) or Aadhar.

Moreover, there is a need to build more gender focus in financial inclusion initiatives. In rural regions, there is a stark disparity between males and females regarding access to financial services. Cyber security remains a significant issue in achieving the goal of complete financial inclusion. There is a need to build a regulatory framework to supervise and regulate the delivery of financial services through digital mode.

Financial Inclusion in India – A Snapshot

Since the adoption of the National e-Governance Plan in India, The timeline for the implementation of various financial inclusion initiatives is given below:

Nachiket Mor Committee: In 2013, the Government of India established the Committee on Comprehensive Financial Services for Small Businesses and Low-Income Households, headed by Nachiket Mor, an RBI member. An extensive report regarding the same was published in 2014. This Committee made a historic recommendation of providing a compulsory banking account to all adults above 18. This recommendation was later implemented as the PMJDY (Pradhan Mantri Jan Dhan Yojana). The committee also emphasised the importance of UID (Unique Identification Number) or Aadhar card as the primary force behind financialisation.

Payment Banks: Nachiket Mor committee, in his report, also recommended setting up a new category of banks called Payment Banks. On 17 July 2014, the Reserve Bank of India provided the draft guidelines for setting up payment banks in India. Paytm wallet was launched in February 2014, and in 2015, the RBI (Reserve Bank of India) released the list of entities that could operate as payment bank (Table 1).

Policy Ecosystem

In India, proper regulation is lacking to ensure safe digital banking. Several different agencies are involved in guaranteeing digital banking in India. RBI, the central bank, is the apex body involved in regulating payments and ensuring a secure ecosystem. PMJDY (Pradhan Mantri Jan Dhan Yojana) scheme launched by the Government of India has played an essential role in promoting digital finance. The ownership of a universal banking account is the best initiative to promote digital banking. NITI Aayog is the strategic think tank of the Government of India, which devises the digital banking and payments strategy. Digital banking in India is still in the nascent stage. The TRAI functions as a regulator that regulates the screening of users through implementing the KYC (Know Your Customer) norms. From the Government's perspective, MeiTY handles digital transactions in India. NPCI is an intermediary institution set up by the RBI (Reserve Bank of India) and backed by other public sector banks. NPCI provides the essential financial infrastructure required for digital transactions. This body provides the infrastructure in the form of a National Finance Switch and owns various brands such as RuPAY and UPI. Besides, RuPAY and UPI, NPCI has also launched different digital products such as IMPS, BHIM, AEPS (Aadhar Enabled Payment System), and Bharat Bill Payment system. IMPS is a unique technology that allows the accurate-time transfer of cash through bank accounts. It is a substitute for the lengthy transfer process through NEFT. BHIM is a mobile application-based fund transfer system. It works through the UPI interface. If the user does not have a smartphone, then Aadhar Enabled Payment System provides a substitute for the immediate fund transfer through other means. Bharat Bill Payment System aims to enable users to pay their utility bills through this application (Fig. 4).

Transforming India's Digital Payment Landscape

Digital services in India are witnessing a spate of technological innovation. Over the past years, digital payment transactions have witnessed a sudden surge in digital transactions (Gabor & Brooks, 2017). There is a sudden effort to promote financial inclusion. Jan Dhan, Aadhar, and Mobile are three pillars of digital transformation. Digital transactions have seen a sudden spurt through various

Table 1. Temporal Strategy – Description of Turn of Events in Digitisation.

	2014	2015	2016	2017	2018
Jan	Mor Committee releases report			India Post Payment Bank launched Airtel Payment Bank launched	
Feb	Paytm Wallet Launch	Finance Minister made a mention of digitising transactions during the budget speech	Demonetisation	Jio passes 100 million subscribers	WhatsApp pay launched
Mar				mAadhaar pay was launched	
Apr		MUDRA Launched	JAM Linkage launched UPI Launched		Jio Payment bank launched
May		PMJBY & PMBSY launched			Bharat Inclusion was launched by JPMorgan, Dell Foundation, and Omidyar Network

Table 1. (*Continued*)

	2014	2015	2016	2017	2018
June					
July	Draft guidelines for Payment Banks and Small Finance Banks were launched			Fintech payment bank launched	
August	PMJDY launched Licence to PhonePe	Payment bank licence to 11 banks	Committee on digital payments launched		
September	The Centre for Digital Financial Inclusion formed	India joins BTCA	Bharat QR launched Jio launched		UPI 2 launched: Supreme Court ruling on Aadhar India Post Payment Bank launched
October			Catalyst launched		
November	Final guidelines for Payment Banks and Small Finance Banks	Ola Money launched	Demonetisation	Paytm Payment Bank launched	
December		PhonePe begins operation			

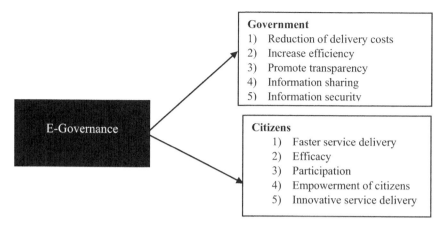

Fig. 3.   Benefits of e-Governance.

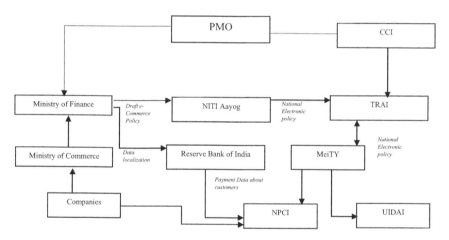

Fig. 4.   Policy Ecosystem for Regulation of Digital Transactions.

initiatives such as BHIM – UPI, Immediate Payment Services (IMPS), Pre-paid instruments (PPI), and National Electronic Toll Collection System (NETC). The volume and value of digital transactions have increased tremendously (Fig. 5).

Fig. 2 provides a description of the value and volume of digital transactions conducted in the Indian economy. In the year 2021–2022, the digital transaction volume went up from 5,554 to 8,840. And the value of transactions went up from 3,000 in 2021–2022 to 3,021 in 2022–2023.

UPI (Unified Payment Interface) is a unique digital platform that has emerged as a payment system to merge multiple banks into a single banking platform. Today, UPI constitutes approximately 40% of total digital transactions. The volume of digital commerce has gone up to 6.58 billion, and the value of digital

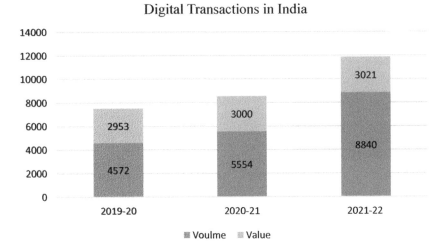

Fig. 5.   Total Digital Transactions in India.

transactions has gone up to Rs 10.73 lakhs. It has boosted the digital transactions done by small businesses and street vendors. Fig. 3 describes the digital transactions conducted by the citizens of India. Digital payments have emerged as the means to receive Government transfer payments and subsidies. Through the analysis of data, the utilisation of digital payments has increased manifold.

In India, digital financial services have grown in three phases. In the first phase, from 2014 to 2016, the growth of transactions was stable at approximately 2% per annum. The payment banks were set up in 2016. Hence, digital transactions through the payment bank channel saw an upward trend. After that, the demonetisation in 2016 led to increased digital transactions. Till 2014, it was debit cards and credit cards, and after 2013 it was transactions through payment wallets that propelled the growth in the volume of digital transactions. 2018 onwards, it is not the debit or credit card but the UPI launched by NPCI that led to increased digital transactions in the country. The UPI launched by NPCI is a significant factor that pushed the volume of digital transactions in 2016. This platform provides low cost and interoperability, leading to an increase in the overall volume of transactions. In 2018, the UPI overtook the volume of transactions using debit, prepaid instruments and credit cards. Thus, from 2018 onwards till 2022, digital transactions saw a significant push. Another factor responsible for the meteoric rise in the number of UPI transactions is smartphone penetration in the interiors of the country. Moreover, the low transaction cost is another reason the UPI transactions saw an upward trend during this period. Over the years, UPI has emerged as the preferred mode of transacting among banking customers (Fig. 6).

Payment Banks in India

Mor Committee recommended the setting up of the Payment Banks in 2014. The objective of this recommendation was to bring Mobile operators, fintech

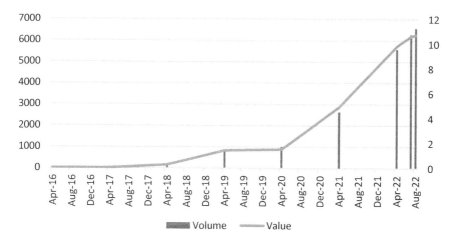

Fig. 6. UPI Transactions in India. *Source:* NABARD.

companies, postal services, and telecom companies into setting up payment banks. Through the existing networks of these entities, payment banks are meant to ensure digital financial inclusion. Payment banks are aimed at providing transfer services and are not meant to provide lending and credit facility to customers. Initially, RBI gave licences to 11 players, including Airtel, Finotech, and Paytm, to set up payment banks. Paytm has emerged as the most significant payment bank. These entities create equity in the market by serving from the wealthiest of the customer to the poorest of the customer. Small Finance Banks are different from Payment banks, as Small Finance Banks were set up with the objective of (1) providing a saving vehicle for the financially excluded people and (2) supply of credit to the small and marginalised sections of society. Small finance banks face a lot of challenge, as they cannot build the liability side of their balance sheet or mobilise enough savings from the investors. They have been able to lend a sufficient amount of money in the form of credit.

Fintech Companies

Demonetisation was at the forefront of the origin of the fintech companies (Mahajan & Singla, 2017; Sahay et al., 2020). Various fintech companies are at the forefront of the financial inclusion programme. These companies include the various payment companies that facilitate retail payments through wallets. The list of Fintech companies haves Paytm, UPI, PhonePe, PayU, MobiKwik, and Freecharge, which are involved in the delivery of financial services and providing payment transfers. These FINTECH companies mainly function based on the digital infrastructure provided by Aadhar. Fintech companies provide payment transfer services at a nominal rate. These companies have several sops and loyalty programmes to retain their customers. This includes back offers and reward points.

Other than demonetisation, e-commerce is another factor that has pushed the fintech growth in the country. The growth of transactions through fintech companies is mainly based on increased smartphone penetration and internet connectivity. The financial inclusion programme in India is implemented through the basic infrastructure, including the unique Aadhar or Unique Identification Number, which includes the India stack. In today's scenario, the financial marketplace has been replaced with the digital financial space.

India stack includes many services, including a comprehensive data identity, payment and management system. In a scenario where most transactions are cash-based, digital finance promotes a faster pace of transactions. Open-access software standards facilitate digital payments. The India stack comprises the digital identification system, with the launch of Aadhar-based identification system. An EMV-based Aadhar identification card is a unique method to establish the user's identity. The Central Bank of India, or the Reserve Bank of India, firmly believes in the capacity of the Aadhar card to transform the banking experience. This Unique Identification Number can reduce fraud in the person's identity. The best fintech companies have launched Payment banks and wallets in the nation. The UPI has facilitated the financial inclusion of the most marginalised section of society in financial inclusion.

Financial Inclusion and Consumer Data Protection

The consumer data about the transactions play an essential role in serving the market's underserved consumers. Globally, the misuse of consumer data is on the rise. In an economy, low-value consumers generally value the protection of data. Consumers are willing to pay an even higher price to seek protection against data threats. In contracts regarding the delivery of consumer services, the consumers agree to strict terms and conditions. Various solutions are being proposed, and one such solution is aggregating the resources to create a regional cybersecurity resource centre. The other foremost solution to the problem is the provision of microinsurance and Agent networks at the last mile. The Government can also leverage the potential of the Agent Networks. The Agent networks refer to the cash-in cash-out (CICO) network to enable the agent's viability in the rural region. Several entities can be enrolled as agents, including mom-and-pop stores, roaming agents, and motorbike drivers. The government should adopt a data-driven strategy to promote agent networks. Overall, the agent network, till the last mile of connectivity, can play a vital role in promoting financial inclusion among the marginalised and the poorer sections of society.

Challenges to the Cashless Economy

A cashless economy is an ecosystem in which physical money is replaced with digital money. In an electronic economy, cash flow is replaced with debit cards, credit cards, mobile banks, and electronic payments. The cash payments constitute approximately 97–98% of the total constructions in the nation. For a cashless economy, a universal banking account is a prerequisite. In the context of the Indian economy, the banking account is made available to all under PMJDY. The challenges to the cashless society are mentioned below:

(1) Financial literacy
(2) Cyber security
(3) Attitude and disposition
(4) Presence of infrastructure
(5) Presence of inequalities
(6) The disintegration of citizen-centric services

In India, a large chunk of the population is financially literate, i.e., they do not have the required skills and understanding to achieve their financial goals (Sangita & Dash, 2005). In terms of cognitive abilities, individuals lack the cognition and mental inputs to achieve their goals. In the Indian context, cyber security remains an essential obstacle to development. Due to a lack of digital literacy, the users are unaware of the perils and basic protocols while using the technology (Nedungadi et al., 2018; Ozili, 2018; Shen et al., 2018). The digital divide is more visible in the context of rural regions. The citizens in the rural area do not have any information about how to use the digital mode of transactions, such as ATMs, credit cards, debit cards, and internet banking. Despite social intermediation, the citizens of India cannot use digital media due to a lack of attitude and dispositions. The rural population has a lot of cultural inhabitations in using technology. In this regard, there is a need for counselling and mindset change to adopt the technology. There is a lack of financial infrastructure in terms of connectivity, data storage, and interface to facilitate resource access.

Moreover, in the Indian context, there are a lot of inequalities between rural and urban people. Thus, there is a need to overcome the critical challenges to ensure the transition to a free economy. Also, the Government of India needs to optimise the digital payment system to drive financial inclusion. It includes integrating the offices of regulators, bankers, payment providers, processors, merchants, and customers.

Digital Capital – Cultural and Social Capital

As per Bourdieu, the key to adopting new technology or innovation in rural India is converting social capital through social intermediation and attitude building. To achieve sustainable development goals, the Government or state has to traverse the barriers of economic gains. Social capital is the soft point in the policy choice available to the state for achieving inclusive growth. The other tools available to the Governance machinery in the arsenal of social capital include social, cultural, symbolic, spiritual, and emotional capital. Through the lens of social constructivist theory, reality is socially constructed. But the socially constructed reality is often biased due to social stereotypes, biases, heuristics, etc. To do away with this shortcoming, we have adopted the theoretical lens of social realism. To achieve a consensus regarding the benefits of digitisation in a complex and diverse society like India, the state will have to introduce social realism. The objective of the *Digital India* programme is to make using digital technology a culture. To transform this type of social capital, it is essential to take care of three things: (1) *Objectify digital cultural capital* – To objectify cultural capital through the creation of works of art, books, paintings, etc.; (2) *Embody the digital cultural capital* – To exhibit this cultural capital in the form of habits, preferences, and mannerisms; (3) *Institutionalise the cultural capital* – To institutionalise the cultural capital in the form of education certificates, training, etc.

Digital Capital – Emotional Capital

When a culture is embodied, it becomes an emotional capital. Then it is institutionalised in the form of *norms or customs* (Lyons & Kass-Hanna, 2021). Emotional capital acts as a catalyst for generating positive dispositions and attitudes among the members. This applies to digital capital as well. The embodiment of digital capital leads to a positive impact and reduces negative effects. The positive outcome leads to higher banking usage of Information Communication Technology (ICT). However, the digital culture can also lead to the risk of cyber security. These risks can be mitigated through the use of social intermediation and training. Digital capital also survives as an emotional capital, which helps the users to withstand disappointments, and failures and improves resilience in the complex environment. Financial exclusion restricts the capacity to act rationally and makes an individual vulnerable leading to poverty. In this situation, digital capital enables an individual to combat the adverse outcomes of financial exclusion.

Benefits of Financial Inclusion and Digitization

The adoption of the technological solution enables the users to avail various benefits. These benefits are mentioned as follows:

(1) *Accessibility* – Digitisation and transformation of the services allow users to access financial services at a significantly lower cost. It provides local access to financial services at the doorstep of the members

(2) *User-Friendly Interface* – Digitisation and financial transformation enable the members to access financial services conveniently through a single interface. NPCI provides a whole pack of interfaces that allow users to access the financial services at their doorsteps at a reduced cost

(3) *Efficiency* – Digitisation and technical transformation of the services enable to increase in the efficiency of the financial systems and ensure the seamless delivery of the financial services at the doorstep at a significantly reduced cost

(4) *Flexibility* – Digitisation and technical transformation provide flexibility in the delivery of financial services to the users. The range of choices available to the users provides the flexibility in the delivery of services.

(5) *Sustainability* – Digitisation of the financial systems also ensures the cost reduction of the services. This further leads to the financial sustainability of the system

(6) *Security* – Digitisation of the financial system and technological transformation further leads to better security for the users. Implementing ICT (Information and Communication Technology) enhances the transparency of the data, and it further leads to better motivation to use the financial system.

Conclusion

As per the study, the Indian state has adopted the vision to be a digital state through technology. This study propagates that adopting technology can help overcome the various forms of exclusion. However, there are multiple challenges, including digital illiteracy and the inability to adopt new technology. Digital illiteracy is a social phenomenon objectified by lending practices from the moneylender and the lenders in the informal sector. And it is embodied in the form of preferences for inferior products and institutionalised in written and debt contracts.

Summary

Money has a primitive history from when Mesopotamia introduced the first coin to the introduction of the paper currency by China. The adoption of digital money, trade, and commerce has achieved vast magnitudes. The first banknotes were introduced in 1661, and the credit cards in 1946. The industrial revolution led to the emergence of the banking system in Britain. Barrings and Rothschild, two prominent families, established the first bank in London. As the first world paved the way for the industrial revolution in Europe, in 1920, the Gold standard was adopted. It was suspended further to pave the way for national currencies based on partial or complete floating. The emergence of digital money is the key to creating equity in a diverse and unequal world. Change management is critical to bring about change. The emergence of the Indian stack programme to introduce NACH and AePS has further led to technological innovation through the financial inclusion programme. The conducive policy environment comprised of various state government entities, payment banks, fintech companies, and financial inclusion has led to the achievement of the goals.

References

Barik, R., & Sharma, P. (2019). Analyzing the progress and prospects of financial inclusion in India. *Journal of Public Affairs*, *19*(1), c1948.

David-West, O. (2016). The path to digital financial inclusion in Nigeria: Experiences of Firstmonie. *Journal of Payments Strategy & Systems*, *9*(4), 256–273.

Gabor, D., & Brooks, S. (2017). The digital revolution in financial inclusion: International development in the fintech era. *New Political Economy*, *22*(4), 423–436.

Lyons, A. C., & Kass-Hanna, J. (2021). A methodological overview to defining and measuring "digital" financial literacy. *Financial Planning Review*, *4*(2), e1113.

Mahajan, P., & Singla, A. (2017). Effect of demonetization on financial inclusion in India. *International Journal of Science Technology and Management*, *6*(1), 338–343.

Nanda, S. (2022). India's e-governance journey: Looking through common service centres. *Indian Journal of Public Administration*, *68*(4), 599–609. https://doi.org/10.1177/00195561221098108

Nedungadi, P. P., Menon, R., Gutjahr, G., Erickson, L., & Raman, R. (2018). Towards an inclusive digital literacy framework for digital India. *Education + Training*, *60*(6), 516–528.

Ozili, P. K. (2018). Impact of digital finance on financial inclusion and stability. *Borsa Istanbul Review*, *18*(4), 329–340.

Ozili, P. K. (2021, October). Financial inclusion research around the world: A review. *Forum for Social Economics*, *50*(4), 457–479. Routledge.

Sahay, M. R., von Allmen, M. U. E., Lahreche, M. A., Khera, P., Ogawa, M. S., Bazarbash, M., & Beaton, M. K. (2020). *The promise of fintech: Financial inclusion in the post COVID-19 era*. International Monetary Fund.

Sangita, S. N., & Dash, B. C. (2005). *Electronic governance and service delivery in India: Theory and practice*. Working Papers165. Institute for Social and Economic Change.

Shen, Y., Hu, W., & Hueng, C. J. (2018). The effects of financial literacy, digital financial product usage and internet usage on financial inclusion in China. In *MATEC Web of Conferences* (Vol. 228, pp. 05012). EDP Sciences.

Chapter 6

Priority in Inclusive Finance

Pradhan Mantri Jan Dhan Yojana

Social Perspective

India has undertaken a famous financial inclusion programme. Within the ambit of this programme, the Government of India aims to provide financial services to all the people at the bottom of the pyramid. The state of India introduced universal banking services in 2014. The objective of this programme is to bring access to financial services, including access to universal bank accounts and financial services. This scheme enables access to credit-related products and services, basic banking accounts, remittance facility, insurance, and pension. This scheme has improved the penetration of bank accounts in India. In addition to the Pradhan Mantri Jan Dhan Yojana (PMJDY), another Bank Mitra or facilitators will be appointed to ensure financial inclusion for all. This programme lies at the core of the development of the philosophy of 'Sab ka Sath Sab ka Vikas'. This project aims to eliminate the money lenders and provide access to financial services through a strong network of banking

Microfinance and Development in Emerging Economies, 119–141
Copyright © 2023 Nishi Malhotra
Published under exclusive licence by Emerald Publishing Limited
doi:10.1108/978-1-83753-826-320231006

facilities through a network of ATMs, a digital platform based on the concept of contact, connect and communication. This initiative aims to integrate all the efforts to achieve the hope of complete financial inclusion collaboratively. Digitalisation has led to the resurgence of economic growth in the post-COVID-19 era.

Introduction

Various challenges, such as the lack of infrastructure in terms of the credit reporting framework, impact India's financial system. These payment systems lead to higher costs of transactions. In the Indian economic system, there are three players, i.e., the financial intermediaries (indirect finance), financial markets (direct finance), and borrowers and lenders. The asymmetric information about the borrowers in the financial markets is a significant obstacle to the financial exclusion of the borrowers. None financial intermediaries, such as banks or formal financial institutions, are willing to lend money to the borrowers. And small borrowers have no choice but to access loans from informal sources, which include money lenders. The priority in inclusive finance is to reduce information asymmetry and introduce new financial products. Group lending is a unique financing mechanism that can ensure financial access for financially excluded entrepreneurs. Since the 1990s, financial institutions have adopted the sustainable finance mandate. It propagates that reducing information asymmetry should reduce the challenges to formal finance. This can be done by using the digital banking mode to reduce agency costs and the cost of borrowing. However, due to a lack of financial literacy, the members might not have the cognitive abilities and the attitude to use this mode of financial access. Digital literacy can help combat this issue and overcome neo-liberal market theory challenges by combating market failures on the demand and supply side. On the supply side, digital banking can ensure access to capital and finance for all the people at the bottom of the pyramid through the low-cost virtual banking ecosystem. On the demand side, financial literacy can help to change attitudes and generate more demand for formal finance. In a joint liability group, the members have prior information about each other, which helps to overcome the financial asymmetry problem. Moreover, members can easily access low-cost funds by pooling resources in a joint liability group.

Financial Systems in India

India's financial system comprises four significant constituents: the borrowers, lenders, financial intermediaries, and the financial markets. The description of the incomplete markets, contrary to Arrow–Debreu hypothesis, is given below. However, in a complete market, under the Arrow–Debreu hypothesis, each portfolio of debt products and investment instruments can be replicated by the use of the assets and collateral. This is akin to the neoliberal market theory in which there is no market failure. But in reality, there is a market failure, and there is a void in the form of asymmetric information about the borrowers to the lenders. Thus, informal finance in the form of group lending can help to fill the void (Fig. 1).

A description of the financial systems is given below:

(1) *Financial intermediaries:* The financial intermediaries refer to the presence of various banks, financial institutions, and intermediaries that enable the borrowers to borrow indirect finance. Generally, financial intermediaries allow borrowers to borrow finance from indirect sources based on information. In the open markets, most financial intermediaries have perfect information about the players through the financial markets. In reality, the neoliberal market hypothesis does not hold. This leads to poverty and imperfection in the markets. In case of a lack of information about the financial markets, the borrowers have to access the finance through informal sources, including joint liability groups. These groups, as a collective, have more information about the borrowers, which enables the borrowers to be financially included in an inclusive financial system. Thus, in the graphical analysis, the third source of finance is introduced as informal finance to overcome the imperfect information hypothesis. The inclusive financial system comprises an additional finance source, joint lending and group lending (see Fig. 2).

(2) *Financial capital markets:* The inclusive financial system comprises an additional player, i.e., the financial markets. The financial markets are the source of direct capital for the borrowers. The markets are a direct finance source and have complete borrowers' information. However, the Arrow–Debreu hypothesis is still not applicable in developing economies. This is

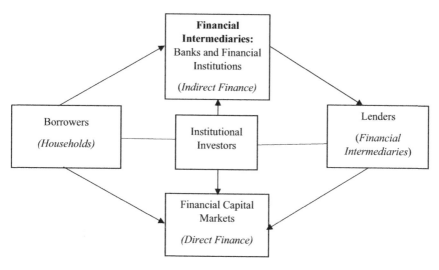

Fig. 1.   Financial Systems.

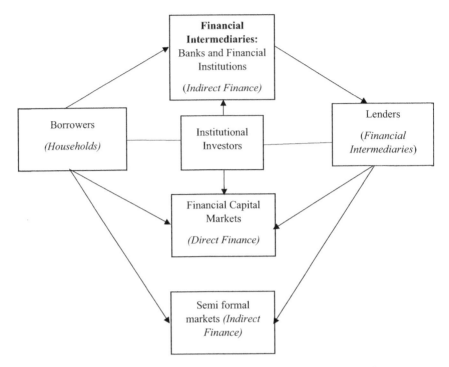

Fig. 2.   Inclusive Financial Systems. *Source:* By the Authors.

because the markets are incomplete, and the existing securities cannot be replicated with the commodities portfolio. This leads to imperfection in the markets. However, the contingent claims and the pricing for the contingent claims can be made using the *Arrow–Debreu* model. Thus, the financial markets are the source of direct capital and finance.

(3) The borrowers generally invest their excess capital in the financial markets. In market-based finance, the borrowers or investors borrow directly from the financial markets by selling the financial instruments, also called the financial instruments and the securities. The financial markets offer the services of payment and settlement. The financial markets comprise the money markets and the capital markets. The money markets allow investors to borrow short-term funds from the markets. The capital markets enable investors to borrow long-term capital from the markets. Regulatory authorities such as SEBI (Securities and Exchange Board of India) regulate the markets' functioning. The macroprudential supervision of the markets is the joint responsibility of the markets.

(4) *Lenders:* The financial system's lenders comprise the lenders or the net savers. These net savers enable the lenders to channelise the funds into the markets. Besides that, the other lenders include households, firms, Government, and non-residents. The financial lenders channel the funds into the

financial markets through direct finance. This finance from the markets is then lent to the borrowers in the form of loans. These loans are extended to households, firms, governments and non-residents.

(5) *Borrowers:* The borrowers in an economy are the net spenders. Borrowers are the net spenders that borrow the funds for consumption and investment. These borrowers are the form of households, firms, the government and non-residents. They borrow direct finance from the financial markets and the funds in the form of loans from credit institutions, monetary institutions, financial institutions and other credit institutions.

(6) *Semi-formal group lending:* Group lending is an informal finance mechanism that enables small entrepreneurs to borrow without paying higher interest rates. The group uses collectivist social capital to allow lending to the borrowers. Small borrowers can borrow money without adequate financial collateral and information about the creditworthiness of the borrowers.

Priorities in Inclusive Finance

The main objective of financial inclusion is to work with financial intermediaries to support the marginalised sections of society and small medium enterprises. The main priority of the financial inclusion programme in India is to strengthen existing financial systems, including financial institutions. The main preferences in inclusive finance programmes are provided as (1) access to financial services, (2) women empowerment and emancipation of women, (3) digital financial inclusion, (4) promoting microfinance and (5) promoting financing for a sustainable climate. The description of the priorities in financial inclusion is given below (see Fig. 3):

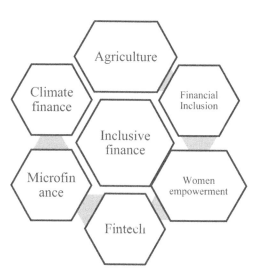

Fig. 3.   Priorities in Inclusive Finance. *Source:* By the Authors.

(1) *Access to financial services:* The priority of the inclusive finance programme is to promote access to financial services. The financial inclusion of the poor helps build assets, promotes income increase, and reduces the vulnerability of low-income families. It also acts as a stabilising force. The financial inclusion programme aims to provide access to financial services for the doorsteps of the poor.

(2) *Women empowerment:* The women empowerment objective of the financial inclusion programme is to empower women, particularly in rural India. Microfinancing helps attract women and retain them through the propagation of finance and credit services.

(3) *Digital Financial Inclusion:* The financial inclusion programme aims to promote the use of technology in ensuring the delivery of financial services. Various financial intermediation initiatives, such as joint liability groups, are undertaken to ensure the digital inclusion of the poor.

(4) *Promoting microfinance:* Globally, approximately 1.7 billion people do not have access to financial services. The financial inclusion programme aims to encourage the use of microfinance through priority lending, joint liability groups linked to bank credit, and microfinance financing. Generally, the poor at the bottom of the pyramid do not have access to financial services due to the lack of collateral. The microfinance programme enables poor members to access finance.

(5) *Promoting the use of climate finance:* UN has adopted the sustainable development goal of preventing climate change. The financial inclusion programme aims to adopt sustainable farming practices in this regard. This includes using green practices such as water harvesting, using green finance and agricultural products, etc.

Particular Focus on Rural Agricultural Finance

One of the reasons for the lackadaisical growth of the agricultural economy is the lack of an institutional credit delivery system. With the increasing role of the non-institutional modes of credit, such as money lenders, and unorganised sector players, such as family, friends and relatives, the small farmer has landed in a cull de sac. To resolve the issue of non-institutional credit and give impetus to agricultural growth, the Government of India has introduced the Kisan Credit Card scheme under the aegis of the Reserve Bank of India. Kisan Credit Card scheme aims to provide timely institutional credit under a single window with the most hassle-free procedure for the farmers. As part of the scheme, Government provides interest subvention and incentives for early repayment of the loans on Kisan Credit Cards. As per RBI, approximately 6.93 crore Kisan Credit Cards are issued to the farmers. Various studies emphasise that the Kisan Credit Card scheme has helped to augment agricultural credit, thereby increasing the farmers' income and boosting crop productivity. Various studies conducted by NA BARD and Reserve Bank of India highlight that despite all the efforts to saturate the farmers with Kisan Credit Cards under the financial inclusion programme, many farmers have still not subscribed to the Kisan Credit Card schemes. Reasons for not subscribing to the Kisan Credit Cards are lack of financial inclusion, lack of literacy, small land holdings, and lack of bank account.

Moreover, the land holding scenario in India is dominated by Small and Marginal farmers, who have operational land holdings of approximately less than 2 acres. These farmers are the most vulnerable to the vagaries of nature and calamities such as floods, droughts, etc. Providing affordable credit to this group of small and distressed farmers to achieve inclusive growth is the way to balanced growth. To address the issue of financial exclusion, NA BARD and RBI have undertaken various programme such as Financial Literacy campaigns and prompt opening of bank accounts to facilitate the issuance of Kisan Credit Cards, waiver of the financial charges, and cross-selling of various products such as health insurance, bank accounts, crop insurance to name a few. The government of India has also introduced multiple features, such as the Kisan Credit Card scheme for tenant farmers, Self Help Groups, and Joint Liability groups. This project aims at understanding the trends in the adoption of Kisan credit Cards across India and various factors impacting the adoption of Kisan Credit Cards in India.

Comparison With the Indian Scenario

The Kisan Credit Scheme was introduced in India in 1998–1999. One of the flagship programmes aimed at providing short-term credit to the farmers by the Government of India. In India, till 2017, approximately 233 million Kisan Credit Cards were issued. India has adopted access to adequate agricultural credit as one of the significant milestones in each five-year plan since independence. Agriculture has been a major source of livelihood for the people of India. One of the considerable obstacles to agriculture-driven economic growth in India has been a lack of institutional credit and farmers' reliance on non-institutional sources of finance. With the adoption of financial inclusion as one of the sustainable development goals, the importance of financial intermediation in the form of policy instruments has increased manifold. One of the significant drivers of the nationalisation of banks in 1969 was increasing access to rural finance and credit for Indian farmers. Kisan Credit Card scheme was a flagship scheme of the Government of India in 1998–1999. This scheme aimed to cut the intricate tangle of unorganised money lenders, who had become a burden to some Indian farmers. Before the Kisan Credit Card scheme, Indian agriculture was predominated by primarily a multiple-agency lending scheme. Most agricultural households in the past used to rely on moneylenders, non-institutional sources of finance.

Indian economy in the year 1951 was predominantly an agrarian economy. At the dawn of Indian independence and the inception of Indian planning, the agricultural yield was 508 Lakh Tonnes which increased to 2,850 lakh tonnes in 2018–2019. In the wake of increasing agricultural production and yield, the Government of India has undertaken massive capacity-building programmes, including farmers training, setting up of the modern e-NAM (e-Marketing), primary health cares to the farmers, automated weather stations and IV-based call centres to provide prompt information to the farmers about the farm product prices. As part of the institutional credit delivery system, the Government of India has introduced 14 different Kisan Credit Cards. To boost the farmers' income, the Government of India has set up an ambitious goal of doubling farmers' income by 2022. Important in the agriculture sector is the release of advance estimates. The yield as kg/hectare increased to 2,299 kg/hectare in 2018–2019. Department of Agriculture and Farmer welfare has worked tremendously on improving the water storage, increasing the sowed area and providing modern equipment and technology to India's farmers. One of the glaring facts about Indian farmers is the increasing number of suicides. The government has undertaken various initiatives to replace non-institutional credits with banking and institutional credits. In 2017, the Indian economy witnessed record horticulture and agriculture products. Public investment in agriculture and allied activities has increased from Rs 35,696 crores in 2011–2012 to Rs 44,957 crores in 2015–2016 (Rajkumar, 2021).

Agricultural credit plays a significant role in reducing the distress of Indian farmers. In June 2004, the Indian Government doubled the agriculture credit flow and reduced it. Since 2004, the flow of credit to agriculture has consistently exceeded the target. In India, there are two seasons of farming Kharif and Rabi. For the Kharif crops, the Indian Government has provided crop loans of up to Rs 3 lakhs at an interest rate of 7%. The Government of India provided an additional % interest subvention to the farmers for the early repayments as per schedule in the year 2009–2010. This interest subvention has been increased substantially from 1% to 2% to 3% p.a. This brings the effective rate to 4%, which is extended as pre-harvest loans by commercial loans and private banks. In the case of post-harvest loans, the credit will be available for negotiable warehouse receipts, and loans are provided at market rates. However, to mitigate the woes of the small and marginal farmers, the Government of India introduced the Kisan Credit Card scheme in the form of post-harvest loans, which will be available at the same rates as the negotiable warehouse receipt and will pass on the benefits of interest subvention to the farmers. The Government of India has increased the limit of collateral loans from 50,000 to 100,000. The Government of India has further upgraded the Kisan Credit Cards as ATM RuPay Cards (Rajkumar, 2021).

MNAIS (Modified National Agricultural Insurance Scheme)

This is a Government of India scheme to provide financial insurance and financial support to farmers in the event of prevented sowing and failure of any of the notified crops as a result of natural calamities, to promote progressive farming practices and use of high inputs and to stabilise the income of the farmer's income. The Agriculture Insurance Corporation and private insurance companies provide this scheme. All the loanee farmers are compulsorily covered under this scheme, and non-loanee farmers are covered under the voluntary component.

This scheme covers food grains, oil seeds and commercial crops based on past yield estimates. This scheme covers all the farmers including individual owner cultivators, tenant farmers, sharecroppers, contract farmers, crop grower associations and self-help groups.

Rashtriya Krishak Vikas Yojana

Under the XIth five-year plan, Additional Central Assistance was extended to the States under Rashtriya Krishi Vikas Yojana under the aegis of the National Development Council. This scheme aimed to provide an additional 4% annual growth in agriculture through the growth of agriculture and allied activities. To increase agriculture productivity, the states are eligible for assistance under RKVY on the basis of the average expenditure incurred on various activities for the past three years. Under this programme, the states are free to select the activities to which the state wants to allocate the funds. This scheme is an umbrella scheme, allowing the state government to choose as per the geographical region. This scheme aims to maximise farmer returns, reducing the yield gaps between various regions. Various methods, such as Crop Husbandry, Animal Husbandry, Sericulture, and Soil and Water harvesting, to name a few. Integrated farming, which involves the cultivation of multiple crops such as horticulture, sericulture and apiculture, is the cornerstone of this scheme.

Moreover, this scheme involves the comprehensive funds made available under various fields such as MNREGA, Swarn Jayanti and Bharat Nirman programme me. It is almost similar to bringing the green revolution back to stern India and promoting crop diversification, soil health, good cattle health, and various saffron missions. Overall, this scheme aims to promote rural employment, capacity building, and infrastructure development, promote agri entrepreneurship, and create post-harvest infrastructure. This scheme has been further upgraded as RKVY RAFTAR.

Price Support Scheme and e-NAM (National Agricultural Markets)

One of the major challenges facing Indian agriculture is the lack of fair prices available in the agricultural markets. The Government of India announces minimum support prices for the 25 major crops in both seasons to ensure remunerative prices to the farmers, with a lower cost of inter-mediation. Moreover, to facilitate fair prices, the Government of India has introduced e-NAM (digital markets), which facilitate auctioning of agricultural products. This initiative aims at reducing the number of intermediaries and brokers that can impact the prices available to the farmers.

ATMA

This programme aims at agricultural extension and technology through capacity building, a judicious mix of physical outreach of personnel, domain expertise, interactive methods of information dissemination, public-private partnerships and the use of ICT and mass media under various schemes of the Government of India. Various central sector schemes include mass media support to extension programme me, Agri clinics and Agribusiness centres, extension to central institutes, and strengthening information dissemination under the Kisan call centres. It is a linkage programme that aims to connect Krishi Vigyan Kendra, State Agriculture Universities, and National Agricultural Research System. This is a district-level programme that aims at operationalising the extension programmes at the district level. This scheme's governance mechanism comprises a State Level Sanctioning Committee that is set up under the Rashtriya Krishi Vikas Yojana. District Farmers Advisory Committee is set up to advise the farmers. There is a block-level committee and a village friend that helps to implement this scheme. This scheme's major focus is ensuring ICT connectivity and information dissemination through mobiles, vans, Pico Projects, e-Panchayats, common service centres, radio stations, Kala Jathas and various road shows.

Pradhan Mantri Fasal Bima Yojana

Pradhan Mantri Fasal Bima Yojana is to support sustainable production in Indian agriculture, encourage farmers to adopt innovative practices, promote the financial support to farmers suffering from crop loss, stabilise the income of the farmers and ensure the flow of credit to the farmers. Insurance will be compulsorily provided to the loanee farmers, and for the non-loanee farmers, the insurance will be provided on a voluntary basis. All the farmers, including the sharecroppers and tenant farmers growing in the notified area, are eligible for this scheme. This scheme covers the following risks, namely, prevented sowing, planting, germination risk due to weather conditions, comprehensive scheme from covering yield losses due to non-preventable hazards such as droughts, flood, inundation, post-harvest losses, losses due to localised wealth calamities, crop loss due to wild animals. The government of India has designed an insurance portal to ensure coordination between various stakeholders, such as insurance companies, banks, and farmers. Through SMS and this portal, the relevant information is provided to the farmers about this insurance in each of the seasons.

Indian Agriculture

Agriculture has a major role in the Indian economy and is the major source of livelihood for the people of India. As per the 2011 census, approximately 55% of the workers are employed in the agriculture and allied sectors. The size of the land holdings in agriculture has been a major concern in the Indian agriculture scenario. Indian agriculture is a major source of wage earning for the rural population in India. Approximately 52% of India's wage earners depend on agriculture for their earnings. The rural economy is the primary source of food security in India. Despite all the technological advances, Indian agriculture is suffering from various challenges, such as lack of rainfall, underemployment, low productivity, poor diversification and a low level of agro-processing. Although agriculture's mechanisation ushered in an era of rural prosperity, more than 55% of the land is still irrigated with tube wells, mini reservoirs, pumps, etc. Not only is there a lack of irrigation facilities and dependence on monsoon, but also due to small land holdings of less than 2 hectares, the mechanisation is unable to reap the benefits.

Institutional Credit

Since independence, agricultural credit has become a catalyst in promoting growth in the agriculture sector. In the year 1960, Cooperative Banks, including Primary Agriculture Cooperatives (PACs), District Central Cooperative Banks (DCCBs), State Cooperative Banks (SCBs), and Agriculture and Rural Development Banks Land Banks have been playing a significant role in the development of this sector. Institutional credit growth gained further momentum with the nationalisation of the banks in 1969. Further, in the year 1975, Regional Rural Banks were set up to give a boost to agricultural credit. As per the 70th Round of NSSO (National Sample Survey Organization), approximately 69% of the farming households in rural India have land holdings of less than 1 hectare. Only 0.4% of the population has a land holding of less than 1 hectare.

Subsidy Linked Schemes

With the participation of the commercial banks in 1969, many subsidies linked to the Government of India implemented credit schemes for the benefit of the farmers. This credit has been divided into (1) crop loans issued for expenses on the cultivation of crops, (2) term loans (3) loans for the purchase of agricultural machinery and capital equipment.

Issues in Indian Agricultural Credit System

As per the NAFIS report 2016–2017, approximately 72% of the credit requirement was met through institutional sources and a flat 28% of non-institutional sources. In various studies conducted by the Reserve Bank of India, the intermediaries and commission agents still play a major role in the agriculture of India. Besides the presence of the intermediaries, another factor that leads to the woes of Indian agriculture is the inefficient collateral systems. To overcome these issues, Indian Government introduced the Kisan Credit Card system to address the problems of collaterals and intermediaries involved.

Indian agriculturists need finance for different purposes, including harvesting land, irrigation, seedling, fertilizers, pesticides and weeding. These include expenses for other purposes, and the banks decide the Scale of Finance (SOF). Generally, the banks will grant finance equal to two third of the total agricultural expenses. The Kisan Credit Card scheme was introduced to replace the existing web of non-institutional credits. Further, this scheme can be renewed after three months. This instrument will enable the farmers to borrow the loan for 12 months or more, and the rate of interest and security margin is to be decided by the banks in India. Further, this scheme will also provide the farmers with Personal Accident Insurance up to Rs 50,000.

Inputs and types of resources impact agricultural productivity. These agricultural inputs include land utilised, credit and other things. Out of all these inputs, financial credit or bank credit is extremely important. Farmers take loans at the stage of Pre harvesting; Post harvesting and agricultural productivity depend on the availability of bank credit. The Kisan Credit Card scheme provides short-term credit for purchasing agricultural inputs, which helps to increase yield and agricultural production.

One of the emerging trends in Indian agriculture is the widening gap between the Short-Term Loan and Investment credit. Various studies indicate that most farmers need the working capital to purchase seeds, pesticides, fertilizers and other inputs. These short-term credit requirements are met in the form of crop loans, which have been extended in the form of the Kisan Credit Card since 1998. Another interesting fact about Indian agriculture is that crop loans have increased faster than the Consumer Price Index for crops.

Rural and Urban Divide in KCC (Kisan Credit Card Ownership)

CMIE (Centre for Monitoring Indian Economy) People Pyramid dx highlights glaring differences in Kisan Credit Card ownership among the Rural and the Urban regions.

Literacy and Its Impact on Kisan Credit Card Ownership

The dataset for the 4-month cycle from Jan 2014–Apr 2014 to Jan 2020–Apr 2020 reveals an emerging gap in KCC ownership between people who are literate and who are not literate.

Bank Accounts and Kisan Credit Cards

Kisan Credit Card adoption is highly correlated with Bank Account ownership. Data from CMIE (Centre for Monitoring Indian Economy) reveals an inherent relationship between Bank ownership and KCC Accounts.

Kisan Credit Card Ownership and Land Holdings

NABARD, in its survey, concluded that there is a vast difference in KCC (Kisan Credit Card) ownership among various groups of farmers. A trend analysis of the KCC (Ownership) by different kinds of farmers highlights that organised farmers is far more likely to own Kisan Credit cards than small farmers. NABARD survey highlights that non-ownership of land holdings is one of the primary reasons cited by the bank for not granting Kisan Credit Cards.

Formal Versus Informal Sources of Finance

As per the RBI (Reserve Bank of India, Handbook of Statistics, 2017), by the year 2010–2011, approximately 85% of the land holdings in India are Small and Marginal land holdings, which are less than 2 hectares. Despite this, the share of Small and Marginal farmers in the total operated area is approximately 44.6%. This category of farmers cannot access markets and has to sell their products through the adatis (commission agents) and the middlemen. Trapped in the web of intermediaries and rising CPI (Consumer Price Index) of agricultural inputs, these small and marginal farmers need loans and credit to operate. Generally, loans are required for cultivation and investment.

However, due to their small land holdings and lack of market access, these small and marginal farmers are the most vulnerable to credit risk. The financing system in the Indian agriculture setting comprises Informal and Formal sources. Generally, Commercial Banks grant loans to the farmers based on proof of land holdings, NOC (No Objection Certificate) from lenders, invoice of purchase cropping pattern, and estimated fund requirements for the seasonal crops based on the scale of finance, as assessed by the District Level Technical Committee. Hence, it can be concluded that there is a massive gap in the Indian Rural Credit system in India, and there is a need for financial reforms to address the woes of the Small and Marginal farmers in India.

Farmer Producer Companies and Organised Farmers

To address this issue of unorganised vulnerable sections of small and marginal farmers, Farmer Producer Organizations (FPOs) were introduced by the Companies Act 2013. Producer Companies or Primary Agriculture Cooperatives (PACs) provide the bargaining power to these unorganised farmers. In the case of PACs, despite elaborate Annual Credit Limit procedures imposed by the Commercial banks, society takes care of all the financial requirements.

Organised Farmers

Companies Act 2013 was a watershed in the history of Indian agriculture as it led to the birth of the Producer companies. The data shows that approximately 33% of the agriculturists in the dataset of around 23,000 farmers are organised farmers. Despite the structural rigidities in the formal credit evaluation systems, Cooperatives and Producer companies provide a panacea to the farmers, who can rely on the PACs (Primary Agriculture Cooperatives) to take care of the bank formalities for the grant of loans.

Small Farmer Coverage (Issue of Lack of Coverage of Small Farmers)

Since 2014, when the 'Equity Grant and Credit Guarantee Scheme' was introduced, the borrowings of FPOs (Farmer Producer Companies) from the banks have increased steadily. For Small and Marginal farmers, there are many obstacles in the form of structural rigidities and formalities to seek a bank loan. With various Interest subventions and debt waiver schemes, the Government of India tried to give a push to agricultural credit for Small and Marginal farmers. Different subsidy-linked insurance schemes, including Personal Accident Insurance Scheme and Rashtriya Krishi Vikas Yojana, have been introduced to give an impetus to Formal agriculture credit.

Despite all efforts, due to the lack of land records and the Scale of the Finance based credit system, borrowings by the Small and Marginal Farmers saw a downward trend. Besides this, the Agricultural Labourers, who form 19.99% of the total dataset, are marginalised and have to rely on informal sources of finance to meet their credit needs. Another issue with a bank loan is that it is a season-based lending system leading to various obstacles in meeting the goal of financial inclusion. Demonetisation in the year 2016 was followed by a financial literacy wave that gave a push to borrowings from banks for all categories of borrowers.

Informal Sources of Finance

Money Lenders
One of the main issues in the Indian agricultural credit system is that while the number of small sizes land holdings is increasing, there is a decline in the number of bank credit accounts held by small and marginal farmers. In the wake of the fact that small and marginal holdings form 85% of total land holdings and commercial banks have the policy to finance only land holdings with a size of more than 2 hectares, the small farmers have to rely on the informal sources of finance, and the formal head of finance becomes unviable. As per the NSSO 2005 survey of indebtedness, approximately 47.3% of the small farmers with land holding less than 0.01 hectares borrow from money lenders, approximately 31.8% of the small farmers with land holdings of 0.01–0.4 hectares borrow from money lenders, 30.8% of the small farmers 0.4–1 hectare borrow from the money lenders and 25.9% of the small farmers with land holdings between 1 and 2 hectares borrow from small and marginal farmers. Till the introduction of the Cash Credit Based system, the farmers, particularly the unorganised farmers, had limited opportunity to access loans from the formal bank systems, which led to the problem of underfinancing. In this background, the farmers had to rely on the informal credit system at extremely high-interest rates to meet the gaps in the funding system.

Borrowings From Self-Help Groups
The 1992 Self-Help Group Bank Linkage programme was launched in 1992 to tap the vast informal financing mechanism and combine it with the formal bank credit delivery mechanism. This scheme led to the acceptance of the informal groups, i.e., the agricultural labourers, as part of the formal bank financing system. SHG Linkage, predominantly called, is a collateral-free lending system that aims to provide finance for specific projects or activities. Around 100 Scheduled

Commercial Banks, 300 District Cooperative Banks, 27 State Rural Livelihood Missions, and 5,000 NGOs are involved in promoting Self Help groups.

Challenges to Inclusive Financial Systems

Access to finance for the bankable poor is fraught with various demand and supply challenges. The demand-side challenges include cultural factors, transaction costs, mistrust of financial institutions, lack of financial literacy, and access to basic financial infrastructure. The supply side challenges include the financial viability of microfinance institutions, real and perceived risk in microlending, institutions, linkages with the formal sector, and approaches and products (Fig. 4).

Demand Side Barriers

(1) *Cultural factors:* Various cultural factors impact financial services and credit availability to the people at the bottom of the pyramid. The people at the bottom of the pyramid, particularly women, are highly marginalised, as they do not have access to financial services. They lack physical collateral, and formal institutions do not have information about the creditworthiness of the poor. Regional or cultural norms impact the financialisation and inclusion of the poor at the bottom of the pyramid. Cultural norms and social attitudes influence the demand for financial services in a developing nation like India. India is a land of diversity, with many diverse tribes and sections of people who are socially excluded. These tribes depend on their ancestral art for their livelihood and do not have access to economic and social capital. There are

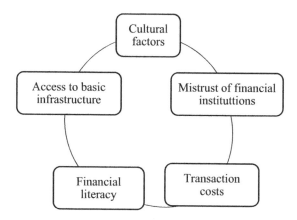

Fig. 4.   Challenges to the Inclusive Financial System. *Source:* By the Authors.

many tribes in India, such as *Paniya, Adiya, Kurichya and Kuruma*, who do not have access to banking and financial services. These tribes are outliers in the social development process and are amenable to the vicious trap of poverty and the perils and pitfalls of the greed of moneylenders. The tribes are a separate human group that is distinct in terms of culture, social background, and historical and cultural origin. In states like Kerala, the RBI and the state Government have undertaken various steps to ensure the welfare of the tribes and the weaker sections of society. The extent of financial exclusion among the poor tribals is very great, and the state Government of India has undertaken various steps such as livelihood programmes for the poor, joint liability groups, and priority lending. But still, many of the socially excluded groups are unwilling to participate in the economic growth story of rural India. This is due to their social disposition and social factors. They are generally marginalised and stay away from the city. Due to their native practices, they are not readily accepted in other parts of India. This leads to the social exclusion of the poor. Many of the women in rural India lack financial decision-making powers. They prefer to leave financial decision-making to their male counterparts. They are not literate, and they lack an understanding of financial independence. Thus, cultural factors such as language, social customs, and practices are the main challenges to the social inclusion of the poor.

(2) *Mistrust of financial institutions:* The poor at the bottom of the pyramid do not have access to financial services. These poor members do not have any collateral, and the banks and financial institutions do not have any information about the creditworthiness of the poor. This leads to mistrust between the financial institutions and the poor. The financial institutions do not find it worthwhile to lend money to the poor at the bottom of the pyramid. This mistrust thus leads to the financial exclusion of the poor. Low-income borrowers generally prefer loans at convenient terms and loans from informal sources such as money lenders, shops, relatives and other informal players. This informal lending puts excessive pressure on the financial system in the country. It also leads to the development of the criminal network and social and financial economic crimes. Due to the bias of the members, the financial institutions are unwilling to lend money to the poor.

(3) *Transaction costs:* Transaction costs of lending to the poor is exceptionally high. The high cost of transactions is the high cost of agencies related to borrowing loans. Financial institutions generally have to spend a lot of money to monitor the self-help groups' members and control their behaviour. Similarly, a lot of money must be spent on screening loan borrowers. Not only this, even their cost related to monitoring the loan provided to the poor. Due to these high costs, granting Banks are reluctant to lend to the poor due to the high cost of screening, monitoring, and enforcing the contract of lending and borrowing money. These increased costs make borrowing from the poor extremely difficult. This is one of the major reasons for the financial exclusion of the poor.

(4) *Financial literacy:* The unbanked poor, without collateral and lack credit-worthiness, lack financial literacy. They lack the financial acumen to make decisions and cannot promote financial savings and borrowings. Due to financial literacy, the poor are unable to avail of financial services and are financially excluded from the financial system. Not only do the members lack the cognition and financial insight to make financial decisions, but they also lack the attitude in terms of dispositions to make a financial decision to achieve financial inclusion. Thus, the lack of financial literacy among the poor leads to poverty among the poor. The members of the group suffer from attitudinal problems. The social and cultural milieu from which they come subjects them to financial exclusion and discrimination in the financial sector.

(5) *Access to the basic financial infrastructure:* To achieve the UN sustainable development goals, it is essential to put in place a basic financial infra-structure to ensure the financial inclusion of the poor. The primary issue with the financial exclusion of the poor is the lack of access to collateral and the lack of information about the creditworthiness of the poor. In order to facilitate the financial inclusion of the poor, credit reporting systems and regulations must be put in place to enforce collaterals and insolvency. Besides, there is a lack of basic infrastructure regarding outreach and access to financial services. The members who live below the poverty line generally lack access to the basic financial infrastructure, including social finance, bank branches, ATMs and internet connectivity. In an interview with the poor members in the remote hinterlands, it became apparent that the poor members lack access to the basic infrastructure, which is the reason for their financial exclusion of the poor. Most bank branches are located at a distance of 10–12 km from the main village. The poor villagers have to walk for kilometres to access financial services and banking facilities. The main fac-tors that impact the financial infrastructure to achieve the UN sustainable development goal of poverty reduction are credit reporting systems, accounting and auditing standards, collateral and insolvency regimes, and payment and settlement systems. The details of the financial infrastructure required to ensure financial access and achieve the UN sustainable devel-opment goals.

a. *Credit Reporting Systems:* One of the primary reasons for not lending to the poor is the lack of information about the creditworthiness of the poor. The banks and financial institutions are unwilling to lend money to the poor due to their lack of creditworthiness. Indian financial system com-prises various public bureaus and private credit bureaus that form the backbone of the Indian credit reporting system. Most corporates and business organisations do not have sufficient retained earnings and have to rely on financial markets or financial intermediaries to access finance. Due to information asymmetry about the creditworthiness and financial performance of small and unorganised businesses, the banks are unwilling to provide credit to these companies. In this scenario, the need was felt for an independent body to assess an entity's investment risk and credit risk and enablesss the creditors to make investment decisions. Initially, the credit rating agencies mainly set the credit risk of the debt instruments, and credit derivatives, and of later, they modified the business model to cover a range of products. Internationally, there are three leading credit rating agencies: Fitch, Standard & Poor, and Moody's investor services. In India, the CRISIL (Credit Rating Information Services of India) was the first credit rating agency that was set up in 1987. In India, there are four major credit rating agencies, namely CRISIL, ICRA, CARE & Brickwork credit rating agency. Credit rating bureaus play an important role in the assessment of the risk and help investors to achieve an equilibrium between risk and return. It also assists the firm in getting access to loans at lower costs.

b. In India, Credit Rating Agencies are generally managed and regulated by SEBI (Securities Exchange Board of India). The credit ratings are used by external regulators such as SEBI, RBI and IRDA for risk assessment and regulation. In India, CRAs (Credit Rating Agencies) play an important role in the regulation of the banking sector. They help in the assessment of the risk of the various products such as money market instruments, pensions and insurance. They also help assess the credit risk in the operation of the banks since the implementation of Basel II capital adequacy norms. The ratings provided by the CRAs are generally mapped into the regulatory risk weights to assess the counterparties' credit risks. While the public credit bureaus mandatorily collect and publish data regarding the financial dealings of the corporates. This data is collected from the regulatory authorities. Private credit bureaus provide a complete picture of the financial dealings of corporate players. These private credit bureaus collect and publish data from various agencies such as retailers, utilities, credit card companies, and mobile users. The private credit bureaus also provide various financial value add services. These agencies play an extremely important role in strengthening the country's financial system. There are various private bureaus that provide a range of value-added activities and financial information about the corporates. They often provide credit ratings and credit scores regarding small and medium enterprises. However, most unorganised small players and business people are not covered by these credit-reporting systems and credit rating agencies.

c. *Regulation of the collateral regime:* The secured transaction system is not well developed in the world's developing economies. The majority of loans in the world's developing economies require some form of collateral. The ability to enforce the collateral agreement and the inadequacy of the creditor's right is one of the most pressing problems in financial contracts involving some form of collateral. The emerging economies lack the legal regulation and framework to enforce the contract for the productive utilisation of movable assets as collateral for obtaining the loan. The essential weakness in the lending mechanism is the registration, enforcement, and sale of collateral. For most of the emerging economies, including India, within a collateral regime, enforcing the creditor's right and the sale of the moveable assets and enforcement of collateral is a problem. The magnitude of this problem is beyond imagination and has been the primary reason behind the financial debacle and the downfall of the major financial institutions in India. Most emerging economies do not have laws and regulations on secured loan agreements. The type of assets that can be used as collateral is minimal. The creation of security interest is an acute problem. Currently, no law regulates the credit agreement, which has no clarity regarding the lender and the creditor's rights. The enforceability of these credit agreements is a problem, and the distinction between the enforcement agreement and the priority of claims is unclear. There is no public policy or regulation regarding the settlement of competing claims against the secured collateral. Due to a lack of agreement about the rights of creditors and debtors and the seizure of the physical collateral in the event of default, the enforcement procedure for collateral loans is costly. The disposition and sale of the collateral assets are a problem as there are delays in selling the assets, leading to the devaluation of the assets. The lack of an insolvency regime and the existing mechanism is the main reason for the failure of the collateral regime in India. Moreover, the rights of the creditors and their priorities are not clear. In developing nations like India, there is a lack of a proper liquidation regime.

Supply-Side Barriers

The supply-side barriers comprise various challenges that include the financial viability of microfinance institutions, real and perceived risk in microlending, institutions and linkages with the formal sector and approaches and products.

(1) *Financial viability of microfinance:* Most of the microfinance institutions in India suffer challenges regarding financial viability. The Government of India has mandated the MFIs (Microfinance institutions in India) to provide credit to the poor. Due to the lack of collateral and information about the creditworthiness of the poor, the bankers are not willing to provide loans to the poor. Thus, microfinance institutions in India face a trade-off between outreach and financial sustainability. In terms of outreach trade-off, the members face a challenge in providing access to loans to the people in the villages of India. Till the 1990s, most of the finance offered by Microfinance institutions was donor or subsidy based. But as the liberalisation of loans took place in the 1990s, microfinance institutions, and banks were given a mandate for priority lending at preferential terms to the micro borrowers below the poverty line. But the financing activity has to be sustainable banking. Thus, donor-based financing has been replaced with sustainable finance. Most microfinance institutions and banks are interested in providing loans only to customers who can pay a higher interest rate on loans. Other

borrowers are denied the bank loan, or impoverished borrowers are denied the bank loan leading to the problem of financial exclusion among the poor.

(2) *Real and perceived risk in microlending:* In most of developing nations, the financial system is not well developed. MFIs (Microfinance Institutions) have emerged as an essential mechanism to ensure access to financial services for the poor. The significant challenges microfinance institutions face in India include the trade-off between outreach, sustainability, and financial sustainability. The major objective of microfinance institutions is to facilitate access to credit and banking services to alleviate poverty and the financial inclusion of the poor. Due to the lack of collateral and information about the creditworthiness of the poor, banks and financial institutions are not willing to provide loans to the poor. Thus, in the case of microlending, there is much scope for policy-making and regulatory changes to ensure access to financial services. There is a need to promote semi-formal finance in form of joint lending to provide access to financial services.

(3) *Linkages with the formal sector:* Most microfinancing institutions do not have any linkage with formal financial institutions. Small and medium enterprises do not have any collateral. Due to a lack of information about the creditworthiness of the poor, the formal financial institutions are unwilling to provide loans to these individuals. Lack of linkages with formal financial institutions leads to the problem of social exclusion and financial exclusion of the poor. The linkages for promoting credit to the rural sector comprise (1) lending to banks and (2) lending to MFIs.

   (1) *Lending to the banks:* Microfinance to the micro borrowers, who do not have physical collateral and information about the creditworthiness of the poor, is not a challenge. The banks do not have information about the creditworthiness of the poor. To facilitate microfinancing for the poor, group lending is aimed at leveraging social capital and peer mechanism to facilitate access to loans. In 1992, the Government of India introduced the self-help group bank linkage programme to facilitate access to loans for the poor at the bottom of the pyramid.

   (2) *Lending by the MFIs (Microfinance institutions):* Microfinance institutions in India provides loans to microenterprises on preferential terms and conditions. Though the banks and formal financial institutions are given the priority mandate to provide microloans to the poor, the microloans and credit needs of the poor cannot be met alone by the banks. Thus, MFIs (Microfinance institutions) are essential in ensuring access to finance for the poor below the poverty line. MFIs aim to provide short loans to the poor at preferential terms. It encourages micro enterprises to become financially sustainable.

   (3) *Linkages with NGOs to promote credit to the poor:* To facilitate the financial inclusion of the poor, the NGOs are appointed to act as facilitators to promote credit linkages with the poor. To ensure the financial inclusion of the poor, NGOs are appointed to serve as SHPIs (Self-help promotion institutes) to facilitate access to credit and finance.

These kinds of linkages are to be provided to link the self-help groups with the bank to facilitate access to loans and credit. NGOs are essential in promoting savings among the poor. To facilitate the same, the NGOs play an important role in training the poor and the micro borrowers. NABARD plays an extremely important role in channelling loans and credit to the poor at the bottom of the pyramid.

(4) *Strategies for inclusive banking.*

The Government of India has introduced various strategies to facilitate inclusive banking. These strategies aim to provide loans to the poor at the bottom of the pyramid. Several measures have been taken by the RBI (Reserve Bank of India) to facilitate the reach to credit and loans for the people at the bottom of the pyramid. The strategies aim to ensure the outreach to loans at the doorsteps of the citizens. The main strategies for financial inclusion include (1) no frill accounts, (2) decentralisation, (3) recognition for RRBs and rural banks, (4) Debt relief and recapitalisation and (4) microfinance.

The description of the strategies for inclusive finance is given below:

(1) *No frill accounts:* The Government of India has introduced the PMJDY (Pradhan Mantri Jan Dhan Yojana) to provide universal banking services to the poor. NABARD has also introduced the KCC (Kisan Credit Card) scheme to facilitate the access to loan for the people at the bottom of the pyramid. Through access to free bank accounts, financial institutions aim to ensure financial inclusion for all, including access to credit at preferential terms.

(2) *Decentralisation:* The decentralised strategy by the Government of India towards financial inclusion aims to provide access to finance and loans to the people at the bottom of the pyramid. The Government of India has initiated the NRLM (National Rural Livelihood Mission) to provide loans. A three-tier body comprising banking committees at the state and district level is established to ensure access to loans. State-level banking committee is responsible for ensuring compliance with the regulations to ensure financial inclusion.

(3) *Recognising RRBs:* In India, specialised institutions such as RRBs (Regional Rural Banks) and cooperative banks have been introduced to ensure the financial inclusion of the poor. Moreover, the Government of India has introduced various practices to provide access to finance for the people at the bottom of the pyramid.

(4) *Priority lending to the poor:* The poor people aim to provide priority lending to the poor. RBI (Reserve Bank of India) and the Government of India have given a mandate to the poor to provide priority lending to the poor. Reserve Bank of India has deregulated the interest rates for the poor, and lending to the poor is to be regarded as priority lending to ensure financial exclusion to the poor. The financial sector supports the financial inclusion of the poor and

more capital is introduced into the microfinance sector through private equity and venture capital.

(5) *Prudential norms for NPAs:* Overall, there are a lot of issues in defining the prudential standards for the NPAs (Non-Performing Assets). A balance sheet of commercial banks is used to conceal many of the facts due to the lack of provision for prudential norms. There is a lack of prudential standards for corporate governance and disclosures. There is a lack of prudential norms regarding recognising income, charging interest rates on loan accounts, or provisioning bad debts. A loan is considered a nonperforming loan if the payment for the interest and principal is not made continuously for 90 days and is classified as a substandard or nonperforming asset. The objective policy of income recognition was introduced based on the record of recovery, classification of bank accounts was made on the classification of assets and the length of time for which the asset is held. After the classification of an asset as substandard, after the 90 days are over, or after losing realisable value, the asset is classified as nonperforming. Proper monitoring and credit appraisal processes should be put in place to ensure access to loans.

(6) *Credit guarantee through SIDBI:* The government operates a credit guarantee scheme to provide credit guarantees to banks for a loan by MSME. This credit guarantee enables loan provision without any collateral or guarantee. For debt restructuring, the Government of India has put in place guidelines. The Government of India has established a regulatory and supervisory body to cull out nonprofitable banks and financial institutions. This scheme is launched to strengthen credit delivery and facilitate the flow of credit to MSMEs (Medium and Small Enterprises). Credit Guarantee Fund has been instrumental in providing a guarantee or collateral for the loans provided to the MSE (Medium Small Enterprise). This scheme has undergone transformative reforms since 2017 to cover NBFCs (Non-Banking Finance Companies) and Small Finance Banks.

(7) *Digitisation and Cybersecurity:* To ensure access to finance, the Government of India has started digitisation of citizen-centric services. The Government has started providing free internet connectivity to the people at the bottom of the pyramid, more commonly called the last mile connectivity. Due to increased digitisation, the members are prone to the risk of data theft and data security. The Government of India has put in place a policy framework to ensure users' cyber security. Cyber security frauds can take many forms: (1) Ransomware, (2) Phishing, (3) Business email impostors and (4) Tech support scams. A brief description of the cybercrimes is given below:

(1) *Ransomware:* It is when somebody in your network gets a fake email. It looks legitimate, and everyone is knocked out from the system when you click on the same. This is a ransomware attack, and attackers can ask for money. Users should be careful against this kind of fraud and cyberattacks.

(2) *Phishing:* This is the email from the vendors, with a link asking the user to click. As soon as you click on the link, it asks you to provide your account details, and then the money is transferred from your account.

(3) *Business email impostors:* The business email impostor gets the email from the email that looks like the business entity. This practice is also called spoofing. To protect from cybercrimes, users need to take cyber insurance. Moreover, there is a need to undertake digital literacy programmes to educate users about cyber fraud.

Conclusion

To ensure inclusive financial growth in India, the Government has adopted various policy measures that include implementing the basic infrastructure in the form of a credit reporting framework, insolvency and collateral regime, and regulatory framework. The priorities of inclusive growth include microfinance, agriculture, financial inclusion, fintech, women empowerment and climate finance. There are various supply and demand-side barriers to inclusive growth. Though digitisation is aimed at mitigating these barriers, it has its perils. There is a need for stricter monitoring and supervision of the financial system.

Summary

Financial systems in India comprise various constituents such as financial intermediaries, who are a source of indirect finance, financial markets as a source of direct finance, financial markets, borrowers, and lenders. The priorities in an inclusive financial system are to ensure access to financial services, women empowerment, digital financial inclusion, promote microfinance and promote climate change finance. Challenges to the inclusive financial system include cultural factors, mistrust of financial institutions, financial literacy, transaction costs, and access to essential services, including credit reporting systems and collateral regimes. The supply-side barriers include microfinance's financial viability, linkages with the formal sector, and lending with banks and microfinance institutions.

Reference

Rajkumar, k. (2021). *Agricultural finance in India: The role of NABARD.* New Century Publication.

Chapter 7

Ensuring Justice and Human Rights

Rehman and His Self-Help Promoting Institute Is Helping to Form Self-Help Groups

Social Perspective

In the hinterlands of Uttar Pradesh, India has a non-government organisation (NGO) involved in solid waste management and cleaning work. This NGO has helped at least 700 women through the self-help group bank linkage programme. The NGO is helping the women involved in solid waste management to form groups. These groups are hence allowed to access bank loans through the self-help group bank linkage programme. Rehman highlights that initially, the group members had difficulty earning money. Before joining the group, the members had a very arrogant attitude towards the management, and they used to be highly disinterested in livelihood. But after joining the group, the members have become highly self-confident. They come regularly, and after coming to the SHPI (self-help promoting institute), they wish each other and have become even more secure about their money. The sustainable development goal of financial inclusion can be easily achieved through

Microfinance and Development in Emerging Economies, 143–159
Copyright © 2023 Nishi Malhotra
Published under exclusive licence by Emerald Publishing Limited
doi:10.1108/978-1-83753-826-320231007

group lending. *This initiative has helped to reduce poverty levels. This initiative is also helping people be financially self-sufficient and empowering women to be efficacious. Thus, it can be included that sustainable development goals can be easily achieved through collaborative efforts.*

Introduction

UN sustainable development goals aim to promote human rights and mitigate global inequalities. The sustainable development goals provide the roadmap to achieve human rights. Human rights include the right to development and social and economic rights. The sustainable development goals are aimed at promoting universal human rights. Human rights are enshrined in all sustainable development goals. The achievement of sustainable development goals leads to the achievement of human rights. More than 90% of the sustainable development goals are embedded as part of human rights. Case studies from all over the globe indicate the need to create synergies between sustainable development goals and human rights. There is a need for political will and cooperation to achieve these synergies. The state governments need to draw a draft road map to achieve sustainable development goals.

In order to achieve economic growth while empowering women, there is a need for vital institutions that ensure adequate implementation. There is a need for strong state machinery that comprises state ministries and central ministries, including the civil society and the parliaments, to achieve human rights. The private sector also plays a vital role in the achievement of sustainable development goals. Globally, governments are playing an exceedingly important role in aligning human rights with sustainable development goals and the states are committing to the achievement of human rights. National Human Right Institutions are being set up to ensure the achievement of sustainable development goals. To achieve human rights, it is imperative to provide education and training to the people. Society should provide adequate support for capacity building. More efforts must be made to enhance the cooperation and linkages between international organizations such as United Nations. The UN Development Group is a consortium that binds over 38 agencies to support the coordination of development policies. The Office of the High Commissioner for Human Rights is the main body that plays an important role in the implementation of human rights and sustainable development goals (Hira, 2012). It helps provide training and capacity building towards achieving human rights.

Human Rights and SDG 1 – Poverty Reduction

UN sustainable development goals have mentioned poverty reduction as the first sustainable development goal. Generally, through the lens of a human right-based approach, it is believed that market failure and the failure of neoliberal policies generally lead to poverty. It is extremely logical to believe that a lack of human rights approach leads to poverty. Considering the argument that market forces cannot achieve the equitable distribution of resources leads to poverty. Due to market failure, it is imperative to introduce the donor or subsidy-based model or moral obligation to participate in the reduction of poverty. Thus, probably one set of theories envisages an enhanced role for the state or public limited companies to reduce poverty. This is often referred to as Welfarist state policy. The neoliberal policy generally prescribes deregulation, privatisation and market reforms. In the 1990s, Bretton Wood prescribed a sustainable growth-based policy framework for the people at the bottom of the pyramid. Many famous social scientists have already objected to neoliberal policies, as they believe that neoliberalism propagates inequality and leads to poverty. They propagate that the neoliberal policies since the 1990s have led to more inequalities and poverty and unwarranted dividends for the rich nations and countries. Proponents of human rights propagate that a balance of welfare state and neoliberal policies can indeed pave the way for poverty reduction, particularly in the context of developing economies like India. The magnitude of this issue can be gauged from the fact that there is vast disparity between the rich and the poor citizens in emerging economies. This is in the context of the per capita income and the access to basic amenities such as the lack of employment, inequalities and uneven and draconian tax policies; all these measures lead to more poverty. Through the lens of the human rights approach, it raises an important question of whether the existing policy frameworks viz the tax policies lead to higher poverty. And is the social discrimination and lattice of power relations enshrined in the civil society framework responsible for the inequitable distribution of resources among the poor? Moreover, it might be that existing institutional policies might lead to more poverty. While discussing the cause of poverty, one cannot overlook the lack of the right to education, the right to health, and the right to a decent standard of living as the main reason for the presence of poverty among the lower sections of society. None of the indexes to measure poverty takes into account the lack of human rights as a dimension to measure poverty; hence, the existing measures are more reactive than preventive. There is a need to design new measures on the basis of preventive measures while taking into account the human rights approach. The presence of tribes in developing countries like India is a grim reality. And the discrimination of these tribes based on caste, creed, race and ostracisation from civil society is a reality. Though the state in emerging nations like India has given recognition and representation to tribes through stratification and the creation of special quotas, there is still a denial of rights. Most of these tribes generally live away from the human settlements in the city and spend their time pursuing their art. Nonetheless, to state that sanitation, education and health in these hamlets are far from satisfactory will not be an exaggeration. Yet another school is duty-based and highlights the need for literacy and attitude change to teaching good habits and attitudes among the marginalised. A hybrid of duty-based and right-based approaches is often sought to reduce poverty among the poor. Various studies highlight the role of differential governance policies on poverty levels among different regions and groups. In one of the interviews with the self-help groups that have been working together as Dhokra artists for years, it came to light that despite the state support in the form of training and access to livelihood opportunities, the group of Dhokra artists is unable to combat poverty. This is because the members of this community generally spend inconsiderate resources on drugs, liquor and unproductive purposes. This leads to social exclusion and poverty among the poor. From a rights perspective, even when they are provided access to credit, and basic amenities like health, banking and education, they are unable to prosper. During the interview, it came to the fore that they, as a group, are not duty based and spend unreasonable resources on unproductive uses. Thus, regarding eradicating social problems like poverty, there is generally a debate between the right-based and duty-based wings. The rights-based group of social researchers generally propagate that the poor should be given representation and a voice in matters important to them. Moreover, resources should be redistributed from the rich to the poor. The recognition and representation of the marginalised sections of society as a separate class in government jobs and facilities is a part of the rights-based approach to poverty reduction. While at the same time, resources should be redistributed from the rich to the poor. This includes the implementation of various social schemes, such as *direct benefit transfers and subsidies*, to provide access to resources for the poor. Though social researchers propagate the use of redistribution of resources as a human right, they often assume. In this framework comes the question of what can be the solution to this issue. The creation of *Responsibility* is the solution to this paradox. Along with recognition and voice, while redistributing the resources, it is important to create responsibility for the welfare of the poor. A case in point is the famous *self-help group bank linkage*, designed to promote access to financial resources for the people at the bottom of the pyramid. Existing studies highlight the lack of formal institutions that promote the eradication of poverty through the redistribution of resources and the recognition of the rights of the poor. The private enterprises will not be interested in the welfare of this marginalised section of people due to the lack of financial sustainability and return on investment for the poor. There is a need for an increasing role for the state and the corporates, but after the 1990s, with the adoption of sustainable finance, there is a need for more innovative policies and solutions. This includes adopting Information and Communication, Technology for implementing such policies. Technology adoption and digitisation can surely be a solution to mitigate poverty.

Case Study on Poverty Reduction in Akodara Village, Gujarat

The Akodara village in Gujarat, India, has played an important role in eradicating poverty by digitising the town. This is a Smart village that provides free internet connectivity to all the villagers in Akodara, Gujarat, India. Access to technology has helped individual villagers to get access to livelihood and financial services. The village boasts a fully automated RO water system, a digital banking system, and a digitized mode of payment in all retail shops. There is complete subsidy distribution system automation and a separate hostel for the animal cattle. Access to computers in the ICICI Bank branch has helped women and senior citizens in India to get transfers to the transfer payments. It has helped the men in the village to get access to a livelihood. This has enabled the villagers to combat poverty through the financial inclusion programme. Thus, the modernisation and digitisation of villages have helped the villagers fight against poverty. Under the Sarv Shiksha Abhiyaan, all the students can send their children to school. This allows them to exercise the fundamental right to education for all children up to 14 years of age.

Further, providing free scholarships to all minority children and army families has improved the living standard of the people at the bottom of the pyramid. The wave of digitisation has increased the inclusion of the poor in the financial systems. It is an entirely digitized village, with various micro-ATMs (Automated Teller Machines) set up to provide multiple payment services. There are many facilities to ensure direct benefit transfer, and an LCD and Projector is provided in each village school to ensure brilliant school and education for the students. This has helped improve the livelihood levels in the village and ensure access to financial services. Creating an integrated ecosystem with a rights and duty approach is the way forward.

Human Rights and SDG 2 – Right to Health and Social Security

The literature refers to the gross violation of human rights regarding the right to good health and social security. Overall International Labour Organization (ILO) has highlighted that 71% of the global population does not have access to health amenities. Similarly, there is a gross disparity regarding access to the right to social security options. Most people worldwide have to pay for their medical expenses from their income. This leads to gross inequalities and imperfections in terms of the distribution of resources among the members. These human rights are provided in the *Universal Declaration of Human Rights* and the *International Covenant for Economic, Social, and Cultural Rights*. In the current scenario, much more attention is being given to the right to health and social security. This right has now become enforceable even in the legal courts of law. The *Universal Declaration of Human Rights* has emphasised that the citizens of the member nations are entitled to health and mental wellness standards of the highest degree possible. In most nations, the National Health Systems are not well developed to ensure equal access to health services and mental health support. It is also important to provide constitutional remedies to the citizens of the member nations to reinforce their right to proper medical and mental health. In most emerging economies, citizens do not have access to the social protection system or insurance coverage. The citizens can avail of the insurance facilities from the public and private players. In emerging economies like India, most public companies are not providing access to health services and retirement benefits. In such a scenario, the government has introduced various social protection schemes, which include the Pradhan Mantri Jeevan Beema Yojana (PMJBY) and Ayushman Bharat. These schemes ensure that the people at the bottom of the pyramid have access to public health services. One of the major challenges to implementing these programmes is the lack of information about the rights of the citizens of India. In this regard, it becomes important that the government conducts various literacy and awareness programmes to ensure the social inclusion of the poor in the social protection systems. Thus, the right to good health, education is the fundamental social right for the people at the bottom of the pyramid. Besides social exclusion from the health system, the other major lacunae are the presence of a large informal sector. In developing economies like India, many individuals are employed in the informal sector. This informal sector further accentuates health woes and leads to the violation of human rights. In many circumstances, the state does not have sufficient funds to finance social health activities. To a certain extent, the market's failure is the reason behind the refusal of the private parties to provide social security to the people at the bottom of the pyramid. Despite introducing corporate social responsibility, not many corporates are interested in providing insurance facility to the people at the bottom of the pyramid. Hence, it becomes important for the state to adopt welfare practices to promote good health among the people at the bottom of the pyramid. The state must educate the members at the bottom of the pyramid to provide literacy to the poor people who are not covered by health insurance. The right to good health is simultaneously linked to the attainment of other rights, including the right to food, security, housing, and non-discrimination against the rights of the upper class. To achieve the implementation of human rights, ensuring good governance in the nation is extremely important. India is at the cusp of ensuring the right to health for all. In this regard, the Indian Government has adopted the Universal vaccination campaign to ensure good health for all. This massive vaccination drive has enabled the nation's citizens to achieve protection from the pandemic. Also, the provision for free drinking water, i.e., '*Jal Jeevan Mission*' for all and toilets for all, under the '*Swachh Bharat Mission*'. These social security programmes will play an important role in promoting good health and social security for all the citizens of India. Thus, a hybrid approach to achieve the socially sustainable goal of good health for all through a robust social protection system contributes to the welfare of the general health of the nation's citizens. The government is financing the social health programme by tapping the resources from the *Corporate Social Responsibility* fund and *non-resident sources*. The government can also provide capital to fund social protection and health programmes. Further, the government of India has the mandate to levy cess and taxes to fund various social protection programmes. There is a need to develop more innovative solutions to combat health issues and sanitation issues among India's citizens. And the Indian state and Government have done a laudable job of providing health and sanitation facilities to the people at the bottom of the pyramid.

Case Study of Initiatives in the Domain of Health and Social Security

The main feature of the social security programme in India is the safety net policies and programs, and social security in the unorganised sector. The new set of initiatives in the domain of social protection and healthcare has transformed the landscape of the Indian rural system. In the 11th Plan, India adopted the Common Minimum Programme, which has introduced various social protection initiatives. These initiatives include programmes to institutionalise legal rights (Mid-day meal programmes, Social pension, MNREGA). The Government of India has also introduced the Rashtriya Swasthya Bima Yojana (RSBY) for BPL households. The main feature of the Social Protection System is (1) promotional measures, (2) preventive measures and (3) protective measures. Promotional measures refer to the measures that aim to improve income in the long run. The key measures in this regard are to build capacity and invest human capital. These measures include stipends, mid-day meals, conditional cash transfers, and targeted credit and livelihood programs. Preventive measures are aimed at enabling households to manage risks and shocks. Protective measures allow the members to be economically safe against the perils and risks existing in the system. Within this ambit is the famous PDS (Public Distribution System) that aims to deliver most of the state's subsidised wheat, rice, and kerosene. MNREGA (Mahatma Gandhi National Rural Employment Guarantee) programme aims to provide 100 days of work in rural districts to unskilled and low-skill personnel. SGSY (Swarn Jayanti Gram Swarozgar Yojana) seeks to provide targeted credit for groups and individuals. This scheme aims to provide subsidised bank credit to the groups.

Besides, the Indira Gandhi Old Age Pension Scheme (IGNOPAS) aims to provide the non-contributory social pension to the poor. This scheme aims to give the monthly cash benefit to the people at the bottom of the pyramid. The Indira Awas Yojana (IAY) is a novel programme for targeted rural housing. The mid-day meal scheme aims to provide free meals to children below 14. Aam Adami Bima Yojana (AABY) aims to provide free insurance to provide cover against natural death, disability, and accident cover for the rural poor. There is a specific urban housing programme for the urban poor. This includes the programme called targeted urban housing (VAMBAY).

Human Rights & SDG 3 – Women Empowerment and Gender Equality

The sustainable development goals highlight the need for women's empowerment and gender equality. Gender inequality is embedded within the lattice of power relations that women share with society. These relations are marked by the stereotypes or the traditional typos through which society portrays the role of women in India. The achievement of women's rights is in itself a goal, as it is a driver of other sustainable development goals such as democracy, sustainable development goals, poverty reduction and peace. The socially constructed roles and images of women are far away from the social reality. To ensure women's equality in society, there is a need to transform power relations. In the eyes of the law, equality of women needs equal access to education, resources, and cultural and social rights. The right to education is a fundamental right that ensures that women have an influential role in the decision-making in the setup they operate from, whether it is an organization, workplace or home (Reifner & Schelhowe, 2010). Women's rights are essential to achieve inclusive and equitable growth. Education is the key to ensuring adequate opportunities for women.

Moreover, the women should be able to enjoy sexual rights and should also get freedom from violence of any kind. To empower women, it is essential to give women the right to access financial resources and control their sources of funds and finances. As per the various studies, in a household, all the financial decisions are generally made by the husbands. More disparity exists between men and women in rural areas. From the human rights perspective, there is a need to empower women to provide them the right to make financial decisions.

Moreover, there is a need to eradicate violence against women in all forms. All women in civil society should be free to work and manage their finances. It is essential to ensure the active participation of women in all decisions. Success in achieving sustainable development goals depends on women's equal participation in the labour force and providing freedom from The research studies show that stereotypes regarding gender roles and women's duties lead to unequal distribution of power, thus impeding freedom. In order to eliminate gender disparity, it is extremely important to provide adequate sanitation and health facilities. There is a need for constitutional reforms to facilitate women's empowerment and equality of rights for women. There is a need for reforms to ensure the financial inclusion of poor women in the financial system. To ensure a universal bank account for all women, it is essential to educate women. The Government of India has undertaken various initiatives for empowering women, including the dowry prohibition act of 1961, and the national plan for the girl child National commission for women protection from domestic violence act of 2005. Maternity benefit act, 2017, women's reservation bill, national policy for empowerment of women, Beti Bachao Beti Padhao, One-Stop Centre Scheme, Women Helpline, Ujjawala, Working Women Hostel, Nari Shakti Puruskar, Stree Shakti Puruskar, Rajya Mahila Samman, Mahila Police Volunteers, Mahila Shakti Kendras and Nirbhaya Fund.

Similarly, to ensure the financial inclusion of poor women, it is essential to provide digital and financial literacy to poor women (Arthur, 2012). Despite various schemes, the women members cannot access finance due to inadequate training and rigid attitude (Bernheim & Garrett, 2003; Hamilton & Darity, 2017; Henry, Murtuza, & Weiss, 2015). For women's empowerment, it is extremely important to involve them in decision-making. It is essential to sensitise women to their rights and duties. Unless and until women are aware of their rights, they cannot be empowered. For a peaceful, prosperous, and sustainable society, it is essential that women are sensitised about their fundamental rights.

Regarding the financial empowerment of women, the central issue that crops up is the lack of finances and pay for women's work in the house. There is a need for aggressive action to ensure women's freedom from the clutches of tyranny, exploitation, and social injustice. Even during COVID-19, women were the worst hit as they lost more jobs. During this period, the Government of India allowed various types of financial support to the women through the self-help group bank linkage programme to facilitate access to credit to the men during the pandemic. This programme aims to ensure that no women are left behind in the process of financial inclusion. Besides, that women are underrepresented in all spheres, and in many places, women are subject to violence. There is stark inequality among men and women worldwide regarding labour participation. For women, it is extremely important to ensure inclusive and equitable growth. The law states that all women and girl children should complete primary and secondary education. There is a need to sensitise society regarding the rights of women. The state needs to support measures that lead to property rights of ownership and entitlement for women. It's essential to create the right to work and get paid for women. There is a need to improve the sexual education of women to facilitate empowerment. There is a need for international commitment to protect women from forced marriages and exploitation. Women empowerment in itself leads to the development of the family and other members. However, as per the literature, women's empowerment can occur on various dimensions, namely the personal level and social empowerment assignment in other people's beliefs. To empower women through the changes in their personal beliefs, it is important to undertake financial literacy training and change women's attitudes. Besides, there should be policy initiatives to change the social attitude through various programs. Community-led endeavours that voice women's concerns regarding their rights are more effective in ensuring the financial inclusion of the poor. This includes self-help groups with bank linkages. Financial empowerment can be achieved by providing access to financial resources to women. Still, to achieve complete empowerment, policy initiatives must be undertaken to empower the community.

Case Study of Women Community Group

The government has introduced the SHG Bank Linkage programme. Various community leaders highlight that to make the group sustainable, and it is essential to organise some form of schedule. To reduce poverty, the NGO Leader stated that homogenous members are grouped to form a group. In a group, the liability of the members is joint. They take a group loan, and if one members out of the 10 members does not make the repayment, then all the members go to the defaulter's door, and the other member pressurises the defaulter to repay the loan. Initially, the members know about the creditworthiness of other group members. There is a practice of inter loaning among the members. The initial period of internal loaning and repayment of loans is beneficial for building a practice of interloaning. All the members who are part of the loan have skills in their hands. In our group, all the members pursue Sujani and Madhubani paintings. These paintings are extremely popular among all the citizens. The Government of India provides marketing support to all enterprises and microenterprises. On an international level, this art has a lot of importance and relevance. Social media play an essential role in credit generation, inter loaning. These measures help reduce poverty and promote prosperity among the group members. India is a diverse country, and one standardized social protection programme is not sufficient to meet the diverse needs of the Indian population that is spatially widespread. The basic structure of this programme has many lacunae, and there is a need for improvising this programme. Moreover, there is a need to

*introduce the PPP (Public Private Partnership) of service delivery to enable the
social inclusion of the marginalised in the social safety net.*

Human Rights & SDG 4: Climate Change

In the context of the Indian economy, the suitable bearers highlight the key
human suitable risks that the citizens of the nation bear (Queralt, 2016). Climate
change is soon becoming a reality, and the government must take sufficient steps
to mitigate climate change risk. Towards achieving the Sustainable Development
Goals 2030, Governments globally should mobilise the funds to minimise the risk
of climate change. The '*Paris Agreement*' is a convention aimed at mitigating the
risk of all kinds of climate changes and environmental damage. Various human
suitable risks are associated with the climate change. Miscellaneous institutions in
the international, public, and private sectors should undertake various measures
to mitigate climate risks. There is a need to design various instruments aided by
the public, private, and international players to minimise climate risks. The
changes in the climate seriously challenge human rights. The measures to mitigate
climate change can also challenge substantive human rights. Climate change can
lead to the infringement of the human rights of individuals and communities to
access information, participate in decision-making, and enjoy livelihood and
lands, culture, and determination. There is a need to integrate human rights into
the policy measures to ensure sustainable development goals. The convention on
human rights says that the government bodies like the police, and the state
government, when taking action, should take into account the rights of the local
communities, migrants, children with disability, vulnerable situations, and marginalised women communities, to name a few. The Paris Convention and the
Vienna Convention, which included approximately 171 nations, had the agenda
around democracy, participatory and mutually reinforcing goals.

Indigenous People's Right to Self-Determination

The tribal people have the right to information in case of adaptation and mitigation rights. Tribals often feel neglected that they are not consulted before
undertaking extractive mitigation projects. The individuals and communities are
impacted by the mitigation and adaptation projects which include the nuclear and
hydropower plant. There is a need to develop respect for the rights of individuals
and communities. The right to be informed and consultation of the local communities in making decisions regarding the adaptation projects that lead to
climate change is significant. Many of the non-renewable projects lack commitment and consultation before starting the project. The UN human rights and
opinion leaders in civil society have not been consulted while formulating and
setting up sensitive projects. Simultaneously, land ownership and tenure rights are
also not considered before undertaking projects that can impact the climate. It is
often argued that modern-day capitalism is destroying the social fabric and
ancestral culture cherished by the indigenous people. Modern-day capitalism in

the form of industrialisation and modernisation is destroying the symbiotic relationship between nature and the indigenous people. The traditional customs, practices, and knowledge of local indigenous people like Adivasis and Tribals enable the government to conserve nature.

Case Study of Kuttanad, Kerala

Kuttanad, Kerala, is an important heritage agricultural system due to the research study published by M.S. Swaminathan Research Foundation. This unique wetland is situated around the Vembanad Lake system. This agrarian system was initially referred to as the region's rice bowl. The waterlogged agricultural system is spread over 110,000 hectares of land. From this, approximately 50,000 hectares remain submerged in the water. This is the only region where farming is done below sea level. This agricultural system is also called the deltaic wetland, formed by the confluence of five major rivers: Achenkovil, Pampa, Manimala, and Meenachil. Traditionally, the clayey soil in this delta is rich in deposits brought about by the silt of the marshy rivers and is fit for the cultivation of the paddy field. However, the excessive forestation in this area has led to a change in the ecological replenishment of this place. The committed, entrepreneurial farmers have reclaimed this land. It is reclaimed land supported by dikes from the vast amount of water.

Due to climate change, many farmers are abandoning the place. The reason for leaving this place is that the waters of this place are turning hazardous for the native people of this place. The local people's houses remain flooded with water for most of the year. They are known as climate refugees, and the lack of river management and backwater protection has led to misery in their lives. In the words of the local people, the Dalit workers who work in this place remain slaves of the landlords, and these people manually drain the drain swamps. The building of big bunds, massive roads, and bridges has disrupted the lives of many in these villages. There is a need for flood management to ensure the security of the people and their households. This wetland has supported the livelihood of diverse ethnic communities engaged in fishing, mussel harvesting, coconut farming, toddy extraction, and traditional crafts like basket weaving using Pandanus. This is a unique wetland where paddy cultivation is done below sea level. Earlier, Kuttanad was given the GIAHS status for recognising indigenous farming practices. As per GIAHS norms, there was a requirement to document the traditional practices. Conservation programmes should be undertaken to preserve the unique wetland and biodiversity. However, due to the complex socioeconomic conditions, there are many challenges to achieving this goal of sustainable development. Over the years, the Kuttanad wetlands that once used to be the heritage of the unique agricultural practices of the local people and community have been transformed into a farming system marked with capitalist relations. In the earlier time, farming was ecology-based, and the farming system was based on the local cycle. Before the Green revolution, salt incursions were allowed in the fields and were considered essential to enhance the soil fertility of the place. But with adopting the green course, the region has started facing many ecological catastrophes. Due to mechanisation and new land tenure systems, the farmers are more interested in profits and not in maintaining the place's environmental stability. During this period, no required steps have been undertaken to conserve or rebuild the wetlands. Indeed, the GIAHS status conferred upon the Kuttanad wetland is an opportunity for the historical knowledge of the indigenous people and tribes to rebuild this vulnerable wetland in the region. As per the Centre for Water Resources Development and Management (CWRDM) in Kozhikode, the unplanned infrastructure development has destroyed the fragile ecosystem of this place. This has made the climate condition worse. Thanneermukkam bund and other modern structures have destroyed the scenic beauty, and the backwaters are suddenly disappearing. To protect the fragile ecosystem, there is a need for re-planning and reconstructing this place by using the indigenous agricultural practices.

Initially called the saltwater barrier, this Thanneermukkam bund was constructed in 1951. The bund was built to stop the saline water intrusion into the paddy fields during the high tides. The fisherman in this region has consistently opposed the construction of this dam. The dam was closed and opened on 15 December and 15 March, respectively. However, sometimes the dam is closed for a more extended period. The environmentalists argue that if the wetland remains closed for a more extended period, the aquatic life cannot immigrate, and the pesticide and fertilizers applied to the paddy crop remain static, leading to high-level pollutants that are harmful to the life of flora and fauna. Similarly, the *Thottappally Spillway was* constructed to facilitate the flushing away of the extra flood waters from the *Pampa, Manimala, and Achenkoil* rivers into the Arabian sea before it floods to Kuttanad. This spillway has added to the ecological concerns in this place. Other than this 24 Km long Alappuzha Changanassery Road in 1957. These roads lead to blockage in the water flow, which leads to flooding in the region.

Human Rights Approach to SDG: Indian Perspective

The Bruntland commission, in 1987, highlighted the need for sustainable growth with development with environmental sustainability. Human development should be achieved by ensuring that the resources are not depleted for future generations. Though the environmental resources are depleting, sustainable growth and development are needed to ensure economic development is achieved easily. The Declaration for the unrestricted right to development emphasises that each citizen should have the right to development. More emphasis should be placed on freedom of speech and expression in a developed society.

Moreover, there is an interrelation between environmental laws and human rights. Globalisation, liberalisation, and industrialisation led to ecological changes that are detrimental to human rights. The environmental changes are visible in the form of climate change, excessive pollution, extinction of the biosphere and biodiversity, and health issues for the country's citizens. Various international conventions, treaties, and statutes have been put in place to safeguard the interests of poor or marginalised people. These declarations include the Stockholm Declaration, 1972, and Rio Declaration, 1992. Article 21 of the Constitution of India highlights the need for the Right to a safe environment as the Right to Life. Article 48a propagates the right of the state to protect the environment. Article 51(g) highlights the role of the citizens of the nation in protecting the environment.

Similarly, the tribunal courts have a vast role to play in the sustainable development of a region. The Indian Government has undertaken various projects to ensure sustainable development in the nation. Many smart cities and villages have been set across the length and breadth of the country. This has further led to the reduction in poverty levels and the creation of livelihood for the citizens at the bottom of the pyramid. The Indian village system has improved drastically, and there is electrification in all the villages. Under the Shyama Prasad Mukherjee Rural Urban Mission (SPMRM), the basic village infrastructure is being provided to ensure reasonable living standards for the people at the bottom of the pyramid. The basic objective of the rural development programme is to bridge the rural and urban divide, simulating the development by generating more job opportunities.

Initiatives for Climate Change

The Indian Government has taken several measures to mitigate the impact of climate change. The Cabinet chaired by Shri Narendra Modi has approved the national determined contribution to the UN Framework Convention on Climate Change (UNFCCC). At the 26th session of the Conference of the Parties (COP26) in Glasgow, United Kingdom, the government presented to the world five nectar elements (Panchamrit), including promoting the electricity generated from the non-fossil fuels, reducing the emission intensity of GDP (Gross Domestic Product) and reduce the creation of excessive carbon sinks. LIFE is called a one-word movement by the Government of India; the Prime Minister of India gave the mantra of Lifestyle For Environment to combat climate change in India.

Government Action for Poverty Reduction

As part of the New India Strategy 2022, the Indian Prime Minister unveiled the initiatives for poverty reduction. The government aims to reduce poverty by emphasising the sectors such as electricity, drinking water, health, education, etc. The government has introduced various programmes and schemes such as Deen Dayal Antyodaya Yojana, National Livelihood Mission, Pradhan Mantri Gram Sadak Yojana, Pradhan Mantri Awas Yojana, MNREGA, Skill Development Programme, Shyama Prasad Mukherjee Rurban Mission, National Social Assistance Programme, etc. To reduce poverty, the government has to emphasise various priority sectors, which include education, skill development, bank credit, water conservation, health and nutrition, electricity, housing, ODF, waste disposal, road, internet, LPG, DBT, social protection of elderly, widows, disabled, sports, youth club, non-agricultural activities in rural areas.

Government Action for Health and Social Security

The government of India has launched the National Health Mission (NHM) to ensure health insurance and coverage for all eligible households and individuals in the country. In the health sector, the lack of inclusion of the poor in the social security scheme has led to the vulnerability of the general population and increased out-of-pocket expenditure for households. In India, approximately 30% of the people and 40 crore individuals who are not covered by the social security schemes are called the missing middle. In September 2018, the government of India introduced Ayushman Bharat – Pradhan Mantri Jan Dhan Yojana and the state Government extension schemes. Another low-cost health insurance product is Arogya Sanjeevani. To include low-income groups of people in the social protection systems, there is a need to create financial literacy and reduce insurance costs.

Moreover, there is a need to reduce adverse selection. There is a need to improve the self-efficacy of the investors and consumers in the social protection systems. In India, the spending on health and social protection is as little as 1.5% GDP, i.e., the lowest in the world. In India, approximately 70% of the population, nearly 95 crores, is lower. The government subsidised provides partially or fully subsidised insurance to segmented sections of the people. The poor in the informal sector are covered under Ayushmaan Bharat Pradhan Mantri Jan Arogya Yojana to approximately 10.9 crores families. Many of the states have adopted state schemes.

The Government of India has introduced various Social protection systems as compulsory contributory health insurance schemes for organised sector employees. Employee State Insurance Scheme is the most significant scheme. Another social health insurance is the Central Government Health Scheme (CGHS), run by the Union Government for its employees with an enrolment of around 40 lakhs. In India, the private health insurance sector is extremely well developed. Approximately 7% of the poor are pushed into poverty due to insufficient health insurance. The citizens excluded from the social health insurance coverage include the self-employed, informal, and semi-formal occupations in rural areas. The Government of India has introduced various standardized insurance products, including the *Aarogya Sanjeevani* insurance policy. This insurance plan is an indemnity and is available to the group and individuals. On the supply side, the major obstacle or challenge faced by the government in ensuring access to health services is the identification of and outreach to consumers.

Due to this reason, insurance coverage for the poor has not been realized. There is a need to push for significant outreach through enrolment in the insurance plans. The lack of data regarding the eligible people who should be covered under the social protection programme is the main reason for the exclusion of the poor. In this scenario, the government has planned and designed the databases for National Food Security Act (NFSA), Pradhan Mantri Suraksha Bima Yojana, or the Pradhan Mantri Kisan Samman Nidhi (PM-KISAN) for agricultural households. This database can be shared with private insurers to ensure the enrolment of the poor. The government has created many standardized products for the social inclusion of the poor into the health and social protection system. There is a need to develop a robust infrastructure to ensure the inclusion of the marginalised into the social protection system.

Government Action for Women's Empowerment

The Government of India has introduced various schemes for women's empowerment through the social, educational, economic, and political uplifting of the poor from the circle of poverty. To enhance the employability of women, the government has undertaken various training through the network of Women's Industrial Training Institutes, National Vocational Training Institutes, and Regional Vocational Training Institutes. To ensure women's economic independence, the Government of India has introduced the Skill India Mission. The National Skill Development Policy has focussed on inclusive skill development. Pradhan Mantri Kaushal Vikas Kendras is a programme that aims to create additional infrastructure for the training and apprenticeship of women in India. In addition, various schemes such as Pradhan Mantri Mudra Yojana and Stand Up India, Prime Minister's Employment Generation Programme (PMEGP) are aimed at building women's enterprises. Pradhan Mantri Ujjwala Yojana (PMUY) aims to safeguard women's health by providing clean household fuel. Various changes have been made in the regulatory provisions of multiple acts to enable the security of livelihood and employment for the poor. Mahatma Gandhi National Rural Employment Guarantee Act, 2005 (MGNREGA) further mandates that jobs for the poor should be provided. The initiatives taken by the government to empower women and girls include POSHAN Abhiyaan, Anganwadi Social Service, Pradhan Mantri Matru Vandana Yojana, Beti Bachao Beti Padaho Scheme, One-Stop Centre, Universalisation of the Women Helpline, Child Protection Services, Scheme for Adolescent Girls, Swadhar Greh Scheme, Ujjawala Scheme, and Working Women Scheme. The government has set up a special Nirbhaya Fund under which the Bureau of Police Research and Development (BPR&D) undertakes various initiatives for the welfare of the poor. The Ministry of Women and Child Development has engaged the services of the National Institute of Mental Health and Neuro Sciences (NIMHANS) to provide various health services to the poor.

Challenges to Ensuring Human Rights for All Citizens

Human rights in India suffer from various social challenges. These challenges include poor education, gender inequality, corruption, discrimination, and poverty. A brief description of the challenges to human rights faced in India is given below:

(1) *Poverty*: Globally, there are 1.7 billion people that do not have a bank account and do not have access to financial services. They do not own any assets, and financial institutions are unwilling to provide them with loans. Due to poverty, the citizens are unable to access education and unable to enjoy the benefit of good food and clothing. Thus, poverty is one of the major challenges facing the citizens of India.

(2) *Inequalities*: In India, gross inequalities exist between the males and females, upper caste and lower caste, different religions and sects, etc. There is stark inequality among the various sections of society regarding consumption and access to resources. In the workplace, female members or women generally suffer from gross inequality. The participation of women in the workforce and their access to resources is very uneven, and similarly, the women members suffer from gross inequalities in terms of wages, income, and access to financial services.

(3) *Corruption*: Corruption is one of the major social evils prevailing in society. The government offices in India are fraught with corruption, and they suffer from bureaucratic delays and red tape.

(4) *Social Discrimination*: In India, there is stark discrimination on a social basis between various sects, castes, religions, and males and females. Members of society face a lot of social discrimination. The people practice violence and perpetrate multiple kinds of crimes against the people. This discrimination could be in the form of caste discrimination, social ostracisation, and not allowing the members of society to use public places. This leads to social discrimination (Zauro et al., 2020).

Conclusion

India has adopted the sustainable development goal of poverty reduction, zero hunger, equality for women, access to health and social security systems and protection against climate change. In this regard, several steps have been taken by the Indian Government. These goals are very closely aligned to ensure human rights for all citizens. In this regard, the right-based approach becomes essential for achieving social justice and development.

Summary

UN Sustainable development goals propagate human rights. Ensuring human rights for all is the way to achieve Sustainable Development Goals. A robust institutional framework is needed to ensure the achievement of the SDGs. The first SDG of poverty reduction depends on how duty-based and rights-based approaches to human rights are propagated. Direct Benefit Transfer and subsidies ensure the achievement of human rights. The Government of India has introduced many schemes, such as

Ayushman and Swachh Bharat, to ensure good health and women's empowerment and depend on financial literacy and empowerment. Various measures need to be undertaken to protect from climate change to grant rights to local communities. There is a need for an integrated approach to achieve Sustainable Development Goals through achieving human rights.

References

Arthur, C. (2012). Consumers or critical citizens? Financial literacy education and freedom. *Critical Education, 3*(6).

Bernheim, B. D., & Garrett, D. M. (2003). The effects of financial education in the workplace: Evidence from a survey of households. *Journal of public Economics, 87*(7–8), 1487–1519.

Hamilton, D., & Darity, W. A. (2017). The political economy of education, financial literacy, and the racial wealth gap. https://doi.org/10.20955/r.2017.59-76

Hastings, J. S., Madrian, B. C., & Skimmyhorn, W. L. (2013). Financial literacy, financial education, and economic outcomes. *Annual Review of Economics, 5*(1), 347–373.

Henry, T. F., Murtuza, A., & Weiss, R. E. (2015). Accounting as an instrument of social justice. *Open Journal of Social Sciences, 3*(01), 66.

Hira, T. K. (2012). Promoting sustainable financial behaviour: Implications for education and research. *International Journal of Consumer Studies, 36*(5), 502–507.

Queralt, J. (2016). A human right to financial inclusion. In H. Gaisbauer, G. Schweiger, & C. Sedmak (Eds.), *Ethical issues in poverty alleviation* (Vol. 14). Studies in Global Justice. Springer. https://doi.org/10.1007/978-3-319-41430-0_5

Reifner, U., & Schelhowe, A. (2010). Financial education. *JSSE-Journal of Social Science Education.* https://doi.org/10.4119/jsse-517

Zauro, N. A., Saad, R. A. J., Ahmi, A., & Mohd Hussin, M. Y. (2020). Integration of Waqf towards enhancing financial inclusion and socio-economic justice in Nigeria. *International Journal of Ethics and Systems, 36*(4), 491–505.

Zauro, N. A., Zauro, N. A., Saad, R. A. J., & Sawandi, N. (2020). Enhancing socio-economic justice and financial inclusion in Nigeria: The role of zakat, Sadaqah and Qardhul Hassan. *Journal of Islamic Accounting and Business Research, 11*(3), 555–572.

Chapter 8

Role of Government to Ensure Economic and Social Welfare

Mid-Day Meal Scheme – A Social Scheme

> That government is the strongest of which every man feels himself a part.
>
> –by *Thomas Jefferson*

The mid-day meal scheme is a government scheme to provide a free meal to all school-going students. The objective of this scheme is to boost attendance in the classroom and improve the nutrition of the students. This scheme provides a mid-day meal with 500 calories and 12 grams of protein to all school-going children. This scheme has a lot of social value, as it promotes socialisation among the school-going children in classes 1–5 in the Government and Government aided schools. It aims to create equal opportunities for all. The aim is to help the children to attend classes regularly and help them increase their concentration. Despite all efforts, the school-going children lag on social parameters, and this scheme ensures that the children achieve a certain level of nutrition and nourishment. This scheme has been

Microfinance and Development in Emerging Economies, 161–188
Copyright © 2023 Nishi Malhotra
Published under exclusive licence by Emerald Publishing Limited
doi:10.1108/978-1-83753-826-320231008

highly successful in combating classroom hunger and has brought about the large increase in the enrolment of the students in the classroom.

Introduction

India has the largest population of poor people and the largest number of malnourished children in India. More than 15% population in India is below the poverty line. Indian economy is mainly agricultural, fraught with various challenges such as over-dependence on monsoon, absence of Agri extension services and lack of markets and infrastructure. The Indian constitution provided for the welfare state. The state government runs more than 1,000 welfare schemes. These schemes include Public Distribution System (PDS), MNREGA (Mahatma Gandhi National Employment Guarantee Act), mid-day meal scheme, Integrated Child Development Scheme and Cash Benefit scheme. Cash transfers are of three kinds conditional, unconditional and stamps/vouchers. In India, cash transfers are generally conditional and unconditional. The State Government, the Central Government, or both can launch the welfare schemes. The Government of India has introduced various social welfare schemes and sets of policies and programs to protect the poor and marginalised against poverty and social exclusion. Indian Government has introduced various right-based schemes and entitlements to enhance the welfare of the poor and marginalised people. Social welfare schemes include the Mid-Day Meal Scheme, Public Distribution Scheme and National Rural Employment Guarantee Scheme. These schemes respond to all the shocks, community-level shocks, natural disasters and pandemics. These social schemes are helping the nation achieve a high economic growth and development level. These schemes are funded either by the state government or the central government. These schemes help to bridge the gap in the investment infrastructure. These programmes aim to scale development to improve connectivity, provide housing and bridge the gender gaps to achieve sustainable development. It aims to cater to vulnerable people who lack access to development opportunities. The main reason for the vulnerability and marginalisation could be social caste discrimination, gender and old age. The social schemes aim to provide equal opportunities to all in society. Some people may be marginalised compared to other members of society. To address this issue, there is a need for additional infrastructure and monetary investment to promote growth and development. Special emphasis should be laid on removing the obstacles and barriers to promoting access to financial services. More emphasis should be laid on promoting the right to education; providing clean drinking water, health and livelihood; and raising awareness about the rights of the poor and marginalised section of society. Among the poor sections of society, women are often considered to be the most vulnerable sections of society. Several social schemes are being implemented to promote the security of women in society. The various sections of society exploit tribals, and the youth is vulnerable to raging depression and society. There are various challenges to the implementation of social reforms, and these challenges include a lack of infrastructure and a lack of regulations. In the last decade, there has been a drastic change in governance in India. The government aims to ensure an irreversible turnaround in the provision of welfare schemes. The state has adopted a saturation approach to providing basic services such as free clean drinking water, LPG connections and electricity in the nation's rural regions. India, as a nation, has emphasised its commitment to the social welfare of the citizens of India. The Constitution of India aims to provide fundamental rights and Directive principles to the nation's citizens. The state and central level legislations aim to provide services to the people at the bottom of the pyramid. The state or the government is assumed to be the agent of socioeconomic change in society. The complexity of the social structure further highlights the need for the state's role as an agent. The welfare state should be established to play an important role in distributing resources to the nation's citizens. The mention of the Indian welfare state is given in the Indian scriptures, which include the sutras, the dharam shastras and the epics. The meaning of social welfare changes according to the context, geographical terrain or region. The economic and social welfare of the citizens in a nation is propagated through laws and regulations. Social welfare comprises the institutions and the framework through which the social well-being of the members of society is promoted. This includes the organisations such as NGOs, Women's Welfare Institutions, state agencies for the protection of the marginalised sections of society, etc. Then there are personal and social relationships in the form of mandals, groups, networks and squads that improve society's social welfare. An example is Women Vigilance Squads, which are run by the National Commission of Women to promote and ensure the security of women in India. The social activities aim to improve the social welfare of the individual members and the communities. The basic fabric of social activities should ensure women's cohesion and promote national unity for all the country's citizens. Social welfare activities help protect society's marginalised sections from further exploitation and help them realise their potential. Thus, the redistribution of economic resources leads to greater equity and social capital among the poor.

Pareto Optimality and Social Evil of Poverty

The Government of India has introduced and implemented many social welfare schemes. These schemes include MNREGA (Mahatma Gandhi National Rural Employment Guarantee Act), Swarnjayanti Gram Swarozgar Yojana (SGSY), National Rural Health Mission (NRHM), Sarv Shiksha Abhiyaan (SSA), Mid-Day Meal scheme (MDM), Nirmal Bharat Abhiyaan, etc. These programmes are aimed at promoting economic growth and development. These social programmes lead to reduced poverty, poor health, and unemployment. The neoliberal approach to economic growth highlights the importance of the equitable distribution of resources to facilitate the freedom of speech, freedom of opportunities, freedom from exploitation and access to property rights. Social welfare has a high social value and utility. The social objectives become significant only when the economic objectives have been achieved. Under the modern capitalist approach, the principles of perfect market and neoliberalism do not apply. Thus, the social welfare schemes and the Government transfer programmes are the missing links between the neoliberal market principles and market failures like poverty.

The corporates are profit-making machines not interested in the social welfare of the economy. However, the Government of India has undertaken various measures to propagate equality and the interest of the people at the bottom of the pyramid. The root of the problem of poverty is that economic resources are limited, and the wants of human beings are unlimited. To meet these unwanted needs, there is a need to redistribute resources. Thus, it is apparent that the market-oriented economic machinery cannot achieve the general population's social welfare objectives. Two of the most important goals in social welfare are fairness and social justice. In a pluralistic society, it is extremely important to ensure social justice by redistributing the economic resources to the people at the bottom of the pyramid to achieve social welfare. In this regard, the critical question that needs to be answered is whether the existing regulations are sufficient to ensure the redistribution of resources to the poor. Habermas has highlighted three basic principles of social welfare: efficiency, stability, and justice. For social welfare, social regulation must be inclusive. The general principle of reciprocity that ensures the redistribution of resources in a social contract generally does not apply to social welfare. Through the lens of the Agency Theory, the elected representatives by the people act as the agents of the general population, and their moral code is to ensure the equitable distribution of resources. Poverty is an exceptional social injustice in which self-interest binds the members. Most of the social activities are illegitimate as the resources devoted to the social welfare activities act as a deterrent to the profitability objective of the corporates. The corporates deem it highly unlawful to devote resources to the cause of social welfare. Religious activities can play a vital role in the equitable distribution of resources. There is a need for an integrated approach to ensure the equitable distribution of resources to ensure social welfare. Social welfare activities are often referred to as the government and state welfare programmes that lead to the redistribution of resources among the poor. Poverty is a case of market failure because the market forces cannot achieve the equitable distribution of resources among the poor sections of society. Through the lens of the Pareto optimality, when some people cannot be made better off without making other people worse off, the markets are essentially incomplete.

Externalities

In a developing economy like India, the negative externalities of population growth are rampant. The development of the population leads to reduced economic growth. The rapid increase in population leads to unequal distribution of resources and can exacerbate the problems for the poor. Externalities are the costs or benefits arising from economic activities that impact people other than those engaged in the activities. Similarly, there are considerable economic and social gains from the welfare programmes, including mid-day meal schemes. Micro-finance programme also has positive externalities for society in general. The earlier social research has established that social welfare activities and programs aimed at achieving sustainable development goals have a positive social impact that is more than the economic impact. Most social welfare programmes, such as Poverty reduction through the mid-day meal scheme and direct cash benefit transfer, have created a critical mass of the population that has traversed the levels of poverty, created an equitable society, and reduced gender bias. The benefits of social activities and community participation are both positive and negative. Positive externalities are embedded in the form of increased community awareness and better citizens' participation. The various indicators of the social activities are given below:

Positive Externalities

- Participation of marginalised women in social activities
- Access to the services at the bottom of the pyramid
- Effective utilisation of resources
- Transformation through agency
- Implementation of the welfare activities
- Gender equity
- Promoting community-based organisations
- Enhancing human capabilities and human transformations

However, it is not that the literature only mentions the positive externalities. There are also some negative externalities, which include social tensions, displacement of the social structures and leaders who claim unequal benefits.

Social Costs

Difficulties arise when one individual's economic activity in consumption impacts another's consumption. The private costs of the activity, together with the personal benefits, diverge from the social costs of the project. Due to the project's mutual effects, it is viable to take only a one-sided conservationist view of the project and consider the project's mutual impact. E.g., In the case of the construction of a dam project, which obstructs the free flow of water and the flow of fish across the rivers, however it protects the water from turning saline, there is a need to weigh the social costs against the social benefits of the projects. And extreme care should be taken to mitigate the social costs. It is essential to compare the marginal price of the project with the marginal benefit of the project. This existence of social costs indicates the presence of transaction costs.

The Issue With the Business Decision

The major problem with business decisions regarding investment is that most projects are evaluated based on the project's economic returns. The independent projects are evaluated in terms of profit and cost. Only the projects with higher returns, Internal Rate of Return, or Payback are considered suitable. The social costs are not taken into account. Essentially, the private costs and the personal benefits determine the scale of operation. In a development project, for evaluation, the first step will be to determine the property rights, the nature of the externality, and the number of bargainers. In the case of the negative externality, it is essential to decide who has the property right to pollute or not to pollute the waters or who has or does not have the right to obstruct the clear waters in the river.

The transaction cost will be highly high without adequate legal institutions. There is a need for social insurance. The primary issue with the project involving negative externalities is that the vested interest generally tends to maximise its benefits. The interventions that mitigate the social costs are inherently costly, and the basic premise of welfare economics or developmental finance is that no one should coerce another individual. In a nutshell, for adopting a social welfare activity, generally, two views are taken into consideration, one is the social view, and the other one is the economic view. The economic view is concerned with the economic efficiency of the projects. The other view is the normative view, i.e., social efficiency projects. The economic efficiency of the projects is that it aims to maximise the income distribution from the projects, and the social view seeks to maximise the social welfare by reducing the social costs of the project.

Externalities of Self-Help Groups

Negative externalities refer to the negative impact of joint liability groups on a group's financial health and well-being. In the case of the self-help group (SHG), due to the joint liability, there is a likelihood of strategic default if the members' output is less than the liability of the individual defaulting member. One of the SHGs is involved in Dhokra Art, and the artisans manufacture the handicraft for daily use. The artisans in this domain do not have access to the tools and tool kits required for manufacturing handicrafts. The artisans also need exposure to the markets. In a SHG, the members are generally from the same profession and are homogenous. All these artisans are linked to the bank linkage and financial activities such as insurance, banks, etc. The government has introduced various social schemes for the poor sections of society, and the NGOs highlight the issue of corruption and inequalities in the redistribution of resources through the state machinery. There is a lack of sustainability in this programme and monitoring of these activities. After taking the credit, the members waste their resources in non-productive and consumption activities. In an unorganised sector and the presence of the informal sector, including all the members in the development process is tough. All the members in the SHG are scheduled caste and scheduled tribes. Due to caste discrimination, SHG members are socially excluded and cannot participate in social activities. The

Government forms the handicraft cluster, and the leaders in the cluster implement the programme, and there is no follow-up in the activity. The members of the group lack access to financial services. More, the governance and the regulation of the activities are fragile. The members are not literate and thus face many social pressures and problems. When the members form the group, they do not have information about the other members of the group. Due to the lack of information, the adverse selection in the group is extremely high. The members are extremely short-sighted, and they look only at their benefits. At the time of the formation of the group, it is extremely important that members know about the other members. Generally, the members look only at the immediate benefit due to forming a group with the family members. This leads to bias and subjectivity in the operation of the group. Most of the groups operating in this region are quite good; they sell their commodities fairly and maintain their livelihood properly. Most of them have membership cards. If the group cannot pay the loan, then a warning is given to the members. In the case of the Dhokra artists, many of the members do not have a card, and the Government provides funds to provide marketing support to the poor members of the group. But the go-betweens divert the funds and use them for ulterior motives. Due to aggression and mafia don, there is a lot of violence and diversion of funds for non-productive purposes. There is a lack of monitoring and follow up of the group members' activities. In addition, to that member of the group are not digitally literate. Digital literacy can improve the social inclusion of the poor and increase information dissemination. The use of technology can lead to social equality and improve the redistribution of resources. Even some of the Government transfers and subsidies are not being utilised properly. There is the diversion of the funds into purchasing liquor and using the existing infrastructure such as TV installations, to watch the popular programme. The bank officers threaten the marginalised poor sections of society. Many government programmes are being worked out to sensitise the members and make them aware of the Government schemes and transfer payments. Thus, there is a need to create literacy programmes to uplift the poor. It is essential to leverage the professional relationships among the members in the form of social networks. But due to the negative externalities, the members of the groups do not share information about their progress. They should be motivated to work together. A leader has been selected in the group, but in the group as well, there is an agency problem that exists. The leader, as an agent, cannot act for the benefit of the poor, and they sometimes withhold important information and misuse it for ulterior purposes. The continuous sharing of information through meetings is a mechanism to achieve financial control. And the peer mechanism in the group is an opportunity to achieve financial sustainability objectives. In case of default, the group exercises strong pressure on the group members to ensure the regular repayment of the loans. Trust is the basic premise for the achievement of sustainable development groups. To build trust, peer mechanisms and social intermediation are significant factors in ensuring the financial sustainability of the group members. There is a need for product verification to ensure the product design's legitimacy and adequate demand for the products. The Dhokra group members manufacture various artefacts, including the Muzarim, earthen vessels and pots, diyas, animal figurines, and boats. As soon as the raw material is *acquired, there is a need to develop the technology to mitigate the adverse impact of that technology. The manufacturing of Dhokra artefacts is done at 130 centigrade, and by sitting near the fire, the members of the group suffer from various health hazards, including the use of the toxic substance; there is a need for the backward and forward linkages to ensure effectiveness and efficiency in the manufacturing processes. The Government has undertaken various programmes for the training of the artisans. The state Government has various programmes and training modules to train the group members. NGO as a concept is unclear, but the group works on trust, faith, and equity principles. To ensure access to financial services, there is a need to create regular communication and information flow between buyers and sellers. Thus, there is sufficient evidence that without dynamic incentives, the group members will not be willing to contribute towards the payment of the loans. Access to additional loans and social capital are the motivations for paying the loans for the defaulter in the group. Monitoring through technology such as digital reporting and the CCTV can also solve the problem of Moral Hazard in a group due to Joint Liability. If properly mentored, the group dynamics in the form of peer mechanisms can reap benefits in the form of better savings, repayment of loans, etc.*

Measures to Mitigate Negative Externalities

Through the lens of the theory of externalities and social benefits, trade and commerce in a group facilitate the allocation of resources among the users or the individuals who comprise an economy. The distribution of the resources is Pareto efficient if and only if it maximises the social benefits. Individuals compete vociferously to maximise their private uses. If the individual selfish motives or private benefits supersede the community interest, it is an example of the negative externality. In this scenario, more steps should be taken to transform the private benefits into a social advantage. This can be achieved through the redistribution or reallocation of resources. The Indian Government has taken an important initiative in levying the *Swachh Bharat Cess* to prevent the spread of many diseases among the citizens. Another way is to *Recognise* and *Represent* the marginalised sections of society. For this purpose, in a community lending group, if a member achieves a milestone, he is given recognition through higher financial incentives and selection as a leader, and additional bank credit. This acts as a motivation for the group members. Besides, there is a need for regular monitoring and social intermediation in the form of financial literacy training to meet financial obligations. Thus, this is an example of how negative externalities can be mitigated through the institutional mechanism. Besides the institutional mechanism, the peer mechanism can play an important role in mitigating the negative externalities of social welfare initiatives, including poverty reduction measures, etc. The best course to minimise the negative externalities is to punish the individuals leading to negative costs. This includes taxing and debarring the individual from using public facilities and assets for a specified purpose. Thus, the negative externalities can be mitigated through intermediation and counselling.

Approaches to Social Welfare

There are several different approaches to social welfare to achieve social objectives. The institutional framework to achieve the goal is referred to as the institutional approach to achieving social welfare. Besides, in many contexts of the familial approach, the existing social capital of the families plays an essential role in achieving the objectives of social welfare. Families thus play a significant role in achieving social welfare objectives. If the family and market or institutions such as NGOs are unable to lead to equities, in that case, the Government can initiate the action to ensure the equitable distribution of resources among the needy and the poor. Besides, there can be a hybrid of the state and the family or institution-based approach to achieve social welfare objectives. The welfare of the marginalised sections of society can also be promoted through collective action and the pooling of the resources of the poor. The social welfare services consist of various central and state government policies. Marginalised sections of society can find solace in the social policy initiatives driven by the state and the central government. This includes underprivileged groups such as the mentally retarded, beggars, prostitutes, physically and mentally disabled, diseased, destitute, and unemployed. Within the constitution are enshrined various rights and provisions to safeguard the interests of the lower sections of society, including the scheduled caste and the scheduled tribes. It includes the initiatives to propagate action and eliminate untouchability from society. To promote the welfare of the scheduled caste and scheduled tribes, the Government of India has promoted various educational schemes and scholarships, including Government transfer and subsidies. Similarly, a commission is set up for the upliftment of the poor, which includes the Scheduled Caste and Scheduled Tribes. And initiatives taken include financial assistance to the poor in the form of microcredit and financial assistance to the poor, forest rights for the tribes and tribals in the villages of India.

Forest Rights Case Study Koska Village

Social Perspective

Indian forests are known for their history and are integral to the local communities. Ethnic groups and communities are strongly associated with the ecosystem. The forest is the second largest resource in agriculture, and the tribal villages on the outskirts are home to around 300 million tribes. Various regulations and policies have impacted the forests and the landscapes. Since the passing of the first regulation in the 1990s, many more local communities have been involved in forest management. In the colonial past, British rule was responsible for the management of the forests. But in the 1990s, the villagers and communities were involved in forest management. The Joint Forest Management Act and the Communities Rights Under the Forest Act, 2006 were enacted to consider the Government intervention. Another example of community participation in decision-making is the Jamguda located at Barabandha Gram Panchayat, Kalahandi district. In these, most of the villages are engaged in community initiatives. The youth committees formed in the Jamguda village were appointed to protect the forest.

The objective was to stop the illegal cutting of trees and end the smuggling of trees. Besides that, the Joint Forest Management Committee was formed to look into the illegal trading of the plantations. In the case of the Indian forests, wildlife is disrupted due to the negative consequences in most of the woods and states. Overall, there is a frequent decrease in the tiger population in the city. There is a setback to the conservation programs in the nation, and efforts should be made to protect the rights of Wildlife. The Government of India has propagated the need for democratic dialogue and participation to ensure the conservation of the ecological resources in the forests of India. In Nepal, forest management is the most important success story. In Nepal, the Community Forest Management initiative was started to reduce the impacts of deforestation and forest degradation to maintain the ecosystem. Community Forest Management has a significant role to play in forest management and enhancing the role of the conservation of biodiversity. Promoting wildlife and its habitat depends on the management of the forests. The management of the woods leads to the upliftment of the rural communities and benefits the local users and the communities. This also allows rural communities to achieve sustainable development through ecological initiatives. The local community works collaboratively to ensure participation in the needs of the local people. Community community-based orga- nisations are required for the effective and collective management of the forests. Under state rule, the local communities were excluded from managing the forests. But soon, the local communities have been involved in mitigating the impact of deforestation through group meetings, executive meetings, and preparing forest management plans. These forest communities have provided important rights including decision making, empowerment over forest management, and access to the forest's resources. This community forest management has led to an improvement in biodiversity. A study revealed that the carbon stock is quite high in the natural forests and the local communities are promoting ecology and conservation through the use of forest watchers. Community forest management has been successful in the conservation of plants and wildlife. Sarv Shiksha Abhiyaan is a programme that aims at providing free and compulsory education to people and children in the age group 1–14 years of age. This scheme aims to promote and propagate the Right to Free and Compulsory Education for school-going children. The Government has also taken up the challenge to provide free education to the children of the migrant workers. Similarly, the Government of India has undertaken the initiative to maintain a clean India or Swachh Bharat along with a clean drinking water supply and sanitation. Thus, involving the people from the bottom of the pyramid is the basic premise of all social welfare programmes.

Social Policy for Developmental Projects

Social policy is an instrument for development. In a developing economy like India, the neoliberal economic principles do not work, leading to gross inequal- ities and market failure. And the social policy works in tandem with the economic and political context to further the cause of development. Social policy is often defined as a social contract between the people's labour, mainly in the unorganised sectors that do not have a voice in the economic growth stories or political milieu, and capital, which is primarily owned by the state or the collectives in a democratic setup. Social policies define the capability of a governance mechanism to absorb the cost of modernisation and development. In a country like India, with many tribes and local communities, social policies can ensure modernisation by leveraging the social capital of these communities. There are instances where for the cause of development, the interests of the local communities in terms of cultural rights are compromised to meet the demands of modernisation and development.

Similarly, many development projects lead to the displacement of the natives geographically, and social policy can ensure the development through negotiations and social capital. Mainly, concerning peasants and educational ventures, where people comprise today's consumption for future consumption, there is a need for social policies to provide basic needs and social services to those deprived of consumption. Though development propels the economic growth cycles, it also leads to gross inequalities among people. To cushion these shocks, the government has to bear the brunt of economic shocks in the form of fiscal deficit. There is a need to develop policies for sustainable growth by developing a partnership with the local communities, marginalised and disciplining them to achieve higher economic growth and freedom from poverty. Moreover, social policies should not only play a protective role by providing an economic cushion in the form of transfers and public goods for the marginalised, but they should also lead to an increase in labour productivity by enhancing and promoting education. There should be an effort to develop skills and obliterate the thin divide between the organised and unorganised sectors through education and health expenditure. A case in point is industrialisation which not only propels development and modernisation but also leads to higher employment and political voice for the displaced. Thus, technological innovation can be a pathway to achieve the equilibrium between the demand and supply of labour and capital, leading to balanced growth. Social policy also helps mitigate the negative externalities of developmental projects by compensating the natural harm to the ecosystem.

Fig. 1 highlights that to achieve modernisation goals through development, there is a need to enhance labour productivity and capital by leveraging the social capital of the local communities, unorganised sectors, and the local community. For the local community, there is a need for introducing social interventions in the form of education, basic need fulfilment through the provision of food and clothing, and shelters for providing economic support to the people at the bottom of the pyramid.

Challenges to the Social Welfare Scheme

The welfarist state is critical in the given times. Due to globalisation, there is a possibility of the rolling back of the welfare state. Around the world, economies are engulfed in gross inequalities. This refers to the redistribution of resources. State governance is fraught with severe injustices and material inequalities. The

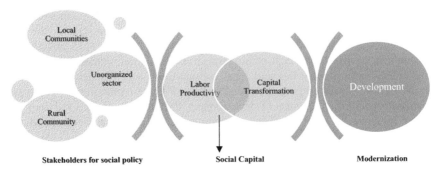

Fig. 1.   Social Policy and Its Importance for Modernisation. *Source:*
By the Authors.

legitimacy of state policies is under threat because of the increasing gulf between the demand and supply of resources. In this scenario, it becomes essential to legitimise the social and welfare activities by including all the sections of society in the welfare schemes run by the state. Public goods and social welfare activities are the two basic requirements for the welfare of society. There is a need to create durable public goods to ensure the social welfare of the poor and marginalised sections of society. Thus, there is a need for the welfare state to propagate an egalitarian society. Democratic state highlights the need for the welfare of the various sections of society. The main reasons for the low level of social welfare are as follows:

(1) Poor governance
(2) Lack of performance incentives
(3) Financial exclusion
(4) Widespread leakages in the system and opting out of the system
(5) Inequalities within the welfare system
(6) Lack of funds and resources
(7) Lack of appropriate laws and regulations

A brief description of the reasons for the low social welfare is given below:

(1) *Poor governance*: In most developing nations, the level of governance is inferior. In developing and emerging countries, weak governance and corruption create obstacles to the efficient delivery of government services to the citizens of India. The failure of power and corruption present a lot of challenges. The existing research highlights that poorly governed states are impoverished. Institutional determinism leads to the underdevelopment of the economy. The conformity with the rules. This conformity essentially does not lead to efficiency. Thus, the problem of poor governance stems from the

excessive attempt to gain legitimacy through adherence to the existing rules and conformity bias. Isomorphic behaviour is at the heart of such a bias. In the hinterlands of India, rural people still lack access to electricity, clean drinking water, and basic amenities, leading to lower social welfare. Lack of infrastructure and the lack of internet connectivity can lead to financial exclusion and, thus, poor governance. This further leads to a lack of social welfare among the citizens. To realise human rights, there must be good governance of the various Government schemes being run in India. Exceptionally well-designed strategies benefit from good corporate governance, accountability, and disclosure practices. There is a need to take an integrated approach at the systems level to ensure commitment to achieving social goals. Good governance is essential to provide high coherence and coordination, financial, fiscal, and economic sustainability, accountability, transparency, predictability and equal treatment, participation and adaptability, dynamism and responsiveness to the social welfare mechanism.

(2) *Lack of performance incentives*: In developing nations, organisations generally do not have enough incentives to promote social welfare. Organisations must trade between attaining profitability through higher Return on Investment and financial sustainability. Due to the lack of performance incentives, firms and corporates generally cannot obtain the goal and objective of social welfare. The organisations do not have enough motivation to promote activities for the welfare of the individuals. In an organisation, due to institutional determinism, there is an emphasis on more rewards, and rewards essentially do not motivate the employees or the members to perform better than the rest of the members of the society. Corporates are entities that have the sole objective of earning profits. The organisations show isomorphism, are similar in construct and result from imitation of other organisations. This coercive and mimetic isomorphism leads to a static culture and standardisation. They do not find it profitable to pursue social objectives. Through laws and regulations in the form of CSR (Corporate Social Responsibility Act), organisations can be motivated to provide funds for social welfare. To gain legitimacy, the firms will adhere to the regulations.

(3) *Financial exclusion*: The low quality of service leads to a lack of social welfare. Generally, in service organisations, there is no way to ensure quality levels in the Indian service industry. Financial exclusion refers to debarring citizens from availing the financial services. Most of the citizens of India, at the bottom of the pyramid, do not have access to financial services, which leads to low social welfare. The financial inclusion programme is aimed to create a trickle-down effect and percolate the economic benefits to the people at the bottom of the pyramid. The inclusion programme plays a crucial role in promoting economic growth. Most of the citizens at the bottom of the pyramid suffer from the lack of access to and use of financial services. This financial exclusion leads to the degradation of the people's quality of living. Financial exclusion is rampant among unemployed people who cannot work during illness and are downtrodden. This leads to a decline in the welfare of the people at the bottom of the pyramid. The people at the bottom of the

pyramid do not have access to finance and credit, leading to a decline in social welfare. Poverty is the cause and consequence of financial exclusion and far exceeds individual costs. Exclusion from the mainstream financial stream and the financial system forces poor individuals to rely more on informal sources of finance, such as money lenders and shops. This social exclusion forces people to adopt informal sources of finance and leads to a decline in individual assets. Thus, financial exclusion leads to rampant misery and poverty in those excluded from the financial system. Most financially excluded people live in areas with higher rates of misery, poverty, and low income. Most poor people do not have access to bank accounts. The prerequisite for getting a job is having. Thus, people who lack bank accounts cannot reap the benefits of social welfare and social advantage. To access suitable employment and livelihood, it is vital to have access to savings and credit. Most financially excluded programs do not have access to financial services, leading to a lack of social welfare in the economy. The citizens suffer from the lack of access to economic activities, which leads to a decline in the social welfare of the poor members.

(4) *Widespread leakages in the system*: In our financial system, there are several leakages. These leakages include fritting away the economic benefits for various reasons, such as weak institutions, inadequate payment infrastructure, and poor accountability. Many citizens in the country do not have access to the identification number of identity. Due to the lack of identification, it is tough for the officials to verify whether the benefits are distributed to the right individual. In this scenario, the local officials can manipulate the numbers. Thus, in this way, the leakages in the financial system can lead to a lack of social welfare. Further people in Public services might compromise sensitive information and resources in favour of the people indulging in illegal activities. This leads to a decline in the social welfare of the people and leads to abject poverty among the people who are extremely poor and financially unsustainable. In our financial systems, there is a large-scale leakage in the system in the form of drug trafficking, hawala, etc. This illicit flow of funds from the financial system leads to corruption. It can further lead to undermining the state by lowering the tax revenues, fuelling criminal activity, and leading to the vicious circle of poverty and underdevelopment in the nation. This type of illegal activity also leads to corruption and can lead to global inequalities in the system.

(5) *Inequalities within the welfare system*: There are various challenges in the welfare system. In such scenarios, the power is concentrated in the hands of a few citizens. Power is concentrated in the hands of a few, such as the hands of managers, professionals, experts, and a few other vested interests. The social systems are fraught with various challenges, such as corruption, drug trafficking, and uneven distribution of economic profits. This further leads to disruption and market failure in the form of concentration of economic power in the hands of vested interests and inequalities. In an underdeveloped state, there is market failure, and the demand and supply system cannot ensure the equitable distribution of resources. Moreover, in an

underdeveloped economy, there are stark differences in the ownership of assets and entitlement to rights among the various population strata. The disparity between the rich and the poor, man and female, and rural and urban regions are starkly evident in an underdeveloped social system. This further leads to the deterioration of the social welfare system. There are various challenges in the social system in the form of unequal distribution of resources which leads to the decline of the welfare system.

(6) *Lack of funds and resources*: The welfare states suffer from inadequate funds and resources. Generally, corporates in a capitalist regime are least interested in providing access to financial services to poor people below the poverty line. Due to a lack of ROI, the corporates are not interested in investing in the upliftment of the inferior members. In the post-1990 era, there was a significant thrust on the liberalisation and abolishment of the donor or subsidy-based model of social growth. And the primary emphasis was on sustainable finance, and many social organisations failed in this scenario. The market failure of the social system was apparent in the form of disparities and poverty. In this situation, the growth cycle cannot be completed unless the state creates some intervention or economic and financial support in the form of access to resources. Thus, one of the significant challenges to the growth of a welfare state is the lack of finances.

(7) *Lack of regulations and conducive legal system*: Regulation refers to regulating human behaviour by rules. These rules cover the behaviour of the masses. However, most regulations aim to control private behaviour through demand and supply market forces. Within market failure, the market mechanism cannot efficiently allocate resources to maximise social welfare. Market regulation is needed to protect consumer interests. However, in developing economies, the perfect allocation of resources is not achieved due to asymmetric information. This prevents the market from ideally allocating resources. Thus, to prevent the asymmetries of information through the regulation of the markets. Externalities and poverty are the two indications of market failure. Moreover, the corporates work to maximise profits and enhance the return on investment (ROI); in this scenario, they might not work to promote the social and public good. Thus, the corporates might indulge in anti-competitive practices or dominant practices. This is an example of regulatory failure. Often such regulatory failure might lead to the inequitable distribution of resources. Moreover, the regulations are not sufficient to ensure the promotion of equitable interests. There is a need for significant regulatory reforms through participation to enable the fair distribution of resources among the poor. There is a need for reforming the regulatory framework, and the critical push towards the same can be the political and administrative leadership that can lead to quality improvement in the government and business interfaces. Most businesses in India are not well regulated, and the culture of the Government departments is highly bureaucratic. The work culture of Government employees is an issue. The unhealthy environment imposes various social and private investments. The

economic regulators need to be accountable, and there is a need to put in place a Grievance redressal mechanism to ensure equity.

Social Planning and Social Welfare

Planning is the process of defining the roadmap of action for action to facilitate the achievement of objectives in the future. Planning is about prioritising goals to formulate what is essential and what is not. Social policy is the course of action that defines the overall fabric of quality of life and circumstances of quality of life. It is the integration of all the acts of the Government to improve the welfare and well-being of people. It is a set of deliberate actions, collectives, and government performed to organise services and efforts to achieve a given objective. The social policy ensures the distribution and reallocation of resources to achieve equality and social justice. The social policy envisages a society where inequalities are reduced to the minimum. Social policy aims to maximise welfare while minimising shortcomings and sufferings. It is aimed at improving the quality of life of people. There are various approaches to social policy, such as (1) residual policy to social welfare, (2) industrial achievement and (3) institutional redistribution of resources. Within the residual policy to social welfare, in certain circumstances, the markets do not perform, and this failure leads to various social problems such as poverty. In this circumstance, the state is responsible for defining the policy for redistributing resources to the people at the bottom of the pyramid. The social needs of society should be met through merit and productivity. This is a testimony that, in the long run, merely equalising opportunities is not beneficial. Still, there is a need for positive discrimination by finding equity from discrimination in the form of Government transfers.

Challenges to Social Policy

There are several challenges to social policy, which include (1) lack of political willingness, (2) coalition government, (3) presence of corruption at all levels, (4) financial constraints, (5) red tape, (6) deterioration of moral values, (7) inadequate human resource planning, (8) delay in social justice and (9) absence of training. Social policy aims to maximise opportunities for fellow human beings by meeting all their demands and managing their problems. In a narrow sense, social welfare is defined as meeting the needs of the needy and poor by providing them the charities and social support. Thus, social policy aims to achieve the social welfare of not only the disadvantaged but all sections of society. The social guidelines aim to standardise decision-making, maximise efficiency, and enable organisations to achieve social objectives. These policies are aimed to design to maintain law and order to ensure national defence to protect the environment, foster communication and promote economic growth. It aims to promote better health, housing, education and welfare activities for all sections of society. The social system of the programme to ensure social welfare includes the programmes, activities, services, and benefits that enable the poor people in the nation to achieve their individual social, educational and health needs. The social policy and programmes involve activities by the state and include the actions of volunteers, non-profit organisations, governmental programmes, social workers and professionals, including family and friends. It obliterates the line between private and public funding to achieve the social objective of the redistribution of resources. The critical part of social policy is to transform the policy ideas into programmes and actions by the states. Thus, as an example, the social workers and street workers lead the social policy programme to achieve the objective of social welfare, better health and sanitation for all sections of society. Social policy is formed over the years through a consensus among community members regarding social actions. Thus, social policy is not an outcome of legislation or deliberate political action; instead, it is the result of the actions taken by the members of society. However, to ensure the state's smooth functioning, the state must regulate the activities of private entities. The social context, the cultural factors, the beliefs, and the attitude system existing in a particular society at a specific point in time impacts the social welfare of a particular community. The social policy initiative plays an important role in maintaining society's political stability and social welfare. The policy process has four major components that include (1) formulation, (2) legislation, (3) implementation and (4) evaluation. In a society, there exists a vast rift between the various sections of society. The various sections of society and activities compete for resources.

Similarly, organisations have to compete for resources. Towards this cause, legislation by the state help to achieve the objectives of social welfare by imposing social costs on the misutilisation of resources. The several different stages of social policy implementation are given:

(1) *Formulation*: The think tanks, interest groups and social groups dominate the policy formulation process. Thus, the normal mode of conduct is converted or transformed into legislation and acts.
(2) *Legislations*: The legislation's formulation generally comes from the democratic process of dialog and participation in the social circle. Capital is vital in lobbying and formulating policies for social welfare.
(3) *Implementation*: Inadequate resources for the social programs and social complexity impact the complex relationships among the people and public and non-profit organisations.
(4) *Evaluation*: The evaluation of the social policy and programs impacts how well the existing policy and programs work and provide feedback to the policymakers.

To create the social policy and framework, there is a need to decide the goals and benefits of the social welfare programme, the benefits that the social programme can produce, the eligibility of the programme, and the source of the finances for the programme. Social policy is a joint programme to fulfil the needs of society to achieve the goals of the organisation and meet the requirements of the will of society to live as an organic whole and, indeed, help other people to survive. It is decided by the actions of the other members and individuals in society.

Role of Social Policy in Social

To achieve social objectives, social welfare should give certain rights to the people of the nation. The basic tenets of social policy are democracy, equal opportunities, needs and rights, and the possibility of the people.

(1) *Democracy*: The liberal social policy should intact the fabric of democracy. To achieve social objectives, the resources should be allocated equally. And social welfare includes basic goals such as equality, access and fair results.
(2) *Equal Opportunity*: To achieve the tenets of social welfare, the public should be given an equal opportunity to participate in the social process. This equality of opportunity should be given irrespective of the gender, class or creed of the person.
(3) *Need*: The needs of society should meet adequately. Only when the basic needs are met can we say that the social objectives are met in totality.
(4) *Freedom and Right*: Civil rights and the democratic rights to meet for the achievement of the social objectives include the right to equality of opportunity, the right to primary education, wellness, jobs, housing, and other social programmes and policies. Social policy includes economic policy, industrial policy and social policy. To solve social injustice in the form of hunger, injustice, and lack of education, there is a need to ensure democratic participation, creativity, and invention.

Measures to Mitigate the Social Costs

Social welfare has many dimensions, such as social or ethical perspectives and Economic Perspectives. Social or moral philosophy comprises various dimensions. One such dimension is *individual:* (1) justice, (2) equality, (3) fairness (4), and the other dimension is *social:* (1) *Social costs* – environment, climate change, development costs, costs of social change and mitigation (2) *Social benefits* – Negative private costs (Fig. 2).

At the individual level, welfare costs include ensuring justice, fairness and equity in dealings with others. If the rights of an individual are respected, it automatically leads to social justice. And value and culture are normative concepts. Many times, a normative reinforcement does not work, and at the individual level, it is the negative reinforcement that facilitates the achievement of the group objectives. And at the social level, the two dimensions are the social costs and social benefits. Social costs refer to the cost imposed on the environment, climate change and costs of mitigating negative externalities. The social benefits of the developmental projects include negative private charges. The negative private costs include lowering production costs and raising profits. For could be the measures that improve the well-being of the projects. Moreover, social

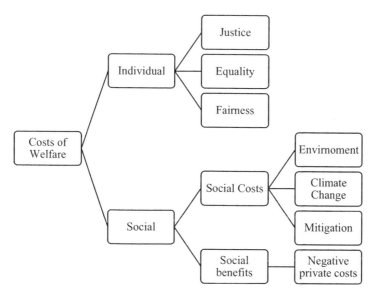

Fig. 2.   Costs of Social Welfare.

institutions and culture can also mitigate the negative impact of externalities. Thus, social capital enables to mitigate the impact of negative externalities. There should be a legitimate acknowledgement that the marginalised sections of society and the older generations have the right to redistributive moral justice. This is the definition of complete justice in a social context.

Principle of Social Values

The stakeholder in the process of social welfare and change experience value. But unfortunately, the social discount is reflected in the prices determined by the markets. The social value is determined by social accounting, audit, sustainability, etc. The changes experienced by the people are referred to as social values. It includes environmental changes, and social value relates to the changes experienced by the people.

(1) Involving the stakeholders
(2) Understanding the changes
(3) Materiality
(4) Avoiding overvaluation
(5) Transparency
(6) Proactive and Responsive

    (1) *Involving the stakeholders*: The first step in determining the social value is to involve the stakeholders. There is a need to identify the

stakeholders and apply these people in decision-making. Stakeholders include the people who will experience a change due to the developmental project or developmental activity.

(2) *Understand the change*: The value is created by the activities, which result from the various stakeholders' contribution. The results should be verified to ensure the changes have occurred.

(3) *Materiality*: The outcomes to be included in the results must be material in terms of the importance of the information and the evidence. Only the relevant outcome and decisions should be included, and the immaterial facts and outcomes should not be included.

(4) *Avoiding the overclaim*: It is essential to create benchmarks and standards. It is also important to evaluate the outcomes against the criteria and standards. Reporting and managing the results leads to a reduction in overclaim.

(5) *Transparency*: It is essential that the outcomes and the results should be transparent and demonstrate the basis on which the analysis has been done with accuracy and clarity.

(6) *Proactive and responsive*: It is important that the social value delivered is optimum and the decision is timely. There is a need to optimise social value by providing the social goals that are agreed upon.

Valuation of Development Projects

It is essential to conduct an economic analysis in the form of cost-benefit research to evaluate the project's social value by Government agencies and international agencies to improve the welfare of a community. For the Government project and the private project that involves state expenditure, there is a need to conduct a cost-benefit analysis to evaluate the project. In these social projects, it is essential to go beyond the financial appraisal of the projects and estimate how commercially viable these projects are. The primary objective of social projects is to optimise community welfare. The social objective of social projects is to do the environmental appraisal and redistribute the economic resources to the particular social project or cause. The cost-benefit analysis estimates the impact of various projects on the community's welfare. Various distortions in the economic markets impact the prices of the commodities in the markets. There is a need to undertake a cost-benefit analysis to determine the costs and benefit to society. To assess the social value of the project, there is a need to undertake the following steps. It includes the definition of the objectives of the colonial project, identification of the project options, and determination of the costs and benefits. The principles of social valuation involve the decision of the economic value of the project before and after the project has been implemented. It should also include the valuation of the social benefits and costs to determine the project's value. There is a need to conduct the social valuation of the product due to the following reasons:

(1) To identify the cost and benefit which can be easily identified
(2) To determine the effects that cannot be identified and measured in economic terms due to the lack of the market signals
(3) To determine the impacts that cannot be economically quantified

For the valuation of social projects, it is essential to include social values as the measure of the objectives achieved within the ambit of the valuation systems. Thus, in the valuation of projects, it is important to include the project's environmental and social impact. In a resource-constrained environment, efforts are made to commit to improving performance. And to make the manufacturing process more efficient and effective. Thus, in the economic decisions about the project, it is essential to include the project's social value. It is crucial to create social value as the indicator of the effectiveness of the developmental intervention. This social value can also indicate the allocation of resources among the various developmental projects. The most crucial issue in the projects' social valuation is measuring the change and the difference made by the multiple tasks. Particularly important in this context is the existing power relations and agency among the various stakeholders in a social system.

Objectives of National Policy

The objectives of a National Policy are to ensure that the projects reflect the correct value of the project. The main goals and objectives of the national policy are:

- To choose the project based on the national impact
- To measure the total impact
- To calculate the correlation between social costs and economic growth

Agency Problem and Social Projects

The agency theory as an approach refers to the process in which the agent makes decisions on behalf of the principal. The implementing agency and social beneficiaries can be regarded as agents and principals. The principal might observe the agents' behaviour or provide the agents with employment contracts. Agency problems can be mitigated by monitoring their incentives or providing commensurate incentives. Some of the significant measures taken by the Government include monitoring costs, that is, monitoring agents' behaviour, bonding costs related to the stimuli, and residual costs. The strategies for reducing opportunistic behaviour include the monitoring and bonding agency charges, whereby there is a trade-off between the monitoring and bonding costs. Monitoring costs are further divided into the Internal Audit costs and Board of Director composition. Internal Audit comprises the mandatory audit of the organisations which are publicly listed. The agents can also suggest an audit. Multiple Performance Evaluation systems can be introduced to monitor the working of organisations. This includes Variance Analysis; Budgeting models can be used to forecast the returns and gauge how the uncertainty affects the use of these tools.

Besides, the Incentive Focussed Strategy can be used to incentivise the agent. This includes the performance-related results, which include the profits and performance bonuses. The author asserts the convergence of interest hypothesis by the interests of all the managers and owners. It argues that as the management shareholding level increases, the managers' cost for not making the value maximising decisions increases in the case of Government companies and departments, the manager increases. There comes the point at which managers become entrenched and make decisions that maximise the wealth as opposed to the wealth of the other shareholders. Also, with the increased ownership, the ability of the managers to monitor declines. Also, as the equity managers' stake increases, their vigilance goes down.

The concepts and principles for the valuation of social projects are:

The Opportunity Cost Principle: The economic valuation of the social projects should be done keeping in mind the cost to society as a whole. It should not consider only the partial view or the cost to the single agency. It should keep in mind the cost to the entire society. The basis for the valuation of the project is the cost of committing the resources or the opportunity costs of the project. Thus, for the valuation of the project, it is essential to consider the non-economic benefits to determine the project's valuation.

Social Benefit Analysis

In the economic valuation of the project, it is assumed that income distribution is the only important issue that needs to be taken into account while determining the value of the project. But most governments and state entities are not only interested in determining the economic value of the project, but there is a need for promoting equity and improving the efficiency of the projects. The social benefit and cost analysis is an important measure to evaluate the project's social value. The basis of the valuation of the colonial project is that the marginal utility of the social projects for a person who receives a low income is higher than the social value of the project for a person who receives a higher economic payment. Financial and economic analysis of the projects only considers the financial appraisal. Similarly, shadow pricing is often used for the valuation of social projects.

Principle to Determine the Benefit of the Social Project

The benefit of the social project to the user can be determined on the basis of the user surplus, termed associo–economic user surplus. This surplus is defined as the difference between what the users are willing to pay, expressed as a shadow price, and the price the user is willing to pay for the social good. Thus, the social benefit analysis can be used to assess the project's marginal social benefit and marginal social cost to evaluate the project's social value. Some externalities exist in the valuation of social projects that are difficult to quantify. It will be impossible to quantify the net benefits without reference to the subjective and qualitative factors. To improve the efficiency of the projects, it is essential to introduce a weighing system based on marginal utilities of income for all individuals. To measure the utility, it is necessary to identify individuals impacted by the project. The poor have a higher marginal utility of wealth, and illiterate people have a higher utility of education. Thus, to resolve this issue, there is a need to introduce weights for poverty, education, and other social factors to determine the cost-benefit analysis for the social projects. Theoretically, society cannot determine how much society will be willing to pay for the social value of the developmental project. Generally, most of the cost-benefit and valuation models are based on the valuation of the immediate payoffs and costs of the project. Thus, maximising economic value or consumption is not ideal for value development projects. There is a need to include the value of marginal social benefits and costs in the valuation to maximise the utility of the projects. To include the social value of the projects, one has to take into account the five basic tenets of social welfare given by *Arrow*:

(1) *Collective rationality*: The social welfare function should propagate a social order.
(2) *Association of social and individual values*: Social welfare should not reflect individual preference in a negative sense.
(3) *Independence of irrelevant alternatives*: The choice between two individuals' id is determined by the community members' preference.
(4) *Conditions of citizen sovereignty*: The social welfare function is to be imposed based on sovereignty and not on the basis of religion, sect, ethics, or race.
(5) *Condition of nondictatorship*: The social welfare and cost are not to be dictatorship based.

Thus, in evaluating social projects, it is tough to estimate the social benefits and costs of the project. No method is available to derive the social welfare function for the project. The project's social valuation is fundamental to making those groups of people valued who have a significant role to play in the welfare of the community. The contrast effect of the social projects depends on whether benefits would have occurred without a social value intervention. The other principle to be kept in mind while valuing social projects is to consider triple-bottom-line accounting, which goes beyond the traditional value of economic profits and costs. It should consider the social and environmental dimensions and be based on the principle of the planet, people, and profits. Accounting based on triple accounting should be used to support the evaluation of sustainability goals. The triple bottom line is based on three dimensions which include social, environmental, and financial factors. Since the social benefits cannot be monetised, creating an index to measure the social benefits and social costs is essential. In the form of an index, the valuation of social costs and benefit enables the maximisation of the social value of the projects. Thus, the way forward towards the social valuation of the developmental projects is to design a social index that considers the achievement of the social parameters that include the indicators of social performance and the viability or financial sustainability of the projects.

Digitization of Social Project Evaluation

Within the purview of microfinance and financial inclusion, women empowerment is emerging as a priority area and one of the sustainable goals to be achieved per the World Bank mandate. Lack of access to Finance services has been identified as a major factor impeding women's inclusion in the development journey. Financial intermediaries through community initiatives such as SHGs are fast emerging as the source of ensuring easy accessibility of credit to poor women in rural India. Lack of financial inclusion and excessive reliance on informal sources of finance has augmented the problem of marginalisation of Women in Rural India. The authors conclude that the broader social context has the most impact on the empowerment of women. In the Asian setting, the author refers to the case of Sri Lankan working women aged 18–33. The author has collected data from the 1992 survey of 1,460 women. A sample of 577 women was selected. The authors have used a mix of Qualitative and Quantitative measures to identify whether social factors of the economic factors impact Women's Empowerment through financial decision-making. The data exhibits that of all the social categories of women, and the Kalutaran women have more impact on financial decision-making. Moors, compared to Sinhalese women, face more restrictive norms. *The authors conclude that there is a need to move from a broad-based conceptualisation of women's empowerment to a specific arena where women can have power. The author laments the lack of sensitivity of the current literature to the social context and overemphasises the role of employment and education in empowering women.* The author highlights the need to focus on structural issues comprised family, social and economic organisation. Despite all policy and regulatory changes, non-monetary incentives and inherent problems of a developing economy like poverty, unemployment, and illiteracy are the precursors of the marginalisation of women. In this regard, microfinance is emerging as a source of empowerment. Morduch (1999) author propagates that microfinance is the movement's legacy in propagating institutional innovation in eliminating poverty. Through various mechanistic designs such as Microfinance Institutions, Grameen Bank of Bangladesh and Village Banks, despite the high transactions cost and no collateral, it is possible to lend profitably. Moreover, by resorting to attractive savings vehicles, one way to address the borrowing constraint of poor households is to address the saving constraints. The microfinance movement has given an uplift to the profile of NGOs. The author argues that with the subsidies, the cost of microfinance can be introduced drastically. With different microcredit mechanisms and subsidised programme, it becomes possible to facilitate microfinancing. The author Rajagopalan's (2005) paper suggests that SHGs significantly lead to gains for women in terms of mobility, self-confidence, access to finance and services, conserving their own savings, competence in public affairs and better status at home and community. Devi (2006) propagates that microcredit is one of the essential features for empowering poor women in rural and urban areas of the Indian state. This paper, through the study of a panel of Indian states for the period 2007–2014, examined the impact of women empowerment of women via SHGs and women's employment opportunities. According to the article, the factors like increasing access to bank loans and female literacy also improve women's empowerment drive. Basu (2006) discusses that women in developing nations live in virtual seclusion and are devoid of any rights. Microfinance focuses on complete women's empowerment and can handle financial matters better than men's. According to this article, SHG helps to improve the financial plight of the women, and findings as per the study show that SHG has a positive impact on the economic impact of SHG (Self Finance Group) members. Meenakshi argues that SHG ensures accessibility to credit to the poor and these entities help ensure access to credit and income generating activities to the people at the bottom of the pyramid. Therefore, according to the paper, poor people should be provided access to finance and additional benefits for the welfare of the poor. Government (2007) defines financial inclusion as ensuring timely access to timely and adequate credit and financial services by vulnerable groups at the lowest costs. Untalan and Cuevas (1989) in their research paper emphasise that the lack of collateral security. Distance from the banks, lack of access, and lack of credit history and documentation were recognised as the main factors limiting the growth of women led SHGs in India. Henceforth, the policymakers have recognised the need for ICT implementation and digitisation of SHGs to facilitate the compilation of a database of women members of SHGs to simplify the granting and availability of formal financial services at the door steps of the members of SHGs. Chakravarty and Pal's (2013) paper has sought to analyse the dismal impact of *Information Communication Technology (ICT)* on SHG in Ranchi District, the capital of Jharkhand state, India. According to the research paper, low literacy level is the main limiting factor that delimits the use of ICT. According to the paper, special emphasis should be placed on educating the dropouts through training. Further, the author propagates that increased ICT will lead to increased awareness and hence ripening the benefits of ready reference database of credit history members of SHGs for hassle-free, collateral-free loans. Moreover, according to the paper, NGOs can play an important role in promoting the use of ICT in the local language. Sakpal (2015) discusses the impact of digitisation through the digital programme launched by the Government of India on the financial health of the SHGs in India. The author argues that rural women in Rural India can use ICT initiatives like *Internet Saarthi* to market the project. According to the article, the SHGs can use the telemedia channels such as television, internet, radio, smartphones with internet connectivity to reach the SHGs. Many of the SHGs are supported by NGOs and private firms. These organisations provide training in the use of ICT and technologies, and many of the members of SHGs are using the ICT to promote the products generated by SHG. Bailur's (2007) paper discusses a participatory approach to ensure ICT in rural

India. According to the paper, *Our Voices* is a participatory radio programme through which the Management Committee is comprised of members of the SHG, which are supposedly good SHGs. It is an ethnographic study of how a community of SHGs is running a contextual radio programme for the members of the village. This case highlights the challenges in establishing participatory and contextual rural IS projects. The relevant questions for research are who defines development? What is contextual? How legitimate is the claim of one community to call the matter relevant, and how does the tension emerge between the groups? Kagwar (2015) discusses the new programme *e-Shakti* that has been launched for digitising all the SHGs accounts. This initiative aims to digitise all the data regarding the e-Shakti SHG and Branches of Banks. The objective of this initiative was to digitise all the social and financial data of the SHGs and the members. It aims at providing easy access to all the information about the SHGs to the stakeholders at their doorsteps. In Phase I, this project was rolled out in two districts, Dhule (Maharashtra) and Ramgarh (Jharkhand). The e-Shakti project has been implemented all over India. As per the study, one of the major challenges facing the SHG was the lack of proper record-keeping. Due to a lapse in the maintenance of the books of Accounts and SHGs, the initiative e-Shakti was undertaken. In the first stage, the Master data was created, and when all the data was uploaded to the server, the SHG was called onboarded. Hence, e-SHAKTI was made operational through Mobile App, and the Go live. This project creates various kinds of data, including member-wise information on SHG savings, the credit history of the members, micro-credit plan of SHGs, Bank linkage details, and other periodic MIS. This initiative allows banks to apply for SHG loans online, provide access to all the information online, and generate reports. According to Kim (2016), the new microfinance in India is indeed a new order of things, including formal, informal, social and financial. That is how it separates the new microfinance from the old one. According to microfinance, the major reasons for this model's failure are the increase in operational subsidies, new information technology, infrastructure investment and a very high rate of interest that is to be paid to the bankers and the lending institutions. The existing model is of promoter bank, in which the promoter lends the money to the SHGs, and the promoters instruct the SHGs to lend the money, and NABARD provides the money to the commercial banks. Panchayati Raj Institution is the other institution that is responsible for Governance. Model 1 encourages banks to form and finance SHGs. Model 2 SHGs encourages NGOs to form groups giving small cash grants and training as an incentive and then link them to the local bank. Model 3 NGOs MFI and Group clusters are banks financed by intermediate loans to SHGs. The bankers have given a model of financial development of group and there are three major phases of financial development. The group chooses a common amount to save each month in this phase. Hence the group opens a savings account at a nearby bank. It leads to the discipline of thrift and the creation of assets. Phase 2: Interlending: This phase deals with savings, the group lends savings members (Charges interest), and basic bookkeeping begins. This way, groups learn to lend and borrow with small amounts of cash at stake, reducing their dependence on money lenders. Phase 3: Bank Linkage: This refers to the within-group saving and lending, and the Group approaches the bank credit up to four times the amount saved. This leads to relationships with mainstream financial institutions, and the group can borrow up to four times savings. Phase 4: Sustainability: The group manages savings, internal lending, bank credit and bookkeeping without subsidised support. The group continues indefinitely (as long as members enjoy benefits). Group linkages bring unexpected benefits to the group members, and the members can motivate the members to lend money. And bankers can lend money to SHGs at a rate much lower than microfinance institutions. NGOs have also started participating in disbursing cash and credit to the people at the bottom of the pyramid. NGOs know what they do not have in terms of good staff, trained in managing cash, conforming to regulations forecasting reserves, and minimising frauds. Poor have a high rate of aversion to risk-taking. Thus, the groups have higher power to bring the news about lower interest rates, affordable insurance, and other financial services to the members of the SHGs. Sustainability is one of the major benefits of SHGs. This involves the quantification of the perceived value of the utility. It is linked to the source of consumption loans, source of production loan, link to get the bank's ability to solve the social and community problem, elevate social status and link to other agencies in the government. This is a case study about Natural Villages defined by watersheds and disasters. In this natural setting, the SHGs can help to mobilise the natural village and lessen the impact of natural hazards. There are numerous examples of SHGs managing disasters in the State of Orissa. Digitisation of the SHG refers to the digitisation of the processes and sub-processes followed by the SHG, which implies installing a digital MIS aided by a technologically advanced banking channel for the members of the SHGs. Currently, all the processes undertaken by the SHGs are manual. But digital SHGs would imply the digitisation of financial, human resources, and marketing modules. In the current dynamic environment, SHGs find it extremely difficult to monitor their activities, including the funds and finances. And the current manual processes are not at all streamlined and need to be integrated into an ecosystem. SRLM and NRLM are the major governance structures that manage SHGs; however, these sub-processes suffer from major inefficiencies and inaccuracies. However, implementing the digital MIS system for SHGs is fraught with major weaknesses. Awareness and access are the two major problems in the success of digital e-markets for the SHG, leading to an extremely high failure rate of the digitised SHGs. There is not much research on the digitisation of community programmes such as SHGs in India. Women's empowerment is defined as the ability to do something and gain strength or powering process from the party who has it to the less powerless. Empowerment is the process through which women gain strength, choice and meaningful control over their lives (O Neil Domingo & Valters). Women empowerment could be of different kinds, which include political power, social power, psychological power, and economic power. The research question to be addressed is how the digitisation of SHGs leads to women's empowerment and why it is important.

Conclusion

Social projects have economic and social benefits beyond the projects' social costs. It is beyond the economic cost of the projects. There is a need to devise methods to evaluate the social benefits of the projects. Economic benefits and costs alone are not enough to evaluate the projects. In order to choose between the various alternatives, it is important to consider the projects' social benefits and social costs.

References

Bailur, S. (2007). Using stakeholder theory to analyze telecenter projects. *Information Technologies and International Development*, *3*, 61–80. https://doi.org/10.1162/itid. 2007.3.3.61

Basu, P. (2006). *Improving access to finance for India's rural poor*. Directions in Development. Washington, DC: World Bank. http://hdl.handle.net/10986/6927

Chakravarty, S. R., & Pal, R. (2013). Financial inclusion in India: An axiomatic approach. *Journal of Policy Modeling*, *35*(5), 813–837.

Devi, N. (2006). Empowering Rural Women. In *The Assam Tribune, II. Guwahati: Patowary*, M. Tribune Press.

Kim, J.-H. (2016). A study on the effect of financial inclusion on the relationship between income inequality and economic growth. *Emerging Markets Finance and Trade*, *52*(2), 498–512. https://doi.org/10.1080/1540496X.2016.1110467

Morduch, J. (1999). The Microfinance Promise. *Journal of Economic Literature*, *37*(4), 1569–1614. http://www.jstor.org/stable/2565486

Rajagopalan. (2005). Microcredit and women's empowerment: The Lokadrusti case. In N. Burra, J. Deshmukh – Ranadive, & R. K. Murthy (Eds.) *Microcredit, poverty, and empowerment* (pp 245–285). New Delhi: Sage.

Sakpal, R. (2015). Creating automated virtual humans. Doctoral dissertation, The University of North Carolina at Charlotte.

Untalan, T., & Cuevas, C. (1989). Transaction cost and the viability of rural financial intermediaries. *Journal of Philippine Development*, *16*(1), 37–87.

Index

Printed and bound by CPI Group (UK) Ltd, Croydon, CR0 4YY

10/03/2024

14467865-0003